CHURCH DOCTRINE

VOLUME I: CANON

CHURCH DOCTRINE

The Faith and Practice of the Christian Community

VOLUME I: CANON

Paul C. McGlasson

CASCADE *Books* • Eugene, Oregon

CHURCH DOCTRINE
Volume One: Canon

Copyright © 2013 Paul C. McGlasson. All rights reserved. Except for brief quotations in critical publications or reviews, no part of this book may be reproduced in any manner without prior written permission from the publisher. Write: Permissions, Wipf and Stock Publishers, 199 W. 8th Ave., Suite 3, Eugene, OR 97401.

Cascade Books
An Imprint of Wipf and Stock Publishers
199 W. 8th Ave., Suite 3
Eugene, OR 97401

www.wipfandstock.com

ISBN 13: 978-1-62032-694-7

Cataloging-in-Publication data:

McGlasson, Paul C.

    Church doctrine : volume one : canon / Paul C. McGlasson.

    xiv + 172 p. ; 23 cm. — Includes bibliographical references.

    ISBN 13: 978-1-62032-694-7

    1. Theology, Doctrinal. I. Title.

BT75 M151 2013

Manufactured in the U.S.A.

To Mickey and Casey, joy of my heart.

Outline of *Church Doctrine*: Volumes I–V

Introduction: Why Doctrine Matters

I. Canon
      1. The Authority of Scripture
      2. Theological Interpretation of Scripture
      3. Proclamation
      4. The Trinity
      5. The Divine Imperative

II. God
      1. The Knowledge of God
      2. The Perfections of God
      3. Election
      4. Love for God

III. Creation
      1. God the Creator
      2. Covenant of Grace
      3. Humanity
      4. The Way of God in the World
      5. Love for Neighbor

IV. Reconciliation
      1. The Incarnation
      2. The Cross
      3. The Resurrection
      4. Justification and Sanctification

      5. Faith
      6. Prayer

V. Redemption
      1. The Gift of the Spirit
      2. The Kingdom of God
      3. The Church
      4. Mission to the World
      5. A New Society
      6. The Return of Christ
      7. The Sacraments
      8. The Joy of Discipleship

Table of Contents Volume I

Preface xi
Abbreviations xiii

Introduction: Why Doctrine Matters 1
    a. The Crisis and Promise of Doctrine 2
    b. The Role of Doctrine 9
    c. The Shape of Doctrine 17
    d. The Goal of Doctrine 22

PART I: CANON

Chapter 1: The Authority of Scripture 27
    a. Scripture as Norm 29
    b. Scripture as Witness 37
    c. Word and Spirit 42
    d. Scripture and Community 50

Chapter 2: Theological Interpretation of Scripture 57
    a. The New World of God 60
    b. The Subject Matter of Scripture 66
    c. Dimensions of Theological Interpretation 75
    d. Faith Seeking Understanding 83

Chapter 3: Proclamation 90
    a. Faith from Hearing 91
    b. The Living Word of God 97
    c. Ministry of the Word 104
    d. The Language of Faith 109

Chapter 4: The Trinity 115
    a. Unity in Diversity 118
    b. Act and Being 125
    c. The Triune God 129
    d. Nicene Faith 135

Chapter 5: The Divine Imperative 144
    a. The Will of God 146
    b. The Commandments of God 153
    c. Conformity to Christ 160
    d. The Rule of Love 164

Bibliography 169

Preface

IN 1618, THE BREMEN theologian Matthias Martini published a fine volume of theology with a lovely title: *Christiana et Catholica Fides*. It was, and is, a beautiful vision: a form of church doctrine (*fides*) that is at the same time true to the heart of the gospel (*Christiana*) and yet also universal in its appeal, scope, and application (*Catholica*). Sadly, Martini's own work appeared the very year the Thirty Years' War began (1618–1648), a war in which Calvinist, Lutheran, and Catholic armies fought each other to the death, largely to the detriment of the civilian population in his German homeland. Their actions were surely neither faithful, Christian, nor catholic; yet the vision of Martini remains valid, and cannot and must not be abandoned. Such concern for church doctrine remains even today a common task of the universal church.

The present volume is the first in a five-volume study of church doctrine. I hope and plan to publish the remaining volumes one per year, and will include comprehensive indices for the entire five volume work at the conclusion of the final volume. I ask the reader's patience; and even more, for those who will, invite their company along the way.

The Introduction included in this first volume provides the theological setting for the entire study as a whole, and I therefore need add little here. Suffice it to say that, like many others, I remain unconvinced by the choice between conventional theologies on the religious left and on the religious right. I have therefore set as my constant endeavor the search for *orthodoxy*, which in my understanding is never a given, but always and ever to be sought again and again in the living reality of the church.

I would like to express my deep thanks to Wipf and Stock Publishers for their willingness to undertake this project; and to my editor, Rodney Clapp, whose theological ear is so very well tuned.

To Peggy, my thanks for everything: the list is surely as close to infinity as we can come in this life. This volume is dedicated to our two wonderful kids, Mickey and Casey (who have taught me far more than I them . . .).

Abbreviations

BTONT	Brevard Childs, *Biblical Theology of the Old and New Testaments*.
CD	Karl Barth, *Church Dogmatics*
CCFCT	Jaroslav Pelikan and Valerie Hotchkiss, *Creeds and Confessions of Faith in the Christian Tradition*
CNTC	John Calvin, *Calvin's New Testament Commentaries*
DP	Otto Ritschl, *Dogmengeschichte des Protestantismus* 1–4.
GCE	Wilhelm Gass, *Geschichte der Christlichen Ethik* I–II/II.
GNET	Emanuel Hirsch, *Geschichte der Neuern Evangelischen Theologie* I–V.
HDThG	*Handbuch der Dogmen- und Theologiegeschichte* 1–3, 2nd edition.
LCC	Library of Christian Classics
LW	Luther's Works (American Edition)
Ptgy	Johannes Quasten, *Patrology* I–IV.
ST	*The Summa Theologica of Thomas Aquinas* I–V (Christian Classics—the Benzinger Bros. edition)
TCT	Jaroslav Pelikan, *The Christian Tradition* 1–5.

Introduction: Why Doctrine Matters

IN THE CHURCH OF Jesus Christ, doctrine *matters*. Doctrine matters to trained theologians of the church, whose work is rooted in the faith of the gospel. Doctrine matters to those who proclaim the gospel from week to week in the Sunday service of worship. Doctrine matters to ordinary Christians, who are baptized in the name of the triune God.

Doctrine matters to the *whole* people of God. An elitist dismissal of doctrine on the grounds that subtle distinctions of the faith cannot possibly matter to the typical layperson overlooks the fact that the creed of the church is burrowed deeply into the heart, mind, and memory of living faith for all Christians. Doctrine expresses the consent of the faithful, which gathers us into one in life and in death.

Doctrine matters to Christians throughout the world, among all societies, and in all nations. Doctrine is a *global* concern. Church doctrine is a burning issue across cultural boundaries, across national boundaries, across racial boundaries, across economic boundaries. Concern for church doctrine as a life or death matter accompanies the gospel wherever it goes throughout all creation.

Doctrine matters in our *contemporary* world. As Christians we embrace the vast variety of changes that have made our modern world: the brilliant growth of modern science, the dizzying pace of modern technology, the all-encompassing network of modern communication, the advent of a new global cosmopolitanism. We live fully in our contemporary world; yet precisely here in modernity we care about doctrine, more than we care about our own welfare, more than we care about our own lives. Church doctrine matters now more than ever.

The purpose of this introduction is *not* to argue that doctrine matters. There is no need for such an argument; for doctrine in fact does matter to all Christians everywhere, in all times, including our own. Doctrine is the treasure of the church, for church doctrine is the doctrine of Christ. Church doctrine is the teaching *about* Jesus Christ; of him who died for our sins and not ours only, but the sins of all humankind; of him who gathers us into his arms when we stumble along the journey of life; of him who, even before the world was made, knew us and called us one by one, each by name; of him who by his resurrection has already made all things new. Church doctrine is the teaching *from* Jesus Christ; who by his Word and Spirit guides his beloved people in every time and age; who freely opens hearts and minds to new insight and fresh perspective, setting us free from the shackles of the past; who guards all that is good in the wonder of truth he entrusts to us, ever enlivening that truth anew in splendor through his present and active rule. Church doctrine—that is, the doctrine of Jesus Christ—is essential to the healthy life of the church, indeed to its very existence.

The purpose rather of this introduction is to propose a set of arguments for *why* doctrine matters. Granted that doctrine matters, why does it matter so much? Why is concern for church doctrine a vital part of living faith in Christ? What role does doctrine play in the ongoing mission of the church in the contemporary world? In what way does doctrine shape practical daily existence for ordinary Christians? Our aim is thus to give a *theological* account of doctrine, not an *apologetic* defense of it. Now, in order to grasp the true import of doctrine, it is essential to face squarely the crisis of doctrine in the mainline church today, and as well to be reminded of its glorious promise.

a. The Crisis and Promise of Doctrine

By the end of 1528, the Reformation was well under way. Toward the end of that year, and at the beginning of the next, Martin Luther visited many of the parishes in Electoral Saxony and Meissen. How had the glorious gospel of justifying faith fared in the churches over the last decade since the onset of a new era for God's people? What was the state of understanding of Christian teaching (*christianae doctrinae cognitio*) among the ordinary people? In the preface to *The Small Catechism*, Luther records his impressions of what he found in the various congregations. He is outraged and appalled at the extremely low level of even basic understanding of Christian belief: "Good God, what wretchedness (*calamitatem*) I beheld!"[1] The conditions in the churches were nothing short of "deplorable" (*miserabilis*).[2] Luther underscores the astonishing lack of knowledge of Christian teaching, an ignorance shared not only by ordinary Christians but also by the clergy as well: "Unfortunately many pastors are quite incompetent and unfitted for teaching."[3] The common people wallow in ignorance, and it shows in their way of life: "They live as if they were pigs and irrational beasts, and . . . they have mastered the fine art of abusing liberty."[4] Luther begs pastors and bishops to take seriously their duty of teaching basic Christian doctrine to the people under their care. Those who refuse instruction should be admonished for their unbelief: "Tell them that they deny Christ and are no Christians."[5] No one should be compelled to believe; yet those who would share in the life of the Christian community should at the very least be able to discern the normative beliefs of the community of faith. There are "standards" of Christian faith and action that all Christians must "learn to know."[6] So, Luther.

Of course we live in the social and cultural world of the twenty-first century, not the sixteenth; of course conditions in the churches of our time are profoundly different in many ways from the days of Luther; nevertheless, the phenomenon of doctrinal illiteracy that Luther laments is surely just as widespread in the church today, affecting laity, clergy (and perhaps even many professional theologians?) alike. Doctrinal illiteracy means a basic lack of understanding of the content and shape of Christian belief. Luther is right: the issue has nothing to do with enforcing belief on others. Long gone are the days when Christians could or should rely upon the state to enforce orthodoxy. The role of the state is to guarantee freedom of religion, not enforce Christian orthodoxy. But that is the role of the state; here we are not speaking of the state, but of the church. The church has both a commission and a need to affirm the basic normative confession of faith by which it lives, and to teach that confession openly and confidently. Doctrinal illiteracy is a fatal contradiction of the very notion of a living church. Where doctrinal illiteracy is rampant, there the very existence of

---

1. Pelikan and Hotchkiss, eds., *CCFCT* II, 31.
2. Ibid.
3. Ibid.
4. Ibid.
5. Ibid., 32.
6. Ibid.

the church is threatened. The great crisis facing the church today is in fact the stunning lack of basic understanding of church doctrine at all levels of the community of faith. Again, Luther, in *The Bondage of the Will*: "Truth and doctrine must be preached always, openly, and constantly, and never accommodated or concealed . . ." (*Veritas et doctrina semper, palam, constanter praedicanda, nunquam obliquanda caelandave est*).[7]

How then are we to come to grips with the crisis of doctrinal illiteracy? What are its causes, and how is it to be solved? Despite a variety of possible historical explanations, some of which may very well have a certain measure of validity, it is essential to start with a theological appraisal. For that, we must turn to the prophetic critique in the Old Testament. The prophet Amos names the crisis of God's people as a famine of God's living word: "The time is surely coming, says the Lord God, when I will send a famine on the land; not a famine of bread, or a thirst for water, but of hearing the words of the Lord." The result of such a famine is rampant, blinding confusion, with no theological clarity in sight: "They shall wander from sea to sea, and from north to east; they shall run to and fro, seeking the word of the Lord, but they shall not find it" (Amos 8:11-12). According to Amos, no greater judgment can come upon God's people than the awful silence of God. God's terrible silence is not the *result* of the people's confusion, but its *indictment*. Amos does not speak such words of judgment as a careful analysis of the contemporary situation, using the latest techniques of socio-cultural inquiry. He speaks because he must. God has made known his eternal will; who can possibly remain silent: "The lion has roared: who will not fear? The Lord God has spoken; who can but prophesy?"(Amos 3:8). The people do not misunderstand *something*; they misunderstand *everything*: God's gracious election, true worship, justice, God's covenant, the sacred promise—and their way of life clearly shows it. "They sell the righteous for silver, and the needy for a pair of sandals—they who trample the head of the poor in the dust of the earth, and push the afflicted out of the way . . ." (Amos 2:7). Their massive failure of social justice is a direct consequence of their unspeakable failure to hear the divine word.

Doctrinal illiteracy is the church's forgetfulness of God. The marginalization of doctrine in the church's life is the attempted marginalization of God, which is death to the church. For God in fact cannot be shunted aside to the margins. The living God is the center of the church, without whom we cannot live. Church doctrine is the lifeblood of the church, through

---

7. Luther, *LW* 33, 56.

which the Spirit of Christ flows into his body. It is through church doctrine that we learn the language of faith; it is through church doctrine that we discover the true identity of God; it is through church doctrine that we find the very meaning of life itself, and each step along life's way; it is through church doctrine that our lives are transformed into the image of Christ. It is through church doctrine that we are taught by the Spirit of God, and come to know the very mind of Christ. Church doctrine is at the center of the church's life because it is taught to us by one Teacher, whom we follow with our whole being, and whose voice we obey with all that we have and are: which is Jesus Christ. To lose our grasp of church doctrine is therefore to walk away from the call of discipleship, which is ultimate folly. Doctrinal illiteracy is truly a famine of the living Word of God.

The source of doctrinal illiteracy in the contemporary church is the marginalization of doctrine by political and cultural ideology. The same holds true on the religious left as on the religious right: political and cultural ideology have driven out the affirmation of doctrine by which the church lives under the rule of Christ. The marginalization of church doctrine by political and cultural ideology—the usual word today is a "worldview"—is the Babylonian Captivity of the church in our time. On the religious right is a cultural ideology of personal ambition through self-reliant individualism; on the religious left is a cultural ideology of inner fulfillment through self-affirmation; on both sides equally, the religious left and the religious right, church doctrine is banished to the margins. Both left and right seek to *enclose God* within the confines of a human political and cultural agenda. In theology, as in life, extremes meet; despite the vastly different conclusions, both the religious left and the religious right agree on the basic approach to theology, including the widespread suspicion and outright dismissal of church doctrine.

The church's answer to both religious left and right can only be the same: the living God cannot and will not be *enclosed* within a political or cultural agenda, even if that agenda or "worldview" is a supposedly Christian one. God is *God*. *His* purposes are not our purposes; *his* ways are not our ways; *his* thoughts are not our thoughts. He is not answerable to us; we are answerable to *him*. To both the religious left and the religious right, our only answer can be the words of Isaiah: "You have turned things upside down! Shall the potter be regarded as the clay?" (Isa 29:16). How perverse, how utterly foolish, to confuse the majesty of the Creator with his creation! "These people draw near with their mouths and honor me with their lips, while their hearts are far from me, and their worship of me is a human commandment learned by rote ..." (Isa 29:13). How completely absurd to confuse the social-cultural maneuvering of petty humanity with the sheer freedom of God who rules all things! "The wisdom of their wise shall perish, and the discernment of the discerning shall be hidden . . . the meek shall obtain fresh joy in the Lord, and the neediest of the people shall exult in the Holy One of Israel" (Isa 29:14, 19). How utterly tragic to discount the living reality of God through political and cultural scheming, he who alone demonstrates his absolute creative power for all creation to see! Only then, when *God* makes himself known, will true knowledge of God be possible: "And those who err in spirit will come to understanding, and those who grumble will accept instruction" (Isa 29:24).

Church doctrine can only begin with the rediscovery of the sheer *incomparability* of God, who is defined only in reference to himself, and whose sovereign claim upon human life is self-validating and self-affirming. Church doctrine is grounded in the inalienable right of God.

Yet how does God exercise that right? "Have you not known? Have you not heard? Has it not been told you from the beginning? Have you not understood from the foundations of the earth?" (Isa 40:21). Jesus Christ himself is the incomparable God; Jesus Christ himself is the sovereign claim of God upon all human life; Jesus Christ himself is God's inalienable right over humanity, a right grounded in his freely electing love for all humankind, a right exercised through the grace of the cross and fulfilled in the radically new life of the resurrection. Jesus Christ is the crisis of church doctrine; but far more importantly he is the one true promise of doctrine and life for the church and for the whole world.

The church lives under the dreadful threat of losing its very identity; but it also lives by the infinitely more powerful promise of God's faithfulness, which cannot and will not fail. Consider: the very year that saw Luther's trenchant lament over the church's dwindling and distorted doctrinal awareness also saw the publication of *The Small Catechism*, and in the next year would appear *The Large Catechism* (1529). Not long after would come *The Augsburg Confession* (1530) among the Lutherans; *The Heidelberg Catechism* (1562), *The Second Helvetic Confession* (1566), and *The Westminster Confession* (1646) among the Reformed; among Anglicans *The Thirty-Nine Articles* (1566); the Roman Catholic *Decrees of the Council of Trent* (1563); and the three great seventeenth-century confessions of Eastern Orthodoxy, *The Confession of Faith by Metrophanes Kritopoulos* (1625), *The Orthodox*

Confession of Peter Mogila (1642), and *The Confession of Dositheus* (1672). All illustrate a constant paradox of church life: times of real growth in the faith of the gospel often only occur at the same time as life or death crisis. Church doctrine does not roll along like a river; it crashes in waves on the sea like a thrashing storm. The same paradox would be in motion again in the twentieth century with the bright light of *The Barmen Declaration* (1934), set against the dark and menacing background of Nazi Germany. The faithfulness of God does not disappear in times of crisis. On the contrary, the church seems always to draw closer to God in such times; or perhaps it is better to say that in such times God himself graciously draws closer to his beloved church.

Once again, we must turn to the prophetic promise of the Old Testament for genuine theological insight. According to the prophet Hosea, the hope of God's people is grounded exclusively in God's utterly miraculous and redeeming love, which simply will not abandon his children: "How can I give you up, Ephraim? How can I hand you over, O Israel? . . . My heart recoils within me . . . I will not execute my fierce anger . . . for I am God and no mortal, the Holy One in your midst, and I will not come in wrath" (Hos 11:8-9). The hope of God's church rests even now upon the passionate loyalty of God, who simply will not let go of his people despite their own disloyalty to him. God is *God*; how can he turn away from his children, even though they turn away from him? Or again, in the midst of devastating and tragic ruin, the prophet Joel proclaims a new day of overwhelming joy: "You shall eat in plenty and be satisfied, and praise the name of the Lord your God, who has dealt wondrously with you . . . You shall know that I am in the midst of Israel, and that I, the Lord, am your God and there is no other . . ." (Joel 2:26-27). The new day of the Lord is a gracious and miraculous eschatological gift, which breaks forth into human life by the mysterious hand of God, through the outpouring of the Spirit (vv. 28-29). Through the joyous gift of the gospel, the eschatological peace of God is already a present reality. In the Bible, crisis is the intersection between the dying of the old, and the birth of the new; the history of church doctrine has repeatedly confirmed this stunning biblical turning point of the times.

Thus, even as we speak of the crisis of doctrinal illiteracy, it is essential to recognize the infinitely greater *promise* of the gospel in the church and the world. Signs of that promise are everywhere evident.

First, despite the massive confusion which has clearly convulsed the theological conversation of the church, the fact remains that ordinary faithful Christians in living congregations continue in the knowledge and service of God in the church for the world. Their words are often softly spoken; their deeds are usually quiet and unassuming. But their words and deeds bear faithful and eloquent witness to Jesus Christ the risen Lord of all creation. The light of the church still shines in the farthest corners of God's vineyard, often far from the centers of ecclesiastical influence and power. The church yet remains the salt of the earth, by its seasoning power preserving and enriching the goodness of life in God's good creation.

Second, we live in a time of *revolutionary* growth in the global church. Seeds that were planted by missions in the nineteenth century and earlier have now sprouted and spread like vibrant wildflowers across the landscape of human need. Mission churches have now become established churches the world over. The language of faith is spoken in countless human dialects, on every continent, among all tribes and peoples. The gospel is celebrated among the nations, in visible fulfillment of the promised outpouring of God's Spirit upon all humankind. The globalization of the church has not set doctrine aside, as many predicted; on the contrary, it has brought a new globalization of church doctrine. Church doctrine was perhaps once centered in western Europe; now it is studied and lived in Africa and Asia, Latin America and the Middle East, studied and lived with searching discovery and intense delight. Church doctrine now matters throughout all creation, and is centered (where in fact it has always been centered) in the one Lord of the church.

Third, the creeds, catechisms, and confessions of the church, despite much widespread neglect, still speak with extraordinary power in the resiliency of truth. These documents contain the memory of the church, which binds us even today with unseen bonds of living community. Their struggles are our struggles; their decisions are our decisions; their faith is our faith. We must press forward to a contemporary and constructive statement of church doctrine, and not simply retreat into the past; however, genuine hope is always based on grateful memory. For those with eyes to see and ears to hear, the creeds and confessions of the church both transmit and guard the faith once for all delivered and cherished by all God's saints.

Fourth, the ecumenical movement of the twentieth century and beyond has thankfully largely replaced the theological rancor of an earlier era. Despite continuing theological differences, which cannot be lightly glossed over by doctrinal indifferentism but must be squarely and honestly faced, the fact remains that a page has surely been turned in the ecumenical relations of the church. Surely it is now long past the time when Roman Catholics, Eastern Orthodox, and Protestants can mutually accuse one another of heresy. The reason for tolerance and affirmation has nothing to do with the modern Enlightenment ideology of pluralism. Pluralism means an affirmation of many gods, a clear violation of the first commandment: "you shall have no other gods besides me." Pluralism is forbidden among those who call upon the risen Lord, who alone rules the church and indeed the entire cosmos. Ecumenism, by sharp contrast, means the recognition of legitimate disagreement, and creative tension, within the one family of faith. The ecumenical movement is a vibrant sign of hope for the recovery of church doctrine.

And finally, and by far the most important sign of hope for the future of church doctrine, the Bible lays open before the church and the world. Doctrinal illiteracy is a necessary concomitant of biblical illiteracy. A true understanding of the content of Scripture will always bring with it passionate concern for church doctrine, just as real understanding of church doctrine will always give rise to renewed passion for the reading and interpretation of Scripture. By contrast, rediscovery of doctrine is a direct implication of rediscovery of the Bible. Church doctrine can only be learned anew from the witness of Holy Scripture. The Bible is the ultimate promise of God's faithfulness to church and world. We turn to the Bible with eager anticipation of illumination by God's Spirit, who freely gives the divine gift of truth and abundant life, even in uncertain times.

b. The Role of Doctrine

A generation after Luther's initial rediscovery of the overpowering truth of the gospel in the church for the world, John Calvin set about in his *Institutes of the Christian Religion* to render the insights of the reformation fruitful for a new generation. In the preface to the 1559 edition (the final in Latin), he admits the long-standing struggle he has waged to find the proper order of teaching church doctrine: "Although I did not regret the labor spent, I was never satisfied until the work had been arranged in the order (*in hunc ordinem*) now set forth."[8] The purpose of such strenuous labor in searching for the right order of presentation over twenty-three years (the first edition of course was published in 1536) has been the same since the very

---

8. Calvin, *LCC* XX, 3.

beginning: the maintenance of "pure doctrine."[9] Doctrine, for Calvin, is not a systematic outline of biblical teaching; that would place the majesty of the Bible *behind* church doctrine, which would in turn then replace the Bible—falsely—as the final word on Christian truth. Rather, doctrine is a summary of common topics (*loci communes*) found in the Bible, whose purpose is to *prepare* preachers and readers of the divine word to understand its genuine content. Above all, the purpose of church doctrine is to point to the one true subject matter (*scopus*) of Scripture, which is Jesus Christ. In the preface to the final French edition (1561), Calvin speaks of his work on doctrine as "guidance," "direction," and as a "path," needed in order to protect the reader from senseless distraction, and in order to lead from the text of the Bible to the risen Lord of whom it speaks.[10] Church doctrine is a rule (*reigle*) for embracing the treasure to be found in every sentence of the Bible. Once again, the point is crucial, and sets Calvin apart from the medieval scholasticism that preceded him and the Protestant scholasticism that succeeded him: church doctrine *precedes* the interpretation of Scripture, rather than following it. The goal of doctrine is fresh insight into Scripture.

Doctrine is at the center of the church's life. Concern for doctrine is a vital dimension of living faith in the gospel of Jesus Christ. The health of the church depends upon the rediscovery of church doctrine in the obedience of faith. Doctrine plays an essential, and indispensable, role in the life of the church. The role of doctrine has several facets, including the following.

I agree with Calvin: the role of church doctrine is not to provide a systematic summary of biblical truth, but rather to lead to a fresh encounter with the living truth of the Bible. That is to say, church doctrine follows a *logic of discovery* rather than a *logic of confirmation*. Were we to use a logic of confirmation, the role of the Bible would be to provide warrants for a system of truths already known: surely in the end a misuse of the authority of Scripture. The Bible would then lie closed, behind the system, rather than open, ahead of it. In using a logic of discovery, the role of doctrine is to invite eager anticipation for the fresh hearing of the divine word. In sum, the Bible does not serve to confirm church doctrine; church doctrine serves to discover afresh the liberating truth of the Bible.

Doctrine provides the church with a theological *pattern* by which to understand the message of Scripture according to the divine purpose. The theological pattern is not imposed upon Scripture, but derived from it;

---

9. Ibid., 4.
10. Ibid., 6–8.

yet the pattern is not identical with Scripture, but is a summary of its true content. The early church spoke of a rule of faith (*regula fidei*), according to which the gospel is rightly understood and lived.[11] Church doctrine attempts to trace the outline of the pattern of faith and life in every new generation of the church. The interpretation of the Bible in the church is a ruled exercise; it involves a discipline of attention and evaluation everywhere and always practiced by faithful followers of Jesus Christ. The theological pattern that doctrine provides is not limited to a specific creed, or confession, though it is embodied in them; rather, it circumscribes a variety of creeds and confessions, showing the legitimacy of flexibility, yet at the same time laying bare the heart of church unity. The theological pattern of church doctrine is a mirror image of the theological shaping of Scripture itself. The majestic *reason* for God's gracious purpose is free and mysterious, ultimately known only to himself; yet the *goal* of God's one sovereign purpose for the world is declared openly and coherently in the message of Scripture: which is the knowledge of God. Church doctrine, in the humility of faith, seeks to discern the mystery of God's one loving purpose for all humanity, even as that mysterious purpose, more precisely, seeks us, and finds us.

Doctrine aids the church in reading Scripture with a *sense of the whole*. From the beginning of the church comes the confession: Holy Scripture is the Word of God. Church doctrine rests secure upon that confession. And yet we read in Holy Scripture itself: "In the beginning was the Word, and the Word was with God, and the Word was God" (John 1:1). Jesus Christ himself is the Word of God. There are thus many voices in Scripture, yet ultimately one divine Word. Now, the point is not to cling to the one content in abstraction from the written word (as in theological liberalism); nor to cling to the written word and ignore the one content (as in fundamentalism). Rather, church doctrine works to understand the whole witness of Holy Scripture in light of the one subject matter of which it speaks: and that is Jesus Christ. Doctrine is a constant reminder to the church that we turn to the Bible to hear the living voice of Christ the risen Lord. He is the object of the biblical witness; but equally important, he forever remains the speaking Subject. The sovereign authority of Christ the exalted Lord is the one content of all Scripture, and the truth by which every passage is rightly understood. Jesus Christ is the one norm for understanding Holy Scripture, the one norm by which the Christian life is measured, the one norm by which the new humanity is illuminated, the one norm to which

---

11. Cf. Andresen and Ritter in *HDThG* I, 85-88.

the church turns in both speech and action. Doctrine protects the church from distraction, and invites the church continually to encounter the One of whom the Bible speaks. Doctrine reminds the church what the Bible is all about, so that the church might not lose its way in unfruitful or even harmful diversion.

Doctrine focuses the attention of the church upon the *content and response* of the faith we cherish. There are two dimensions of faith according to Scripture, both equally valid and equally important: faith as content (*fides quae creditur*) and faith as response (*fides qua creditur*). In his letter to the congregation at Corinth (1 Cor 15:1–5), Paul speaks of the faith which he has "received" and "handed on"; the content of faith is not "Paul's," but is transmitted in a given tradition which is to be guarded and preserved. Yet on the other hand, Paul speaks of taking one's "stand" in this faith, which draws forth therefore a passionate and total life commitment. Clearly for Paul both dimensions—content and response—are equally valid and closely intertwined. Christian doctrine struggles to understand both dimensions of faith, for neither can be neglected where the gospel of Jesus Christ is firmly grasped. Nevertheless, there is a proper ordering between the two: the content of faith determines the response of faith. Said another way, *what* we believe teaches us *how* to believe. The content of faith does not in the least replace the need for a human response; church doctrine rejects a false objectivism just as strenuously as a false subjectivism. It is a question rather of balanced proportion, according to the biblical witness. Church doctrine strives to bring to the attention of the church the content of our common faith. In so doing, it goes against the current of modern thought, which turns faith into a human phenomenon, in abstraction from the object of faith. Church doctrine also calls for a passionate and total response of the whole person. In so doing, it protects the faith of the church from a lifeless set of propositions detached from the life and death struggles of being human.

Doctrine helps the church in searching for the *inner logic* of the subject matter of the Bible. The content of the Bible evinces a pattern of inter-relationship. There is, to use the traditional phrase, an *analogy of faith*; a sense in which the substance of the Bible can be discerned according to its own inner order. On the one hand, doctrine protects against any other access to the subject matter of the Bible than the analogy of faith. When approached on the grounds of human reason and experience; when sought on the basis of the canons of human logic; when measured by the inner resources of cultural ideology, the sovereign reality of which the Bible speaks withdraws in dreadful silence. The reality of the Bible is the living God; the living God can be measured by no one except himself. Every attempt to measure God by any standard of measurement other than himself is fatal to the church. Nevertheless, church doctrine joins the community of faith upon the joyful and exciting search for the inner logic of divine truth, an invitation which comes to us through the Bible by the living God himself. The search for the inner logic of the content of the Bible is at the same time gift and demand: gift, because the challenge is possible only on the basis of God's own self-disclosure; demand, because the search for the living reality of God draws from us the highest reach of human intellect and imagination. The challenge of Paul is to "discern" what is the will of God: an active, not a passive, moment of responsible endeavor (cf. Rom 12:1–2).

Doctrine gathers the community of faith together in passionate *concern for truth*. Truth in the Bible is not a correspondence between human language and exterior reality. Truth is the overpowering reality of divine action confirming the promise of the divine word: "You may say to yourself, 'How can we recognize a word that the Lord has not spoken?' If a prophet speaks in the name of the Lord but the thing does not take place or prove true, it is a word that the Lord has not spoken" (Deut 18:22–23). Truth is God's own entry into the world that he has made, in order to transform it from the inside. In the Bible, truth has a name; Jesus Christ is the truth. Concern for truth is therefore a direct implication of the obedience of faith. Truth is an encounter between Christ the risen Lord and the community of faith which treasures the gospel. There is no valid theological opposition between the living Christ and the passionate concern for truth in church doctrine. On the contrary, we try as Christians to get it right precisely because we owe our truthfulness to the risen and living One whom we serve. The truth of the gospel is worth every effort to find it; every ounce of energy to express and reflect upon it; all courage to defend it; all creative imagination to proclaim it. The church lives by the truth, and cannot for one moment turn its back upon concern for truth and still remain the church of the living Lord. Church doctrine has a role to play in continuously raising the question of truth for the sake of the common good. In doing so, it may raise questions which bring momentary discomfort to some; but it does so only in order to bear witness to the genuine comfort of God given to all humanity.

Church doctrine serves the church in drawing valid *theological boundaries*—taken from Scripture and acknowledged by the universal church—beyond which the gospel is not rightly preached. From the very beginning, doctrine has involved a pattern of both affirmation and negation. That is to say, the church has found it possible to affirm the truth of the gospel only by simultaneously negating the errors that deny it. There are boundaries drawn around the legitimate use of the language of faith, and one role of doctrine is to trace and illuminate the edges of those boundaries. Outside of those boundaries is false doctrine, which is the willful disregard of the content of faith. The creeds of the early church were hammered out against the backdrop of such heresies as Gnosticism, Arianism, and Sabellianism. The Augustinian legacy of church doctrine came with a corresponding rejection of Pelagianism and Donatism. The Reformation cannot be understood apart from the late-medieval errors of Semi-Pelagianism which it combats. Even in the twentieth century, the Barmen Declaration rejects as "false doctrine" the teaching of the so-called German Christians. Affirmation of the gospel requires negation of its denial, however much we might wish it otherwise. The offense of the gospel cannot be removed by general goodwill: "Do not think that I have come to bring peace to the earth; I have not come to bring peace, but a sword" (Matt 10:34).

On the other hand, while it is essential for church doctrine to trace the boundaries of the gospel, it is also crucial to make clear the vast room for *legitimate variety* within those boundaries. If the error of the religious left is typically to deny or override the boundaries, the mirror-image error of the religious right is to draw them where they do not belong. Both are equally wrong. Doctrine has the role of aiding the church in recognizing and enforcing authentic boundaries, but at the same time insisting upon and securing the joyful freedom of the gospel within those boundaries—a freedom which must be celebrated, and which must not be compromised. Sometimes in the Bible the truth comes forth as yes or no; but just as often, the truth is rendered with a great deal of flexibility, not in black or white but in a coat of many colors, which church doctrine must strive to preserve. Nor is the role of theological boundaries to eliminate the need for creative discovery; rather, the purpose of doctrinal limits is to show the church where to look, while still leaving open the process of imaginative theological construction. Needless to say, theological precision in tracing such boundaries is essential, even if often profoundly difficult.

Church doctrine assists the community of faith in a *contemporary* formulation of the gospel. Despite the instructive guidance we today receive from the church in history, we face the challenges of the present, not the past. We live in our contemporary world, and are claimed by the living Lord for the proclamation of the gospel in the world of today. Our language must be appropriate to the extraordinary times in which we live. Doctrine is a testing ground for the attempt to speak the language of faith in contemporary words. Doctrine is a laboratory of proclamation, testing the extent to which contemporary Christian speech and action are a faithful and relevant application of the biblical message. Doctrine also provides suggestions that may hopefully be found useful in the contemporaneous affirmation of the gospel in word and deed. Doctrine also warns against such attempts that are found to obscure, rather than illuminate, the shining light of truth. Which attempts are worthless fads and gimmicks; and which attempts bring home to our present day the overwhelming wonder of faith? There is not only one valid contemporary formulation; but there are approaches that strengthen the task of proclamation, and others that sadly weaken and dilute it. Which is which? Seeking an answer to these questions is one role which church doctrine plays in the service of the church, for the sake of the world. We cannot simply repristinate the past; in living responsibility before the exalted Lord, we today must rethink both the form and the content of the faith we cherish. Church doctrine can do no less, for the whole gospel is at stake in every new generation. As Luther argues in his revolutionary *Lectures on Romans*, each new generation in some sense begins at the beginning: "To stand still on God's way means to go backward, and to go forward means ever to begin anew."[12]

Church doctrine speaks both to and for the whole church. One of the characteristics of false doctrine is factionalism, already encountered so dramatically in the early church (cf. 1 Cor 1:10-17). Factions are groups within the church that speak to and for a special interest or agenda. The churches today are filled with various "coalitions" and "covenants," some representing the typical positions of the religious left, others representing the typical positions of the religious right. Doctrine radically resists all factionalism, and affirms the unity of the gospel in the unity of the church, under the unity of Christ the risen Lord. As Paul reminds the divisive church in Corinth, they are called by God—not as a special faction apart—but "together with all those who in every place call on the name of our Lord Jesus" (1 Cor 1:2).

---

12. Luther, *LCC* XV, 370.

There is not a special "Corinthian Christianity": there is only the one gospel of the universal church, grounded in the one Lord. Nor is church doctrine a sociologically or statistically defined snapshot of church belief. The truth of doctrine is not derived from a poll of Christians, and may at times even call into question majority opinion (as it did, for example, at the time of Athanasius, or during the German church struggle when the majority sided with Hitler). Nor is the truth of doctrine a matter of diplomatic compromise, no matter how artfully derived. Doctrine is not the *vox populi*, even though the truths of doctrine are held as the ultimate comfort of countless multitudes of Christians everywhere. Doctrine speaks not only to the whole people of God; doctrine also speaks for the whole people of God. Doctrine is universal because it is true; contrariwise, doctrine is true because it is universal, not factional. There is no way behind this ultimate paradox; it is known simply in the church's common confession: "we believe . . ."

Doctrine teaches the language of faith by which we know God. Without true doctrine, there is no true knowledge of God; without true knowledge of God, there is . . . nothing at all. That is why doctrine is not a luxury for the church to be undertaken in times of ease; doctrine is an essential activity of the church, all the more important when church struggle threatens to engulf Christian life and witness. The church may be wealthy, but without true doctrine it is unspeakably poor. The church may be influential in society, but without true doctrine its influence is cancerous. The church may luxuriate in extraordinary piety and spirituality, but without true doctrine, its piety and spirituality are an offense to God: "What to me is the multitude of your sacrifices? says the Lord . . . Your new moons and your appointed festivals my soul hates . . . cease to do evil, learn to do good" (Isa 1:11–16). Without true doctrine, the language of faith becomes incomprehensible gibberish: "Therefore the word of the Lord will be to them, 'Precept upon precept, precept upon precept, line upon line, line upon line, here a little, there a little'" (Isa 28:13). By contrast, the church may be utterly poor, but with true doctrine it shines the light of the gospel for all the world to see, giving pleasure to the living God. The church may have little influence in society, but with true doctrine it is the leaven that leavens the whole loaf, the tree in which the birds of the air build their nests. The church may be poor in spirit, but with true doctrine it is filled with all the fullness of the presence of Christ, who reigns supreme over the cosmos.

Church doctrine is not talk about God; doctrine is the church's living *dialogue* with God. Through doctrine, God calls to the church; through doctrine, the church responds in the obedience of faith. At stake in church doctrine is nothing less than the true knowledge of God: "Thus says the Lord: Do not let the wise boast in their wisdom, do not let the mighty boast in their might, do not let the wealthy boast in their wealth; but let those who boast boast in this, that they understand and know me, that I am the Lord; I act with steadfast love, justice, and righteousness in the earth, for in these things I delight says the Lord" (Jer 9:23–4). The dialogue of doctrine may for a time be sent to the margins; but it will always return to the center of the church, where it belongs. Nor will the dialogue ever cease, as long as we live in the time between the times; for the church grows by moving from faith to faith in the knowledge of the living God.

c. The Shape of Doctrine

The first school for disciplined theological reflection on church doctrine was founded in Alexandria, in northern Africa. It flourished during the second and third centuries; and its most influential product is surely *On First Principles*, by Origen. In the preface to this groundbreaking work, Origen sets out his basic approach. Following his teacher Clement, Origen understands the living Christ to be the one true Teacher of the church. Christ teaches through the words of the Bible; not only his own spoken words during his earthly life, but the entire Scriptural witness: "By the words of Christ we do not mean only those which formed his teaching (*doctrina*) when he was made man and dwelt in the flesh, since even before that Christ the Word of God was in Moses and the prophets."[13] Having thus established the basic christological source and content of all true doctrine, Origen proceeds to argue that the genuine content unfolds in a definite shape. Two steps are required. First, certain basic doctrines of the faith found in Scripture are to be identified and regarded as essential: "The holy apostles, when preaching the faith of Christ, took certain doctrines, those namely which they believed to be necessary ones, and delivered them in the plainest terms (*manifestissime*) to all believers."[14] Then second, those basic doctrines derived from the open proclamation of the gospel that is the kerygma of the church are to be thoughtfully explored for the purpose of discerning the coherent shape of their truth: "Thus by clear and cogent arguments he will discover the truth about each particular point and so will

13. Origen, *Principles*, 1.
14. Ibid., 2.

produce ... a single body (*corpus*) of doctrine."¹⁵ To summarize, Origen approaches the Scriptures in the light of their genuine christological content, seeking to illumine the kerygma of the church by coherent explication of the content of the scriptural witness.

In my judgment, Origen correctly describes the basic issues faced by every authentic presentation of church doctrine. What is *church* doctrine—doctrine undertaken in and by and for the church—if it is not ultimately grounded in the proclamation of the gospel? What is church *doctrine* if it does not lead toward a greater understanding of the content of Scripture? Now, there is no propositional system of truth in Scripture. Neither is there only one right way to present Christian doctrine, nor one perfect configuration of doctrinal truth. A variety of options are possible; a variety of methods are available. The ancient dictum remains: *methodus est arbitraria* ("The method used is a matter for decision"). However, the *ultimate* test for any attempt at summarizing church doctrine is the illumination of Scripture it yields. Does it engender fresh insight into the witness of Scripture? Does it open the truth of the Scriptures for a new generation of readers? Does it summarize the teaching of Scripture as a whole? Does it invite the reader back to the Scriptures for fresh and eager discovery? If so, it is useful as church doctrine; if not, it is not serviceable to the church of Jesus Christ. The final criterion by which to measure the truthfulness of church doctrine is Jesus Christ himself.

The present study follows the loci-method, first widely used in the Reformation and post-Reformation era, and then reformulated with fresh vigor in the twentieth century by Karl Barth.¹⁶ Christian truth is divided into five loci, or parts: Canon, God, Creation, Reconciliation, and Redemption. Within these larger parts, the details of church doctrine are investigated according to chapters and sections. Each locus or part stands on its own as an independent sphere of divine truth; yet each part is also interrelated with the others parts, forming a coherent whole. There is no larger systematic principle by which to organize the whole; nor is there a systematic center hidden within. Jesus Christ himself—the risen and exalted Lord—is the one center of all church doctrine.

Part I on canon (the present volume) is logically unique within the wider field of Christian doctrine. We define canon, following the

---

15. Ibid., 6.
16. Barth, *CD* I/2, 853–54, especially 870.

groundbreaking work of Brevard Childs,[17] in three ways: 1) A fixed body of normative writings which are the authoritative Scriptures of the church; 2) the particular theological shape of those writings rendered by Israel and the early church, as a witness to the living reality of God for future generations of the community of faith including our own; and 3) the contemporary task of interpreting the biblical language of faith in the contemporary context.[18] Canon is itself one subject for theological analysis and study as the first part; it is also the comprehensive context for all church doctrine, inclusive of everything. In that sense, the first part on canon replaces the older section on "prolegomena." Theological reflection on canon is at the same time *part* of church doctrine, and yet also the theological context for *all* church doctrine. The first part on canon treats the christological grounds for the authority of Scripture in the life of the church, including the relationship of Scripture and tradition. It also includes the basic rules for interpreting Scripture, or theological exegesis, which opens up the new world of God in the Bible. Canon means the church's living relationship to Scripture, and its use within the community of faith; the part on canon therefore also considers the role of proclamation in the life of the church, which is the living word of God. Finally, already in the first part on canon it is impossible not to speak of the One to whom all Scripture points: which is the triune God. The living God is a relationship of love; the living God above all desires loving relationship with humanity. The part on canon therefore includes the church's confession of the Trinity.

Part II on God summarizes the church's manifold confession concerning the living reality of God. It begins by considering the knowledge of God. The central purpose for God's self-manifestation in the world is that his glory might be known among all nations. What does it mean to know the living God according to his own self-defined and self-revealed reality? Also treated is the identity of God, including what are traditionally called the attributes or perfections of God. Who is God, and what is he like, according to the authoritative witness of Scripture? The part on God includes theological reflection on God's election, or the traditional topic of predestination. Election is not a topic prominent in much modern theology (again with the notable exception of Barth); nevertheless, it is profoundly

---

17. Cf. Childs, *BTONT*, 70–94.

18. I am perplexed that so fine a theological scholar as Robert Jenson continues to define canon as a "fixed body of literature," as if that is the end of the matter. Such a definition could have been used half a century ago; since the work of Childs (and many others) it is now badly outdated. See Jenson, *Canon and Creed*, 13.

central to the biblical witness, and in fact pervades the classical Christian confession of God in all historic Christian communions. Without simply reproducing the theology of the past, we *must* seek a modern formulation of the biblical doctrine of election that deepens our understanding of the grandeur of the gospel, and compels our wholehearted consent.

Part III on Creation begins by confessing God the Creator, for the emphasis of the Bible is not so much on creation as it is on the One who created all things according to his mysterious and gracious purpose. Central to this section are the opening chapters of the book of Genesis, whose rich theological witness has unfortunately been held hostage to stale and unworthy debates between science and "creationism." What do the opening chapters of the Bible say—on their own terms—about God's creation of the world? The part on creation then proceeds to reflect upon the covenant of God with humankind. Creation and covenant are tied together: creation is the outer setting for the covenant, while the covenant is the inner meaning of creation. The third part then narrows its focus within creation to the reality of humanity, both the old humanity cancelled out by the cross, and the new humanity set free by the resurrection. The doctrine of creation then moves to reflection upon the way of God in the world, or the traditional doctrine of divine providence. God rules over all reality; what are the surprising characteristics of his presence and rule? To what extent is his rule manifest to faith; and to what extent is his rule hidden, even from the eyes of faith? It then considers the traditional problem of evil, which in church doctrine means the triumph of divine order over the chaotic forces of evil that threaten the cosmos God created very good.

Part IV on reconciliation begins with the confession of the Incarnation, based on Scripture and attentive to the creeds of the early church. Even here, simple repetition is not enough; what does it mean for Christians today to confess Jesus Christ, truly divine and truly human, before the world? Included in this section is a consideration of the threefold office of Christ as prophet, priest, and king, for in him both the witness of the Old and the New are joined together. Attention is then focused upon the crucifixion of Christ, including the central Christian witness to the mystery of the atonement. From Good Friday, we move to Easter; the part on reconciliation treats of the resurrection of Christ on the third day, "according to the Scriptures." The cross and resurrection of Christ are God's free acts of reconciliation for all humanity, involving justification and sanctification, each in their place and order. God's free gift is received in faith, which is a life-encompassing passion.

Part V on redemption begins with the gift of the Spirit, which is life and joy in the fullness of divine power. It reflects upon the inbreaking rule of God, which comes with overwhelming force and is nevertheless hidden in surprise and wonder. The gospel calls into reality a new community, which is the church of Jesus Christ. What is the church, and what horizons guide its life in the contemporary world? What is the church's mission to the surrounding world, and what challenges does the church face in carrying out its mission in our world today? The church's confession asserts that the gospel has already transformed the whole of creation. Thus, the kingdom of God cannot rightly be separated from concern for a new society. What is the shape of that new society? There is an already to the gospel, but there is also a not yet; as Christians we look for the return of Christ at the end of the age. Freed from the hopeless misunderstanding of speculative timetables, what does it mean to look for the coming of Christ and the final consummation of all things? What does it mean to live by hope in light of the promise of the gospel? The part on redemption also includes the church's witness to baptism as a graphic sign of real unity with the risen Lord; and the celebration of the Lord's Supper, in which the return of Christ is eagerly anticipated.

Can we speak of a larger coherence encompassing the various loci of Christian doctrine? Indeed, we can and we must, in faithfulness to Holy Scripture. As the theological shape of Scripture makes clear, God's one eternal purpose for the world unfolds over time. It begins with creation; it is accomplished once and for all in reconciliation; it is consummated in redemption. The temporal sequence is not historical, in the modern sense of the word; for in each case, the divine acts of creation, reconciliation, and redemption are completely unique, without any possible analogy. They can be known only in reference to themselves, or better, in reference to God himself who acts in them. Nor is the temporal sequence fictional, or mythological; far from it, for God's action shapes all human life directly, with sovereign and unrestrained power. We have "heard . . . seen with our eyes . . . looked at . . . .touched with our hands" the revelation of God (1 John 1:1–5). It is best therefore to speak of the temporal sequence of Christian doctrine as a divine *event*; church doctrine comprises God's gracious action toward humankind. God's action encloses and determines all human history; yet God cannot be known from history. The Bible alone bears faithful witness to God's creative, reconciling, and redeeming event for the whole world. Church doctrine, on the one hand, must be aware of and preserve the temporal structure of Christian truth. Traditional doctrine speaks of the divine "economy," by which is meant the particular ordering of the one redemptive divine purpose for the world. On the other hand, church doctrine also insists upon the ontological unity of the one God who alone guides his active love for humankind, from start to finish. The triune God, and he alone, is the One who creates, reconciles, and redeems; for indeed time itself is his creature, and his servant for our well-being: "In everything God works for good . . . according to his purpose (Rom. 8:28).

While we have spoken of a larger temporal coherence to Christian doctrine based on God's creative, reconciling, and redemptive event, we are not thereby endorsing narrative theology; in fact just the opposite is the case. By definition, narrative theology defines God as an agent rendered by a narrative. That is to say, God is "God" narrated in the text. Christian doctrine, by sharp contrast, confesses at the outset that the divine Agent attested in the text is in fact the living reality of God. "God" is in fact God, the one Ruler of all that exists. We *start* with this confession, which is identical to the faith of the church. Dietrich Bonhoeffer rightly insists: "When Genesis says 'Yahweh,' historically or psychologically it means nothing but Yahweh. Theologically, however, i.e., from the Church's point of view, it is speaking of God. God is the One God in the whole of Holy Scripture: the Church and theological study stand and fall with this faith."[19]

d. The Goal of Doctrine

In his groundbreaking treatise on theological method, entitled *On Christian Doctrine*, Augustine carefully sets forth a series of rules (*praecepta*) for both discovering and teaching the truth contained in Scripture. Church doctrine involves the difficult and subtle task of moving from the witness of Scripture—Augustine calls it the sign (*signum*)—to the reality of which Scripture speaks—which he calls the thing (*res*). Moving from witness to reality, from sign to thing, calls for strenuous reflection, and often enough leaves room for unresolved ambiguity. In such cases, a clear rule presents itself: the true catholic interpretation is that which conforms to "the love of God and of one's neighbor" (*ad diligendum deum et proximum*).[20] The

---

19. Bonhoeffer, *Creation and Fall*, 12.
20. Augustine, *Doctrine*, 88.

twofold rule of love is thus a comprehensive test for valid discovery and teaching of church doctrine. Yet even that is not enough; for what is love, if it is not put into practice? The goal of doctrine is not *assent* but *action*: "But when that which is taught must be put into practice and is taught for that reason, the truth of what is said is acknowledged in vain . . . unless that which is learned is implemented in action."[21] The only goal of truth is obedience; the only source of obedience is truth.

Church doctrine involves a careful attempt at precision and clarity; how can the truth by which we are reconciled to God deserve anything less? Nevertheless, church doctrine is anything but a lifeless deposit of abstract teaching. The gospel of Jesus Christ is God's overwhelming power of redemption for the whole cosmos; the gospel of Jesus Christ has already transformed the entire creation; the gospel of Jesus Christ brings radical transformation into every human life. The goal of doctrine is thus to bear witness to God's own transformation of the world in both word and deed. Rightly to understand Christian doctrine is to be forever changed; changed not a little here and there, but changed at the very core of our being. True affirmation of church doctrine brings new life: new ways of thinking about the world, new ways of making decisions in life, new ways of feeling about ourselves and our fellow human beings, new ways of caring for our own physical well-being and for the rights of others. Church doctrine attests the radical transformation of life under the rule of God in Jesus Christ. The goal of doctrine is thus growth in discipleship.

Church doctrine therefore necessarily includes theological ethics. Doctrine and ethics can never be separated, despite repeated attempts in the history of the church to make just such a separation.[22] What is genuine doctrine, if it does not also involve the claim of the gospel upon human existence in the world? And what is theological ethics, if it is not grounded in the living God of the gospel? Doctrine without ethics is empty; ethics without doctrine is blind. The separation between the two has left the church hopelessly confused, both in terms of a truncated doctrine and in terms of a theologically vacuous ethic. It is essential for church doctrine in our time to recover the living bond of doctrine and ethics for the confessing church of Jesus Christ, who is the one true embodiment of God's eternal will.

21. Ibid., 138.

22. According to Wilhelm Gass, the formal separation of theology and ethics takes place with the publication of Calixt's *Epitome Theologiae Moralis* in 1634. However, the *tendency*—as Gass carefully argues—goes back much further, at least to the time of Melanchthon. See *GCE* II, 278-83.

Therefore, at the end of each part (on canon, God, creation, reconciliation, and redemption) there will be a final chapter on ethics. At the end of the part on canon will be *general* ethical reflection on the divine imperative: what does it mean to live in the light of the divine command, according to Scripture? It is significant that the chapter on the divine imperative directly follows the central affirmation of the Trinity; for in church doctrine, to know God is to do his will. The living God who is in himself an eternal relationship of love desires a living relationship with all humanity in the obedience of faith. At the end of each of the remaining parts will be *special* ethical reflection relevant to the theological substance under consideration. At the end of the part on God will come theological reflection on the first part of the Decalogue, which is the traditional guide to the living response of love for God. At the end of the part on creation will come similar reflection on the second part of the Decalogue, where the church has always found its surest insights into love for neighbor. At the end of the part on reconciliation will come theological analysis of the Lord's Prayer as a general summary concerning the necessary and life-giving conversation with God undertaken by all who love, fear, and trust him above all things. Finally, at the end of the part on redemption, and therefore as the final chapter in church doctrine, is a chapter on the joy of discipleship, based on the Beatitudes. How can we end church doctrine anywhere else but with overwhelming joy?

# Part I: CANON

1

The Authority of Scripture

JOHN CALVIN IN HIS commentary on 1 Corinthians speaks of the architecture of church doctrine. A wise builder (*sapiens architectus*) must accomplish two essential objectives: start with the right foundation (*fundamentum*), and then erect the appropriate superstructure (*superficiem*). Christ himself is the only true foundation, and any theological argument constructed upon another basis must of necessity collapse: "For what is more destructive than confusing believers well grounded in pure doctrine, with a new kind of teaching, so that they are not sure where they stand..."[1]

Theological argument on both the religious left (theological liberalism) and the religious right (conservative evangelicalism) moves from *general* possibility to *particular* reality. Friedrich Schleiermacher's monumental book *The Christian Faith* for example moves in the famous introduction from general anthropology (*Ethik*), to the philosophy of religion (*Religionsphilosophie*), and then finally to specifically Christian piety.[2] A. A. Hodge, in his *Outlines of Theology*, a distillation of Princeton scholastic orthodoxy, likewise follows the same pattern of logic. Hodge begins with the nature of religion in general, moves to the science of religion, followed by theological science, proofs for God's existence, and then finally the inspiration of the Bible.[3] The structural logic of theology is the same in both,

---

1. Calvin, *CNTC* 9, 74.

2. Schleiermacher, *Christian Faith*, 3–128.

3. Hodge, *Outlines*, 15–81. The story on the religious right has changed little. Michael Horton, in his recent book *The Christian Faith*, provides his own summary of the structure of his prolegomena thus (205): "Working our way in concentric circles from

even though of course the conclusions are polar opposites. To return to the metaphor of Calvin, (which is of course ultimately the apostle Paul's, 1 Cor 3:10–15), it is as if the superstructure is erected first, and then the foundation is placed on top. Indeed, "Each builder must choose with care how to build..." (1 Cor 3:10).

The Bible, by sharp contrast, always moves from the *particular* event of God's call to the *general* horizon of human encounter with God. Out of all the nations of the earth, God calls Abraham. It is through this one man, Abraham, that all nations of the world will receive overwhelming divine blessing: "I will make of you a great nation, and I will bless you, and make your name great, so that you will be a blessing. I will bless those who bless you, and the one who curses you I will curse; and in you all the families of the earth shall be blessed" (Gen 12:2–3). Of all the nations of the earth, God elects only Israel to serve as his chosen people (the *particular*); yet through Israel, God's will is made known among all peoples of the world (the *general*): "I am the Lord, I have called you in righteousness, I have taken you by the hand and kept you; I have given you as a covenant to the people, a light to the nations..." (Isa 42:6). Jesus calls the disciples by name (the *particular*), yet gives to them an astonishing commission (the *general*): "you are the salt of the earth... you are the light of the world" (Matt 5:13–14). In each case, the call is particular, while the mission is universal, and the movement is always from the former to the latter.

The scandal of particularity simply cannot be set aside in the confessing community of faith. It is not hard to see that the logical structure of both liberal and conservative theology directly contradicts the inner logic of the biblical witness. Liberalism and evangelicalism move from the general to the particular; the gospel moves from the particular to the general. What is to be done? We can of course try to mediate between the general and the particular; we can try to build some kind of bridge, spanning the gap. Many have tried, and failed miserably, at a so-called mediating theology.[4] Or, we can start again from the beginning.

Instead of trying to fit the gospel into the alien logic of a general ontology or anthropology, we can reorient our theological reflection to the utterly alien logic of the gospel. Instead of beginning where it may be comfortable

---

the widest horizon — namely, ontology to epistemology and then to revelation and Scripture — we now arrive at the nature of Christian doctrine." Horton's book — whether he is aware of it or not — clearly shares more than the title with Schleiermacher's famous work.

4. A good account of mediating theology (*Vermittlungstheologie*) can be found in GNET 5, 364–430.

for us to begin, with the things we know, or think we know, about ourselves and the world around us, we can learn to recognize the hand of God in what is totally marvelous and strange: ". . . strange is his deed . . . alien is his work!" (Isa 28:21). Instead of erecting the doctrine of canon as a superstructure upon a previously derived view of religion as the foundation—as in both modern liberal and modern conservative theology—we can search for a new approach to theology built upon the foundation of the church's confession of canon. Instead of seeking to reform the message of Scripture by the self-validating authority of human religious piety, we can hope and pray for the reform of the church by the self-validating message of Scripture, which is the living word of God. The church at large faces an either/or; church doctrine can either take the easy road, which leads to more of the same; or it can take the hard road, which alone leads to life. We therefore begin, not with religion, but with Scripture, which is the Word of God.

a. Scripture as Norm

Church doctrine *begins* with reverence for Scripture. In so stating, we break radically with the predominate voices of the immediate present in Christian theology, conservative and liberal; nevertheless, we join a chorus of voices from the universal church of all times and places. Consider the following.

Gregory Nazianzus, in the second of his *Theological Orations*, states that the theologian must begin there alone where theological reflection can be fruitful: "Since, then . . . we have broken up for ourselves the fallows of divinity, so as not to sow upon thorns, and have made plain the face of the ground, being molded and molding others by Holy Scripture (*graphe*) . . . let us now enter upon theological questions (*theologias*) . . ."[5] Theology does not begin somewhere else, and then eventually arrive at Scripture; rather, the theological confession of Scriptural authority prepares the ground for fruitful theological labor. Adherence to Scripture *commences* the journey which constitutes genuine theological reflection.

In the opening articles of the *Summa Theologiae*, Thomas Aquinas points out that the appeal to Scripture is the logical foundation for everything else in theological science: "Hence Sacred Scripture, since it has no science above itself, can dispute with one who denies its principles only if the opponent admits some at least of the truths obtained through divine revelation (*per divinam revelationem*) . . . Since faith rests upon infallible

---

5. Gregory Nazianzus, *LCC* III, 136.

truth... Sacred doctrine (*sacra doctrina*)... properly uses the authority of the canonical Scriptures as an incontrovertible proof... For our faith rests upon the revelation made to the apostles and the prophets, who wrote the canonical books (*canonicos libros*)."[6] The affirmation of Scripture is the logical basis for everything else in theology. According to Thomas, we cannot arrive at that affirmation from somewhere else, unless we first begin with it. Confession of canon comes first in a strict logical sequence that cannot be reversed, without surrendering the essence of church doctrine.

Bonaventure similarly states that Scripture is based solely on authority, not on argument: "Therefore, lest Scripture appear doubtful and lose some of its moving power, God has given it, in place of the evidence of demonstration through reasoning, the certitude of authority; a certitude so absolute as to surpass any attainable by the keenest human mind."[7] The Bible may contain numerous forms of literature, including narrative, command, instruction, praise, and so forth; nevertheless, all forms of literature are encompassed by the overall concept of authority: "All these, however, are dependent upon the one principle of authority, and properly so."[8]

Melanchthon begins his summary of Christian doctrine by stressing the theological basis in Scripture. The purpose of doctrine is not to add to the teaching of Scripture, but precisely to direct the attention of the reader to the Scriptures themselves: "I am therefore merely stating a list of the topics to which a person roaming through Scripture should be directed ... I do this not to call students away from the Scriptures to obscure and complicated arguments (*disputationes*) but, rather, to summon them to the Scriptures if I can."[9] Only in the Scriptures does the reader find the certainty which constitutes living faith in the gospel: "There is nothing I desire more, if possible, than that all Christians (*christianos omnes*) be occupied in the greatest freedom with the divine Scriptures alone (*in solis divinis literis*) and be thoroughly transformed into their nature."[10] Such admonitions come in the Dedicatory Letter included already in the 1521 edition of the *Loci Communes*; Melanchthon would not have us arrive at this conclusion, but rather to begin with it, confessing our faith that we might learn to know what we believe.

---

6. Aquinas, *ST* 1, 5–6.
7. Bonaventure, *Breviloquium*, 17.
8. Ibid., 16.
9. Melanchthon, *LCC* XIX, 19.
10. Ibid.

According to John Calvin, the authority of Scripture is based on the inner working of the Holy Spirit, and therefore the message of Scripture validates itself apart from all human rational justification: "Let this point therefore stand (*fixum*): that those whom the Holy Spirit has inwardly taught truly rest upon (*acquiescere*) Scripture, and that Scripture indeed is self-authenticated (*autopiston*); hence, it is not right to subject it to reasoning and proof." The result is a submission of human will to the superior claim of Scripture: "We seek no proofs . . . but we subject (*subiicimus*) our judgment and wit to it as to a thing far beyond any guesswork!"[11] For Calvin then the "beginning of true doctrine" (*verae doctrinae initium*) is nothing other than "a prompt eagerness (*prompta alacritas*) to hearken to God's voice."[12]

In each of these statements from the mainstream of orthodox Christianity, the direction of theological argument moves, not from the *general* (a theory of religion, ontology, anthropology, etc.) to the specific; but rather from the *specific* of the church's special relation to Scripture, to the general task of theological witness. We do not *arrive* at the authority of Scripture from somewhere else; we *begin* here, confessing our faith. If we begin somewhere else, then the authority of Scripture is a function of whatever reason or judgment precedes and grounds it; theology as a whole then becomes a sovereign abstraction, closed off from the living content of the Bible (as Thomas points out, above). Only if we begin church doctrine with our confession of canon is theological reflection truly open to the radically new Voice which speaks through the Bible: which is the voice of Christ, the Good Shepherd, who in fact holds the whole cosmos in is hands: "and the sheep follow him because they know his voice" (John 10:4).

Because the *authority* of Scripture comes logically first; because the content of Scripture is self-validating, Scripture is therefore the norm for Christian faith and practice in such a way that there is no appeal behind, above, after, or around it. Scripture is the active norm in the church, above which no other norm stands supreme (*norma normans sed non normata*). It is not we who measure the Bible, even in our piety; it is the living God of the Bible who measures us. The authority of Scripture therefore at the same time points to the *freedom* of Scripture to maintain its own active witness within the church, free from the all-consuming constraints of human

---

11. Calvin, *LCC* XX, 80.
12. Ibid., 81.

self-interest. Scripture is free insofar as it continually speaks its own Voice, among the many legitimate and necessary voices of the church.

According to the prophet Amos, God himself measures his people by the only true measure, which is his own justice and righteousness: "This is what he showed me: the Lord was standing beside a wall built with a plumb line, with a plumb line in his hand . . . Then the Lord said, 'See, I am setting a plumb line in the midst of my people Israel . . .'" (Amos 7:7-8). According to the book of Deuteronomy, the command of God is sovereign and utterly compelling: "You must therefore be careful to do as the Lord your God has commanded you; you shall not turn to the right or to the left" (Deut 5:32). According to the book of Proverbs, authentic human wisdom is derived only from recognizing the self-validating force of the divine word: "Every word of God proves true; he is a shield to those who take refuge in him" (Prov 30:5). In the Sermon on the Mount, Jesus makes it clear that the normative authority of Scripture remains constant and undiminished: "Do not think that I have come to abolish the law or the prophets; I have come not to abolish but to fulfill. For truly I tell you, until heaven and earth pass away, not one letter, not one stroke of a letter, will pass from the law until all is accomplished" (Matt 5:17-18). The normative quality of Scripture is not an alien authority imposed on the Bible, which somehow offers itself in a different light, such as a religious classic; rather, to adjust our faith and practice to Scripture as norm is to recognize the authority and freedom that it clearly claims for itself. To confess Scripture as canon means to accede to Scripture the intrinsic right to function as norm for Christian life.

As the norm of Christian existence, Scripture exercises both *authority* over, and *freedom* within, the church. The dialectic of authority and freedom is a crucial and delicate balance, and easily comes unraveled, as the history of church doctrine certainly confirms.

The logic of Scriptural *authority* in the church of Jesus Christ has not fared well on the religious left. In his popular handbook on theology, *Faith Seeking Understanding*, Daniel L. Migliore sets himself the task of developing a "liberative understanding of the authority of Scripture."[13] During the time of the Reformation, according to Migliore, the Bible was experienced as a "liberating message"; today, by contrast, the Bible is held to be a coercive authority invoking "terror rather than joy."[14] There is for Migliore an

---

13. Migliore, *Faith Seeking*, 44.

14. Ibid. Terror in the face of Scripture is not a leading characteristic of contemporary theology, in my experience. The domestication of the Bible on the religious left and

either/or; either the Bible retains coercive force and evokes terror, or it liberates and evokes joy. According to Migliore the Bible launches "relentless criticism" against all forms of authority in competition with God, and that includes religious doctrines and traditions, as is evident in the condemnation of the Pharisees by Jesus. In sum: Migliore argues for an "authority of liberating love that creates new community rather than an authority that works by coercive power."[15]

I wonder whether it is really that simple, or simplistic. Did the Reformers truly avoid all talk of the coercive power of the Bible? Surely if any did, it would be Luther; yet what did Luther truly say about the authority of the Bible over Christian life? In his *Lectures on Romans*, Luther speaks of the victorious power of God's Word, which overturns and overcomes all human resistance: "And he is victorious in his words when his word prevails against all who try to oppose it—as it has happened with the gospel, which always is and has been triumphant. For the truth is all-victorious."[16] For Luther there is no opposition between the authoritative power of the gospel on the one hand, and its liberating message on the other; the one merely confirms the other. Does the Bible have no coercive force in our lives? Again from *Romans*: "To change our mind is the purpose of every word of Scripture and every action of God."[17] The whole *point* of the Bible is to reach down into the depths of our existence, overcoming our blindness and obstinacy, making us wholly new. Does the Bible ever tell us something that we do not want to hear? Of course it does, indeed at the heart of the gospel, which is the cross: "Hence, we cling to truth when it has an attractive appearance, but we despise it when it appears to be unattractive—as it always does, as we can see in Christ who 'had no form or comeliness.' So it is the case with every truth that goes counter to our thinking."[18] For Luther, the gospel not only *sometimes* greets us with an alien force of logic, it *always* does; for it tells us that God himself was concealed in the frailty of Christmas morning. It is *we* who must adjust to that alien logic, for only by doing so do we receive the liberating message hidden within this utterly contrary truth. Again from *Romans*: "Therefore, we must always be ready to surrender our own point of view so that we do not stumble on this rock

the religious right has made the Bible quite comfortable indeed.
15. Ibid., 47.
16. Luther, *LCC* XVI, 54.
17. Ibid., 83.
18. Ibid., 96.

of offense, i.e., the truth which in humility stands over against us and is contrary to what we think it ought to be. We are so presumptuous as to believe that only what we think is the truth, and we want to hear and see as the truth only what we agree with and approve. But this cannot be."[19] Indeed, this cannot be, as we must state in disagreement with Migliore. This *surrender* is precisely the "joyful and free willingness"[20] that characterizes genuine discipleship.

More importantly, did *Jesus* condemn all "religious doctrines" as false authority, as Migliore maintains? The key passage is of course the confrontation between Jesus and the Pharisees over the "tradition of the elders" (Matt 15:1-20). The disciples of Jesus are accused by the Pharisees of not following established religious custom; the attack is of course only indirect, for Jesus himself is the real target. If Migliore is right, the response of Jesus should be: you Pharisees are wrong, because God's liberating word is about freeing human beings, not binding them. Is that what he says? In fact, exactly the *opposite* is the case. Jesus accuses the Pharisees of using moral custom as a *shield* from the binding and authoritative force of the divine command: "And why do you break the commandment of God for the sake of your tradition?" (Matt 15:3). It is not at all that the Pharisees are standing for the coercive force of the divine word, while Jesus is defending "liberating love." Rather, the Pharisees are *avoiding* the true requirements of love (in this case for father and mother) by hiding behind their *liberating* moral tradition. Jesus exposes their hypocrisy, not by critiquing the coercive power of the divine word, but by *appealing* to it: "So, for the sake of your tradition, you make void the word of God. You hypocrites!" (Matt 15:6-7). Comments Calvin: "And so the worship of God is vitiated, for its principle and head is obedience."[21] In the Bible, the elements of obedience, surrender, submission to God, service, are hardly missing (as every reader of Scripture well knows), nor do they in any way cancel out the notes of joy. Against Migliore we must affirm: there is a compelling force to Scripture. The Bible may not say what we at first expect, whether our inclinations are conservative or liberal; but it is our expectations that must give way to something *infinitely* more valuable than yet one more liberal or conservative platitude. The Bible may not proclaim what we first desire; but it is

---

19. Ibid., 103.
20. Ibid., 389.
21. Calvin, *CNTC* 2, 156.

our desire that is ultimately absorbed by a divine satisfaction *qualitatively* greater than all possible human fulfillment.

On the other hand, the logic of Scriptural *freedom* in the church has eroded considerably on the religious right. The culprit is the now almost universal notion within conservative evangelical circles of a "Christian worldview" into which the Bible itself is inserted. Though often portrayed as a traditional idea, the fact is clear that the very notion of a "worldview" did not come about until the Enlightenment philosophy of Immanuel Kant. Only on the condition of the possibility of a transcendental Self is the idea of a worldview even meaningful; nor was it ever asserted before Kant. The *first* observation therefore that needs to be made—contrary to expectation, certainly—is that the use of "worldview" language among Christian conservatives is an embrace of the Enlightenment, certainly not traditional church doctrine. Furthermore, the first theologian to teach a specifically *Christian* worldview was the Dutch Reformed theologian Abraham Kuyper (1837–1920). Kuyper argues that Christianity presents a universal, all-encompassing conservative worldview, which is in "mortal combat" with the liberal worldview of "Modernism."[22] Of course his conservative "Christian worldview"—Kuyper is radically opposed to all notions of equality[23]—dovetails very nicely with his political involvement as founder and leader of the Anti-Revolutionary party in Holland. The *second* observation then is that from the very first use of "worldview" language among Christians it is pinned to a conservative, anti-liberal, political agenda.

Just as clearly as we affirm the *authority* of Scripture against the religious left, so clearly must we affirm the *freedom* of Scripture against the religious right. The Bible is the Word of *God*; it cannot and will not allow itself to be enclosed within a "worldview." Worldviews are invented by human beings, and they come and go with the passing fads and gimmicks of the era; the Bible is *God's Word* that endures forever, and speaks afresh with sovereign freedom in each new age of the church. Now, the notion of a "Christian worldview" grew up on the soil of Dutch neo-Calvinism; it is therefore certainly fair to ask: does it represent Calvin's own view?

According to Calvin, first the law, prophets, psalms, and writings of the Old Testament; and then the apostolic testimony of the New; are given to the church as a written standard beyond which the church may not stray: "Let this be a firm principle: No other word is to be held as the Word of God

---

22. Kuyper, *Calvinism*, 11.
23. Ibid., 95.

and given place in the church, than what is contained first in the Law and the Prophets, then in the writing of the apostles; and the only authorized way of teaching in the church is by prescription and standard of his Word."[24] The Word is free to speak its own Voice, and no subtraction or expansion can be allowed. Now, the crucial point is this: Calvin is not insisting upon the absolute freedom of the word against a "secular humanist worldview"; rather, he maintains the exclusive freedom of God's Word against its Christian *religious* distortion: "For sensible men see how perilous it is if men once be given such authority. They also see how great a window is opened to the quips and cavils of the impious if we say that what men have decided is to be taken as an oracle among Christians."[25] To surround Scripture with an all-encompassing religious worldview is to claim for human beings an authority which only God's Word possesses, and thus to open the church to the charge of religious distortion: "They should acknowledge one King, their deliverer Christ, and should be governed by one law of freedom, the holy Word of the gospel . . . They must be held in no bondage, and bound by no bonds."[26] God's Word alone is God's Word; it can and must retain its freedom to critique every "worldview," but especially a "Christian worldview." That is Calvin's view.

Is there a "Christian worldview" in the Bible itself? We return to the same passage expounded above, in which Jesus confronts the Pharisees (Matt 15:1–20), now looking at it from the angle of the *freedom* of the Word. We have argued against the religious left that Jesus most emphatically appeals to the sovereign and compelling authority of the commandment of God. What, we now ask, is the target of his appeal, the object of his critique? The moral customs of the Pharisees (tradition) have been put into place in order to protect the sanctity of the divine will. In modern terms, there is a religious worldview in which God's command is the center. How does Jesus respond? Does he embrace the worldview in order to protect the divine command? Despite their good intentions, the Pharisees not only fail to *protect* the sanctity of the divine will by their moral custom; in fact, they *circumvent* it. "For the sake of your tradition, you make void the word of God" (Matt 15:6). Above we stressed the basis of the appeal of Christ in the *authority* of the divine command alone (against the religious left); here we must equally stress the appeal of Christ to the *freedom* of the divine word

---

24. Calvin, *LCC* XXI, 1155.
25. Ibid., 1164.
26. Ibid., 1180.

over against an explicitly traditional religious morality. The role of the Bible is not to undergird a conservative moral-political agenda; it is rather to contradict, and indeed to overturn it.

There can be no authority of the Bible over the church, where there is no freedom of the Bible within the church; there can be no freedom of the Bible in the church, where there is no authority of the Bible over the church. Or said in a positive formulation: the true freedom of the Bible binds us; the true authority of the Bible sets us free.

b. Scripture as Witness

Holy Scripture is a witness to Jesus Christ. It is not a religious classic; it is not a collection of theological symbols and metaphors; it is not a monument to human piety. Holy Scripture is a living and authoritative witness to the reality of God in Jesus Christ. There is a limit implied in this role that it performs: Scripture is not the reality itself, but points to the reality. There is also a secure and living connection that can never be ignored by the church: Scripture alone is the truthful and reliable witness to God's self-manifestation in Jesus Christ for the redemption of the world. The role of witness is not conferred on Scripture by the church; rather, the church recognizes the role that Scripture as witness to Jesus Christ plays in the ongoing response of faith. The role of witness is built into the theological shape of Scripture itself, and corresponds as well to the subject-matter of which it speaks. Of course, Scripture can be read in many other ways, for example as a source for the understanding of ancient religious history. Church doctrine has no interest in denying other uses. Nevertheless, the confessing faith of the church insists that the role of witness corresponds to the self-presentation of Scripture itself. Scripture *functions* as witness in the church because Scripture *is* a witness to the risen Lord of whom it speaks. That is true of its final form; that is also true of earlier written and oral levels of tradition. Scripture as a whole is kerygmatic: "You search the scriptures because you think that in them you have eternal life; and it is they that testify on my behalf" (John 5:39).

The role of Scripture as witness is tied to the Incarnation of God in Jesus Christ. God entered time and space; God became a human being, without being any less God. All time and space are not a revelation of God; rather, God entered a specific time and space, in the full reality of life: "And the Word became flesh and lived among us . . ." (John 1:14). Even here a response of faith is required: when God entered the world, only the shepherds in the fields received the revelation of God's overwhelming glory in this birth, while all in the nearby city slept the night away. God is hidden, even in his self-revelation. Expected eagerly in the Old Testament, remembered gratefully in the New Testament, the time and space of God's Incarnation retains the offense of particularity, which cannot be erased. We were not there; others were not there. The apostles and prophets were there, and bear witness to the One whom they have seen and touched: "We declare to you what was from the beginning, what we have heard, what we have seen with our eyes, what we have looked at and touched with our hands, concerning the word of life . . ." (1 John 1:1). The biblical witness points to the fulfilled time of God's self-demonstration for the joyous redemption of all humanity: "this life was revealed, and we have seen it and testify to it, and declare to you the eternal life that was with the Father and was revealed to us . . ." (1 John 1:2).

The role of Scripture as witness is a direct implication of the astonishing form of God's self-revelation in Jesus Christ. Witness and Incarnation belong together. God's self-revelation did not end during the earthly life of Christ; Christ continues to rule his church, continues to make himself known, continues to govern all reality. God is known only in self-revelation, then as now. Nevertheless, now the exalted Christ makes known his grace and peace through the witness of the prophets and the apostles, chosen for that purpose by him. The apostles and prophets speak only because they are *called* to speak; only that *commission* authorizes the divine truth of their open speech to the community of faith and to the world. We are not apostles or prophets; we therefore learn Jesus Christ through the witness of Scripture, as we are taught by him: "But as for you, continue in what you have learned and firmly believed, knowing from whom you learned it, and how from childhood you have known the sacred writings that are able to instruct you for salvation through faith in Christ Jesus" (2 Tim 3:14–15). As disciples we learn Jesus Christ in the witness of Scripture.

We must distinguish between the *witness* of Scripture and the *reality* to which it points. In his now classic work *The Nature of Doctrine*, George Lindbeck offers a "postliberal" vision of Scripture in which all truth is *intrasystematic* in nature. Doctrine regulates truth claims, it does not make them. Thus, the Nicene Creed is not a first-order affirmation about the reality of the Triune God, but a rule concerning how speech about God ought to be conducted.²⁷ Doctrine makes no assertions; it only speaks about the meaning of assertions.²⁸ Scripture itself is "intrasemiotic or intratextual,"²⁹ (which of course is very different from the *intertexuality* of Scripture). Scripture is a "semiotic world" which is able to "absorb the universe."³⁰ Now, no one should doubt Lindbeck's commitment to the church, and to the truth of the gospel; no one should dare fall short of his love for the ecumenical catholicity of the church and the doctrine which it cherishes. The serious question remains however whether he has too quickly solved the problem of ecumenical *consensus* by a theory of doctrine that no *participant* in that consensus can fully affirm.

The fact is, self-referentiality is not a feature of the canonical biblical witness, and has never been recognized as such by ecumenical church doctrine. In the Western church, Augustine makes fully clear in his classic work *On Christian Doctrine* that there is a necessary distinction between sign and signified, grounded in the witness of faith: "All doctrine concerns either things or signs."³¹ There is therefore a subject-matter (*res*) to which the biblical witness points as a sign, and that requires careful theological reflection to discern. Similarly, in the Eastern church Athanasius in his *First Letter to Serapion* explicitly insists that the language of faith is not self-referential, but points to the living reality of the triune God: "It is a Triad not only in name and form of speech, but in truth and actuality."³² Again, in the Protestant tradition, Luther in *The Bondage of the Will* insists upon the distinction between text and reality, which must be maintained at all costs (here against the humanist Erasmus): "God and the Scripture of God are two things, no less than Creator and creature."³³ We are not redeemed by a text, but by the Redeemer of whom the witness of Scripture speaks; we are not baptized into a text, but into the Lord of whom the Bible testifies; we do not eagerly await the return of a text, but the coming One whose return the Bible promises in hope; we are not transformed by a text, but by the Spirit of Christ the true Lord of life, as attested in Scripture. We do not live in the

---

27. Lindbeck, *Nature*, 19.
28. Ibid., 69.
29. Ibid., 114.
30. Ibid., 116–17.
31. Augustine, *Doctrine*, 8.
32. Quoted in Quasten, *Ptgy* III, 67.
33. Luther, *LW* 33, 25.

world of the text, but in the flesh and blood world of creation of which the Scriptures speak, and which Christ himself entered making our lives whole.

Church doctrine cannot go the direction of postmodern theology in collapsing the subject-matter into the text itself. Interpretation of Scripture then too easily becomes simply an expression of underlying power relations, unchecked by the overwhelming force of the living substance of the Bible. Postmodernism is theological anarchy, a grasp of power against power: "all the people did what was right in their own eyes" (Judg 21:25). The church of Jesus Christ by sharp contrast lives under a gracious rule, which is the radically new reign of God in Jesus Christ. The rule of Jesus Christ over all creation is the one substance of the Bible, whose role as witness is grounded in his absolute authority. The rule of Christ the risen Lord is the one authority upon which Scripture itself is gounded, and by which Scripture of both Testaments is rightly measured and understood. If we take away these affirmations we take away the gospel. Luther rightly points out against Erasmus: "Nothing is better known or more common among Christians than assertions. Take away assertions and you take away Christianity."[34]

On the other hand, there can be no *separation* between the witness of Scripture and the living Lord of whom it speaks. We must therefore reject just as decisively the modern project of historical-referential reading, whether in its conservative-apologetic form, or in its liberal-reconstructive form.[35] To interpose the reason and experience of the reader between the meaning of the text and the reality to which it points, whether to separate them further (the liberal agenda) or to show their mutual fit (the conservative agenda), is a false move for church doctrine. Scripture alone, and not human reason and experience, truthfully bears witness to the risen Christ. Church doctrine rejects ostensive reference—with its talk of "claims" and "evidence"—just as clearly and decisively as it rejects self-referentiality in its affirmation of the authority of Scripture. Scripture makes *assertions*, not claims; it rests on divine truth, not on rational evidence. Through the active presence of the Spirit, the voices of Scripture are the voice of Jesus Christ himself. The truth of Scripture is the truth of Christ; the comfort of Scripture is the comfort of Christ; the instruction of Scripture is the instruction of Christ; correction by Scripture is correction by Christ. We cannot say that

---

34. Ibid., 21.

35. The story of that separation between meaning and truth is told with luminous clarity in Hans Frei, *The Eclipse of Biblical Narrative*.

Scripture created the world; but we can and must say that Scripture *alone* faithfully testifies to the one Creator of the heavens and the earth, whom no eye can see, no ear can hear. We cannot say that Scripture reconciles us to God; but we can and must say that Scripture *alone* bears the message of reconciliation, by which we live joyously in the world. We cannot speak of a hope for redemption by Scripture; but again we can and must say that our living hope is grounded *solely* in the biblical promise, which is more true than our own experience of life itself. There can be no separation between the witness of Scripture and the reality of which it speaks. When the Scriptures speak, God speaks, as Luther states: "Neither councils, fathers, nor we, in spite of the greatest and best possible success, will do as well as the Holy Scriptures, that is, as well as God himself has done."[36] A distinction is theologically essential; a separation is theologically catastrophic.

Because Scripture is a witness to Jesus Christ, it becomes clearer that the authority of Scripture is in fact christologically based. The authority of Scripture as witness is derived from the absolute authority of the One to whom it bears witness. This is not a limitation of Scripture's authority, but quite the contrary its only true significance. We ascribe authority to Scripture in the church because we worship Jesus Christ. We adhere to the authority of Scripture because we are bound to Christ, in life and in death. The authority of Scripture is as wide as the rule of Christ, which is universal over all reality. The authority of Scripture extends as far as the rule of Christ, which pervades all creation, and governs all nations and peoples. The authority of Scripture is based upon the rule of Christ, for it is Christ himself who chose these witnesses then, and uses these witnesses now to make known his will through the gift of his Spirit. The Bible must be received by the church in its proper role of sacred Scripture, and it is received in a confession of faith; but the church's reception does not *create* an authority which is otherwise absent. The church's reception of Scripture *recognizes* an authority that is itself grounded elsewhere: namely, in Jesus Christ himself. "Whoever welcomes you welcomes me, and whoever welcomes me welcomes the one who sent me" (Matt 10:40). So says Christ to the apostles, and so says the same Christ, crucified and risen, to those who receive the prophetic and apostolic word even in our world today.

---

36. So Luther, in his *Preface to the Wittenberg Edition of Luther's German Writings 1539*, LW 34. Cf. Luther, LW 34, 284.

c. Word and Spirit

Church doctrine of all times and places confesses that Scripture is the word of God. God is the author of the Bible. Hidden within this confession is a mystery which the church of Jesus Christ has always refused to unravel.

On the one hand, the Bible is written by human beings, indeed fallible human beings. Both the Old and the New Testaments make no attempt to conceal the sheer humanity of those who bear the divine word to the community of faith and to the world. In many cases the human speakers are carefully noted: "These are the words that Moses spoke . . ." (Deut 1:1); "The words of Nehemiah, son of Hacaliah . . ." (Neh 1:1); "The proverbs of Solomon son of David, king of Israel . . ." (Prov 1:1); "The vision of Isaiah son of Amoz . . ." (Isa 1:1); "The words of Jeremiah son of Hilkiah . . ." (Jer 1:1); "The Gospel According to Matthew"; "Paul a servant of Jesus Christ . . ." (Rom 1:1); "Peter, an apostle of Jesus Christ . . ." (1 Pet 1:1), etc. Modern notions of authorship are not implied, and in many cases are tangential. Nevertheless, the key point is that the sheer humanity of the Bible is left fully intact by its transmission within the community of faith. Confession of canon means full acceptance of the humanity of the biblical writers.

Yet on the other hand, the church confesses with one voice that the entire Bible, including its message and the words which convey it, is the word of *God*. The Christian Bible makes it abundantly clear that the God of Scripture, both Old and New Testaments, *speaks*. God created the world by speaking (Gen 1:1-3); God announces himself as both the beginning and end of all that exists (Rev 1:8). God's voice summons creation into being, will one day bring all creation to its ultimate fulfillment in him; and between the time of the beginning and the time of the end, speaks within that creation: "The mighty one, God the Lord, speaks and summons the earth from the rising of the sun to its setting" (Ps 50:1). Thus, in making the confession that the Bible is the word of God the church does not act with caprice; rather, it affirms what it finds in the Bible itself. Every faithful reader of the Bible knows by heart the constant refrain: Thus says the Lord . . .

The mysterious link between the human word of the authors and the divine voice that speaks through them is contained in the church doctrine of *inspiration*. Again, in confessing the inspiration of the Bible, the church—which has of course maintained this doctrine in all communions since the advent of the community of faith—is simply honoring the truth of Scripture. The Spirit, according to the Niceno-Constantinopolitan Creed (381), "spoke through the prophets" (*to lalesan dia ton propheton, qui locutus est per prophetas*).[37] Inspiration is universal throughout the Bible, though it is acknowledged in various ways. On numerous occasions, the narrative simply pauses to describe the majestic divine appearance, who speaks. God's words are then to be delivered to the people: "Then I heard the voice of the Lord saying, "Whom shall I send, and who will go for us?" And I said, Here I am; send me!" And he said to me, "Go and say to this people . . ." (Isa 6: 1–12). At other times, common formulae simply record the fact—supreme in its utter mystery—that God has spoken: "Thus the Lord said to me . . ." (Jer 13:1); and, "The Word of the Lord that came to Jeremiah . . ." (Jer 14: 1). Furthermore, the Bible quite often makes it clear that the inspired divine word is written down for the instruction of generations yet to come: "When Moses had finished writing down in a book the words of the law . . . Moses commanded the Levites . . . Take this book of the law and put it beside the ark of the covenant . . . let it remain there as a witness . . ." (Deut 31:24–26). God's inspired word is not only spoken, but written.

The words of the Bible are God's inspired word. Yet how is it possible to receive these fallible human words as the word of God himself? The doctrine of inspiration is only completed by the necessary corollary of divine *illumination*. It is not only because they are inspired by God, through the presence of his Spirit; it is also because the same Spirit even now illumines the community of faith to a fresh hearing and understanding of his word; that the words of the Bible are the word of God. The Bible repeatedly makes it clear that the word of Scripture is not limited or confined to the past: "So we have the prophetic message more fully confirmed. You will do well to be attentive to this as to a lamp shining in a dark place, until the day dawns and the morning star rises in your hearts" (2 Pet 1:19). Through the presence of the Spirit of the risen Lord, the Scriptures continue to serve as a medium through which Christ himself guides his church in each new age through the living word of the gospel: "So that your trust may be in the Lord, I have made them known to you today—yes, to you" (Prov 22:19). God's revelation did not cease with the church's confession of canon; rather, God continues to reveal himself—how else can we know him?—through the divine illumination of Scripture by the Spirit.

The theological affirmation of inspiration is therefore dialectically bound to the equally important affirmation of illumination. The same Spirit who inspired the Bible illumines the reader today to a genuine

---

37. Pelikan and Hotchkiss, eds., *CCFCT* I, 163.

understanding of the divine word. Apart from the miraculous work of the Holy Spirit in the present, the Bible is misunderstood and distorted; only the Holy Spirit makes alive the message of the Bible for every new generation of the church. Not reason and experience, not cultural or political ideology, but the Spirit of God guides the church to a true understanding of the witness of Scripture, sealing on our hearts and minds the living word of Jesus Christ. Affirmation of the present work of the Holy Spirit in illumining Scripture is found in all the major confessional traditions of the Christian community, along with inspiration. Already in the early church, for example, Origen stresses the dynamic connection between inspiration and illumination. He states categorically: ". . . the Scriptures were composed by the Spirit of God." But then he adds the crucial corresponding clarification: "On this point the entire Church is unanimous, that while the whole law is spiritual, the inspired meaning is not recognized by all, but only by those who are gifted with the grace of the Holy Spirit in the word of wisdom and knowledge."[38] Inspiration of the Bible by the Spirit is only affirmed and understood by those illumined by the same Spirit.

Still, it was especially the Reformation which brought more conceptual precision to the doctrine of illumination through their concept of the inner witness of the Holy Spirit (*testimonium spiritus sancti internum*). Indeed, according to Wilhelm Neuser, the doctrine of the inner witness of the Spirit is a genuine creative theological insight of the Reformers, despite its more unreflective presence in earlier sources.[39] While the roots of the full reformation doctrine are clearly present in Luther, the inner witness of the Spirit is most carefully worked out theologically by Calvin. Calvin asserts without fuller explanation the inspiration of the Bible, by which the truth of the biblical word is forever rendered "superior to all opinion."[40] He simply assumes the traditional position hammered out by the church fathers: the prophets and apostles were "sure and genuine scribes of the Holy Spirit."[41] The Word of God given to the prophets and apostles was written down so that future generations might learn the truth from one generation to the next: the word of God written is Holy Scripture. Nevertheless, Scripture must be confirmed among the community of faith; Scripture must be received by those who cherish the message of the gospel.

38. Quoted in Quasten, *Ptgy* II, 92.
39. See Andresen, et al., *HDThG* 2, 244.
40. Calvin, *LCC* XX, 71.
41. Calvin, *LCC* XXI, 1157.

The work of illumination, like the work of inspiration, is the work of the Holy Spirit, and the two movements can neither be separated nor collapsed: "The same Spirit, therefore, who has spoken through the mouths of the prophets must penetrate into our hearts to persuade us that they faithfully proclaimed what had been divinely commanded."[42] Because of the testimony of the Spirit, Scripture cannot be subject to human proof and reasoning, and those who believe do not rest upon their own judgment, nor anyone else's, but above all judgment grasp the truth with "utter certainty."[43] By the power of the Spirit, Christians obey God "knowingly and willingly" in a way paradoxically greater than all human "willing or knowing."[44] Thus, for Calvin as for the other primary Reformers, the stress on illumination by the Spirit completes a circle of miraculous divine action which cannot be broken without distorting the very nature of faith itself.

As we have seen, the church doctrine of inspiration is grounded in the Bible; so too is the equally important doctrine of illumination. According to Isaiah, the sovereign creativity of God is self-grounded, self-moved, and utterly free: "Who has measured the waters in the hollow of his hand and marked off the heavens with a span, enclosed the dust of the earth in a measure, and weighed the mountains in scales and the hills in a balance?" (Isa 40:12). The sovereign work of God includes the movement of the Spirit, which is in no way coordinated with human capacity: "Who has directed the spirit of the Lord, or as his counselor has instructed him? Who did he consult for his enlightenment, and who taught him knowledge, and showed him the way of understanding?" (Isa 40:13-14). God's understanding is unsearchable (Isa 40:28). Yet the same God who is completely inaccessible makes himself known through his word, which is effective and cannot fail: "For as the rain and the snow come down from heaven, and do not return there until they have watered the earth . . . so shall my word be that goes out from my mouth; it shall not return to me empty, but it shall accomplish that which I purpose" (Isa 55:10-11). The word of God is not fleeting, but abides: "The grass withers, the flower fades; but the word of God will stand forever" (Isa 40:8). God's people will be restored only when the Spirit is poured out upon them "from on high," through an eschatological gift, " . . . and the wilderness becomes a fruitful field" (Isa 32:15). The Old Testament may lack the precision of the New on this issue, yet clearly the dynamic

---

42. Calvin, *LCC* XX, 78.
43. Ibid., 80.
44. Ibid.

action of the Spirit in illumination is fully present, and tied closely to the divine word.

In the New Testament, John's Gospel stresses the active role of the Spirit in the ongoing life of the community of faith, in which the Spirit is the living bond between the community and the risen Christ. The Holy Spirit will come to guide the new generation of the community—those who have not seen the earthly Jesus, but must believe—to a true understanding of the word of Christ: "I have said these things to you while I am still with you. But the Advocate, the Holy Spirit, whom the Father will send in my name, will teach you everything, and remind you of all that I have said to you" (John 14:26). The Spirit of truth cannot be received by the world, but leads the new community to a full grasp of the truth (John 14:17). The promised coming of the Spirit will guide the community of faith into all truth, and will point the community to the risen Christ whom he is sent to glorify (John 16:12–14). Furthermore, the apostle Paul stresses illumination by the Spirit as the only source of knowledge of God. What no eye has seen, what no ear has heard, what no human heart has conceived, God has revealed by his Spirit, who alone knows the purpose of God: "these things God has revealed through the Spirit; for the Spirit searches everything, even the depths of God" (1 Cor 2:10). Paul underscores the sheer incapacity for human receptivity to God, apart from the miraculous work of the Spirit: "So also no one comprehends what is truly God's except the Spirit of God" (1 Cor 2:11). Without illumination by the Spirit, human beings can discern nothing of God's will; yet those who are illumined by the Spirit comprehend the very "mind of Christ" (1 Cor 2:16). There is for Paul an absolute contrast between natural human capacity and the eschatological gift of the Spirit, who alone teaches the genuine knowledge of God.

Church doctrine also affirms the dialectical relation of Word and Spirit. We do not know God simply by reading the Bible; Scripture lies voiceless and dark apart from the illumination of the Spirit. Yet the Spirit does not work apart from the text of the Bible; rather, the Spirit gives the knowledge of God through the witness of the prophets and the apostles. The Spirit continues to guide the contemporary church to a true understanding of Scripture, and indeed instructs the church through its living experience with the Bible. The Spirit points to the risen Christ who guides his church in each new generation, and claims his church not only in the past but also in the present. The work of the Spirit cannot be collapsed into the Word; but nor can the Word be separated from the work of the Spirit. Once again, we make our confession in unity with the church universal. Calvin for example insists upon the unbreakable bond between Word and Spirit against the radical fanatics, who foolishly look for the Spirit apart from the Word: "For by a kind of mutual bond the Lord has joined together the certainty of his Word and of his Spirit so that the perfect religion of the Word may abide in our minds when the Spirit, who causes us to contemplate God's face, shines; and that we, in turn, may embrace the Spirit with no fear of being deceived, when we recognize him in his own image, namely, in the Word."[45] In the community of faith in Jesus Christ, we learn only from the Spirit—how else can we know God but by God?—yet we are instructed by the Spirit only through the witness of Holy Scripture.

The church doctrine of Word and Spirit must be affirmed against errors on both the right and the left. Evangelicalism errs by separating inspiration from illumination, grounding inspiration instead on the canons of human rationality and experience. A. A. Hodge, for example, establishes conditions for the possibility of inspiration based on the structures of human moral nature. Only when these conditions are met can inspiration be affirmed, based on "moral and spiritual evidences."[46] Inspiration thus becomes locked into a larger apologetic structure rationalistically defined, and entirely loses the Christological basis of the orthodox doctrine. Inspiration is "evidence" for something else; it is no longer a fundamental confession of faith in the risen Lord. Inspiration furthermore becomes tied to a referential reading of Scripture, including the authority of the "original autographs."[47] Hodge continues to speak vaguely of the testimony of the Holy Spirit, yet even the power of the Spirit is simply one more piece of *evidence*, ultimately based anthropocentrically on "instinctive confidence in the constitution of our own natures."[48] Hodge thinks he is reproducing the thought of the Reformers; but how much further can he be from the vigorous assertion of Luther: "The Holy Spirit is no skeptic, and it is not doubts or mere opinions that he has written on our hearts, but assertions more sure and certain than life itself and all experience."[49] By separating inspiration from illumination via a model of rational evidentiary argument, conservative evangelicalism profoundly undercuts the radically new world

---

45. Ibid., 95.
46. Hodge, *Outlines*, 66.
47. Ibid.
48. Ibid., 470.
49. Luther, *LW* 33, 24.

of the gospel, which we enter only by faith. Faith is a miraculous gift of the Spirit, not in any sense an exercise in human moral or rational capacity. Scripture does not move from human possibility to reality; Scripture always moves from astonishing new divine reality to miraculous possibility.

Nor has the story changed more recently on the religious right. In his comprehensive handbook of doctrine, Michael Horton, while he affirms the need for illumination as well as inspiration, limits the Spirit's illuminating work to the very syllables of Scripture in abstraction from its living content.[50] For Horton, as for conservative evangelicalism generally, revelation has *come to an end*; it is "past."[51] Yet how else can we possibly know God except by his own self-revelation—even now—through Word and Spirit: ". . . and no one knows the Father except the Son and anyone to whom the Son chooses to reveal him" (Matt 11:27). This is not a mere matter of words, but a crucial theological issue concerning the *continuing activity* of God's revealing work today through the witness of Scripture. Calvin is clear: "But the Father, who dwells in light inaccessible and is in Himself incomprehensible, is revealed to us by the Son (*a Filio nobis manifestari*) . . ."[52] The present infinitive makes it fully clear: God is even now actively revealing himself *to us*. Finally, Horton makes what can only be characterized as a catastrophic misjudgment, in my opinion, by committing himself wholeheartedly to the Hodge-Warfield doctrine of inerrancy.[53] This badly misguided commitment forces him to speak, for example, of "original autographs";[54] of "textual" as opposed to the banned "higher" criticism;[55] of the "*ipsissima verba*" of the biblical authors;[56] all profoundly outmoded legacies of outdated debates of the nineteenth century. To his great credit, Horton does his very best to make the Hodge-Warfield model work in something like a modern context; the glaring problem is that the effort is unnecessary and detrimental to faithful confession of Scripture from the outset. It has long since been known for example, at least since the original researches of August Tholuck in the nineteenth century, that Calvin was serenely unconcerned about errors in the Bible. When the Gospel of

---

50. Horton, *Christian Faith*, 168.
51. Ibid., 167.
52. Calvin, *CNTC* 2, 24.
53. Ibid., 176-81.
54. Ibid., 180.
55. Ibid.
56. Ibid., 177.

Matthew wrongly attributes a prophecy to Jeremiah, Calvin is clearly not worried: "How the name of Jeremiah crept in I cannot confess to know nor do I make much of it; obviously Jeremiah's name is put in error for Zechariah. Nothing of this sort is in Jeremiah, or anything like it."[57] Such passages are familiar to any reader of Calvin's commentaries, and stand in the sharpest possible contrast to the apologetic turn of nineteenth-century Princeton orthodoxy. Modern reformed fundamentalism is no match for the true evangelical freedom of the Reformer.

Liberalism on the other simply collapses inspiration into illumination, cutting itself free from the dialectical theology of the confessing church. Certainly the most prominent defense of the liberal Protestant position in recent decades has been offered by David Kelsey in his widely popular monograph, *The Uses of Scripture in Recent Theology*. Above all, Kelsey is concerned to argue that inspiration cannot even *meaningfully* refer to a theological dimension of the text itself, but can only be a second-order description of the *uses* of the Bible in the church.[58] The older theological liberalism would certainly argue that inspiration is wrong; Kesley goes further to argue that it is not even logically meaningful. The authority of Scripture is thus not based on any intrinsic claim of the text upon the church, but rather affirmed because of the function it performs in the life of the community.[59] Based on his reductionist view of functional authority—no one of course denies that Scripture functions as authority in the church, the question is the implication of this fact for the doctrine of Scripture—it is no longer the written word which provides the basic framework for theological coherence, but rather a logically prior act of metaphorical imagination which governs the reading of Scripture.[60] The result of his theological argument is that Kelsey dramatically and fatally reverses the relation of ecclesiology and christology: the church now functionally grounds the reality of Christ. By contrast, church doctrine affirms that it is not the church that grounds the reality of Christ, but Jesus Christ who grounds and governs the reality of the church: "I am the vine, you are the branches. Those who abide in me and I in them bear much fruit, for apart from me you can do nothing" (John 15:5). The church does not create the authority of Scripture by using it; rather, the church recognizes the authority of Scripture in a grateful

57. Calvin, *CNTC* 3, 177.
58. Kelsey, *Uses of Scripture*, 89.
59. Ibid., 47.
60. Ibid., 163.

act of discipleship: "We also constantly give thanks to God for this, that when you received the word of God that you heard from us, you accepted it not as a human word, but as what it really is, God's word, which is also at work in you believers" (1 Thess 2:13). The universal confession of the church does indeed—contra Kelsey—recognize a real theological attribute of Scripture, not based on evidence or rational proof, but solely because it is true. As Barth accurately and powerfully summarizes the position of the church, "Scripture is recognized as the Word of God by the fact that it *is* the Word of God."[61] We affirm this confession solely because it is sealed on our hearts and minds through the presence of the Spirit; whether it is logically meaningful to do so is of course a matter for logicians to decide, but make this confession we must and will. Again, against Kelsey we maintain that the ultimate criterion by which all theological reflection is guided and judged is not an act of human imagination, but the living Lord himself, Jesus Christ, who acts only as self-directed Subject, the "way, the truth, and the life" (John 14:6), and never as an object handed over to the function of church manipulation, whether conservative or liberal. Liberalism is no nearer to authentic church orthodoxy than is conservative evangelicalism; for orthodoxy proclaims the new world of God that transcends the inner conflict of human opinion in the radiant grandeur of truth.

d. Scripture and Community

The church's affirmation of canon involves a clear recognition of the indissoluble relationship between Scripture and the community of faith. By definition, canon includes acknowledgement of the bond that ties together the witness of Scripture and the community that reveres it, and lives by its rule. Canon means written Scripture shaped for the very purpose of serving as the instrument by which the living God instructs and guides each generation of the church. To say "canon" is therefore at once to speak of both the Bible and the community of faith. In that sense, canon certainly includes a functionalist dimension of authority. On the other hand, the church's affirmation of canon also draws a firm and irremovable line between *Scripture* and all later *interpretation* of Scripture. Indeed, the very writtenness of Scripture serves as a check against every attempt to absorb the text into the community. Scripture alone is the word of God; all later efforts of interpretation are to be carefully distinguished from the witness of

---

61. Barth, *CD* I/2, 537.

the text itself. The community of faith itself openly confesses that authority in the church lies in Scripture, as grounded in the exalted Christ.

Scripture and community belong together. In the Book of Deuteronomy, Moses convenes the new generation of Israel, a generation not present at the original events of exodus and Sinai. He declares however that the covenant of God given at Sinai *includes* the gathered community ready now to enter the promised land: "Not with our ancestors did the Lord make this covenant, but with us, who are all of us here alive today" (Deut 5:3). Moses repeats the Ten Commandments, enjoining upon the gathered community diligence in learning and observing the commandments. Moses emphasizes the careful requirement of obedience that flows from the divine command to the living community: "You must therefore be careful to do as the Lord your God has commanded you; you shall not turn to the right or to the left. You must follow exactly the path that the Lord your God has commanded you, so that you may live . . ." (Deut 5:32–3). The words recited by Moses are to be memorized, and handed on from each generation to the next; they are the constant guide for the life of the community, for God's abundant blessing enters their life together only in careful obedience. To speak of Scripture is to include the community that lives by it; to speak of the community is to point to the written Word that guides every step. Similarly, after the return of the exiles, and the completion of the wall, Ezra summons the people together in the public square. Ezra brings forth the book of the Law given to Israel. He reads the Law to the entire gathered people from a specially constructed platform so that all can hear and understood his speech; the people listen attentively, and weep as they hear the words. Others add interpretation so that the people can understand what is read: "So they read from the book, from the law of God, with interpretation. They gave the sense, so that the people understood the reading" (Neh 8:8). Scripture and community belong together in the living event of interpretation. Or again, according to Psalm 1, even the devout individual *within* the community has the same living relationship with the Scriptures. The one who takes delight in the Law of God is supremely blessed. Like a tree, planted by a flowing river, is the one who gives one's whole being to the understanding of God's revealed will: "on his law they meditate day and night" (Ps 1:2).[62] The Lord watches over the way of the blessed, whose life is filled with abundant and timely fruitfulness. In summary, a living relationship with Scripture is of

---

62. The Hebrew of the verse is of course singular, not plural.

the essence of the community of faith; and guidance in the community as the divine norm of life is of the essence of Scripture itself.

On the other hand, there is a sharp awareness in the Bible that the divine word must not be swallowed up by the agenda of the community. According to the biblical witness, this is the essence of false prophecy, which is not a straightforward unbelieving rejection of the word—that would be too easy, too obvious—but a distortion through the refracting power of human religiosity. Deuteronomy warns the community against divining prophets who would lead the community astray by false speech, even when their miraculous portents are successful (Deut 13). When such prophets come, the community must understand that their exclusive and total love for God is being tested, and the only genuine response is utter obedience to God alone: "The Lord your God you shall follow, him alone you shall fear, his commandments you shall keep, his voice you shall obey, him you shall serve, and to him you shall hold fast" (Deut 13:4). Jeremiah denounces the false prophets of hope where true peace is absent, who prophesy nothing but the delusional visions of their own minds (Jer 23). They are not sent by God; they do not speak the word of God; they are not to be heeded; they tell the people only what they want to hear, and not what God himself declares. According to Jeremiah, God himself hears the false prophecy that flows from them: "Who can hide in secret places so that I cannot see them? says the Lord. Do I not fill heaven and earth? says the Lord. I have heard what the prophets have said who prophesy lies in my name . . ." (Jer 23:23–25). The dreams of the false prophets are in sharp contrast to the authentic word of the faithful: "Let the prophet who has a dream tell the dream, but let the one who has my word speak my word faithfully" (Jer 23:28). There is no divinely mandated abstract ideological agenda or cause, no "burden of the Lord" for the community of faith; there is only the concrete word of God that must be obeyed. The apostle Paul chides the church in Corinth for thinking that the gospel can be specially trimmed to fit the needs of the Corinthian "context": "For who sees anything different in you? What do you have that you did not receive? And if you received it, why do you boast as if it were not a gift?" (1 Cor 4:7). The link between Scripture and community is inviolable; but so also is the proper proportion, which gives absolute priority to the former, though without in any way calling into question the integrity of the latter.

The error of the religious right is clearly to separate Scripture from the living community of faith. Karl Barth once made the charge that Protestant scholasticism turned the Bible into an abstract textbook of revealed propositions apart from its living use within a community of faith.[63] His charge was instantly pilloried by modern conservative evangelicalism—most recently by Michael Horton[64]—but the fact remains that Barth's observation must certainly be sustained on historical and theological grounds. The issue is most clearly evident in the Protestant scholastic doctrine of the Bible's spiritual effectiveness even before it is heard in the community (*efficacia extra usum*), a view which emerged during the Rahtmann controversy in the seventeenth century.[65] Early Lutheran confessional orthodoxy certainly retained a role for the church in relation to Scripture, although of course it was carefully circumscribed in light of Roman Catholic polemic. Leonhard Hutter in his well known textbook of doctrine, *Compendium Locorum Theologicorum* (1610), ascribes to the church the position of witness (*testis*) in relation to Scripture, but denies it the role of judge (*Iudicis*).[66] Scripture and church belong together; the church must be witness. A dramatic shift occurs marking the transition to high Protestant scholasticism. Hermann Rahtmann—a Lutheran pastor in Danzig—argued, clearly under the influence of emerging Pietism, that Scripture in itself, apart from the cooperation of the Spirit, is ineffective: "God did not reveal Holy Scripture, that it should remain outwardly, on paper, a mere letter; but rather that it should be living in us, spiritually . . ."[67] Johannes Quenstedt wrote the definitive orthodox response in a withering essay, *De Efficacia Verbi Dei* in which the thesis is defended: "The Word of God has, by the ordination and will of God, both before and outside of its legitimate use, intrinsic, divine, and sufficient power and efficacy for a spiritual and divine effect . . ."[68] Now, the theological problem is clear: of what use is it to speak of a "spiritual effect" apart from a community of faith? Even a sensitive and sympathetic

---

63. Barth, *CD* II/1, 514–26; Childs makes a similar charge in his *The New Testament as Canon*, 26.

64. Horton, *Christian Faith*, 181–84.

65. For a good, brief treatment of the Rahtmann controversy, see Lohse, *Short History*, 222–23.

66. Hutter, *Compendium*, 2. It is no different on the Reformed side. Wollebius refers to a twofold witness (*Testimonium . . . duplex*). The first is primary (*principale*), which is the testimony of the Spirit. The second is subordinate (*ministeriale*), which is the testimony of the church. Like Hutter, Wollebius insists that the church receives Scripture as witness. See Wollebius, *Compendium*, 3.

67. Hirsch, *Hilfsbuch*, 319.

68. Quenstedt, *De Efficacia*, 1.

expositor of Protestant scholasticism such as Bernhard Lohse is unconvinced: "The truth is that Orthodoxy, in spite of the greatness which must be attributed to much of its theological work, never satisfactorily solved the problem of the development of the doctrine of Holy Scripture, though this was a problem which had been peculiarly its own."[69] The Protestant scholastic notion of the Bible's *efficacia extra usum* drove the Reformation Scripture principle into the cul-de-sac (unnecessarily) of an abstract doctrinal system, where sadly their modern conservative progeny remain, unable to find an exit point.

Yet on the opposite end of the spectrum, Migliore clearly collapses the authority of Scripture into its use within the community, the very issue the Reformers were so concerned to "protest" against! According to Migliore, "the Bible is the Word of God only in a derivative sense."[70] That is to say, the Bible is not authoritative "in itself," but only as it "functions in the community of faith."[71] Of course it functions that way insofar as, and only insofar as, it speaks a "liberating" message to the world.[72] As with Kelsey's "imaginative construal," Migliore has decided in advance what the Bible is/must be about, and therefore that in which its authority must consist. If theological conservatism has distorted the Reformation Scripture principle into an abstract system of revealed propositions by its doctrine of the *efficacia extra usum*, theological liberalism has rendered mute the living voice of the gospel that encounters the church with a sovereign divine word of judgment and grace: "prepare to meet your God, o Israel!" (Amos 4:12). Despite Migliore's misleading appeal to the Reformers, Calvin's defense of Scriptural authority remains definitive. For Calvin, Scripture is not the Word of God in *any* derivative sense, but plain and simply: "Hence the Scriptures obtain full authority among believers only when men regard them as having sprung from heaven, as if there the living words of God were heard."[73] Moreover, while the Scriptures *function* as an authority in the church, the *basis* of that authority rests elsewhere: "But a most pernicious error widely prevails that Scripture has only so much weight as is conceded to it by the consent of the church. As if the eternal and inviolable truth of

---

69. Lohse, *Short History*, 223.
70. Migliore, *Faith Seeking*, 51.
71. Ibid.
72. Ibid.
73. Calvin, *LCC* XX, 74.

God depended upon the decision of men!"[74] Indeed, one is forced to question how such "liberation" as Migliore offers is distinguished from a new *tyranny* by the church itself.

The contemporary theological affirmation of canon overcomes the theological stalemate between the Reformation and Roman Catholicism on the issue of Scripture and Tradition. A modern convergence of positions on both sides has now made a unitary ecumenical position entirely possible and meaningful, not in the name of doctrinal indifferentism, but in the name of ecumenical truth. The early Protestant position was that Scripture alone is the source of our knowledge of God, *sola Scriptura*. The Counter Reformation position was that Scripture and Tradition together are necessary in the divine instruction of the church. How is the tension to be overcome? The key lies, I believe, in the distinction made by the historian Heiko Oberman between Tradition I and Tradition II.[75] Tradition I does not posit a second source of revelation apart from Scripture; it does however argue that Scripture is rightly understood only in the church. The history of obedient interpretation of Scripture is tradition. Tradition II does posit a *second* source of revelation alongside Holy Scripture. The mainstream of ecumenical church doctrine holds that Tradition I is valid and necessary; while Tradition II is invalid, and should not be sustained. Affirmation of canon means acknowledgement of the necessary link between Scripture and Tradition (understood as Tradition I), and at the same time the strict insistence on Scripture alone as the instrument by which the risen Christ guides his church (against Tradition II). There is thus a way forward beyond the two opposing historic formulations. In the context of debating any who would *separate* the Bible from the church, church doctrine stresses Scripture and Tradition; in the context of debating any who would *collapse* the Bible into the church, church doctrine stresses *sola Scriptura*. Both have their place in the divine economy of instruction: "Therefore every scribe who has been trained for the kingdom of heaven is like the master of a household who brings out of his treasure what is new and what is old" (Matt 13:52).

We will give the last word to the Eastern Orthodox theologian Theodore G. Stylianopoulos, who speaks in my opinion not only for his own tradition but for the church ecumenical: "The Bible as the supreme record of revelation is the indisputable norm of the Church's faith and practice.

---

74. Ibid., 75.
75. Oberman, *Forerunners*, 53–65.

The scriptures thereby bear God's authority and challenge the church, making it accountable to the revealed will of God . . . Everything in the Church must be in harmony with the scriptural witness."[76]

---

76. Stylianopoulos, "Scripture and Tradition," in ed. Mary Cunningham, et al., *Cambridge Companion to Orthodox Theology*, 25.

2

Theological Interpretation of Scripture

NOT LONG AFTER HIS revolutionary confession at Worms, Luther was brought to the Castle at Wartburg. Among other items on his feverish work agenda was a series of sermons based on the Gospels and epistles, ultimately known as the Wartburg Postil. Luther published the set of sermons at Wittenberg in 1522, and appended an introduction: "A Brief Instruction on What to look for and Expect in the Gospels" (*Eyn kleyn unterricht, was man ynn den Evangelijs suchen and gewartten soll*).

Luther begins his brief instruction by pointing out the common practice of numbering and naming the four Gospels, and simply leaving it at that; with the result that the gospel cannot be read in a "profitable or Christian manner" so that "people remain as pagan as ever."[1] The problem is profound; for the fact is "one should realize that there is only one gospel, but that it is described by many apostles."[2] Despite being narrated in different ways by the four canonical evangelists, there is only one gospel: "There you have it. The gospel is a story about Christ, God's and David's Son, who died and was raised and is established as Lord. This is the gospel in a nutshell. Just as there is no more than one Christ, so there is and may be no more than one gospel."[3] This one gospel of Christ is to be received first as a gift, and only then followed as an example: "This means that when you see or hear of Christ doing or suffering something, you do not doubt that

---

1. Luther, *LW* 35, 117.
2. Ibid., 117.
3. Ibid., 118.

Christ himself, with his deeds and suffering, belongs to you."[4] First comes promise, then command, and only in that order. Only so can we have a "proper grasp of the gospel."[5] Sadly, according to Luther, Christians no longer understand how to read the four Gospels; no longer know "what to look for and what to expect" in them.[6] The fact is, the Gospels were written for "this very purpose"; they "want to be our guides" in showing us the one gospel of God's free love in Jesus Christ.[7] All Scripture "tends toward him," who must be "comprehended" (*Vorfassett*) as he is presented in Scripture.[8] In sum, the gospel itself is our "guide and instructor" in reading Scripture.[9]

It is crucial to observe the brilliant dialectical thrust of Luther's argument. It is one thing to acknowledge and affirm the *authority* of Scripture. That much can be done, and yet the Scripture, even as the norm of church doctrine, can still remain an ultimately closed book. It is quite another thing to confess that Scripture *interprets* itself; that is, that the normative quality of Scripture includes the theological *framework* of Scripture. To use Luther's example, it is not enough simply to believe that the four canonical Gospels are the norm in the church, though that is certainly true. It is likewise essential to embrace the way in which the four Gospels all point to *one* gospel, which is their true and genuine theological context, as given in Scripture itself. Without recognizing the theological framework of Scripture—how Scripture itself guides the church to a true understanding of its content—only error emerges. For example, the deeds of Christ are interpreted first of all as examples to follow, which, says Luther, empties the promise of God of the certainty of truth. Instead the deeds of Christ are first of all a *gift* of mercy, and only then an example to follow. Luther's point is not that his is one "interpretation" of the Bible as opposed to another; Luther is emphatically *not* fighting for the freedom of interpretation, as he is so often portrayed in modern liberalism. Rather, his point is that Scripture itself is theologically shaped as a *guide* to interpretation, and only when that guide is followed is true, as opposed to false, understanding of the Bible attained. In summary, for Luther (and for the remaining Reformers) the *that* of Scriptural authority is always confessed in dialectical unity

---

4. Ibid., 119.
5. Ibid.
6. Ibid., 122.
7. Ibid.
8. Ibid.
9. Ibid., 123.

with the *what* of Scriptural truth; norm and interpretation mutually imply and condition one another. Sacred Scripture is its own interpreter (*sacra Scriptura sui ipsius interpres*).

Two and a half centuries later, the story is very different, though the difference is much easier to see now than it was to the participants at the time. In 1761, Johann August Ernesti published his *Institutio Interpretis Novi Testamenti*, which ran through numerous editions (I have in front of me the fifth). Not unlike Luther, Ernesti points out that interpreting the Bible is the "highest and most difficult task of the theologian."[10] All knowledge of divine truth comes, according to Ernesti, from a "right understanding and interpretation of the Scriptures."[11] Without question then, Ernesti agrees with Luther this far: Scripture is the *norm* of church doctrine. Yet that is where the agreement ends; now is where the open breach occurs, though unrecorded, unobserved. When it comes to *interpreting* Scripture, according to Ernesti, theology must rely, not on the theological framework of Scripture, but upon the *science of hermeneutics* (*hermenuetice*—Ernesti has of course Latinized the ancient Greek).[12] The science of hermeneutics contains the general principles for interpreting languages and texts; and interpretation of the New Testament must follow these general rules. Principles of interpretation are the same, whether the writing is sacred or profane; only "fanatics" (*fanatici*) try to separate the Bible as a sacred book from other human writings in the act of interpretation.[13] Ernesti's argument is clear: if a special guide is needed for understanding the Scriptures, then they do not communicate to humanity; only if they communicate in the universal language of rules of general interpretation, can they rightly be called a true "revelation."[14] All appeals to the Spirit, to the analogy of faith, to church doctrine, as guides to interpretation, must be abandoned forever. So Ernesti.

Clearly a radical shift has occurred in these pivotal two centuries. Luther holds the authority of Scripture as norm, and the interpretation of Scripture as content, *together* in the one act of confessing faith. Ernesti, by sharp contrast, tears them *apart*; the norm can be held, but the framework of interpretation of Scripture is no longer embraced in the confessing faith

10. Ernesti, *Institutio*, 2.
11. Ibid.
12. Ibid., 11.
13. Ibid., 25.
14. Ibid., 28.

of the church, instead it falls under the general rubric of human understanding. The story has changed little since Ernesti, on both the left and the right; the divorce between norm and interpretation remains firm. Our argument in this chapter will be straightforward: there can be no affirmation of the authority of Scripture as *norm*, which does not at the same time follow the theological framework of Scripture as *guide*. Norm and content belong together. But how?

a. The New World of God

On the first day of the week, two disciples are traveling along the road from Jerusalem to Emmaus (Luke 24:13-35). They converse together about the amazing events that have just transpired in Jerusalem, concerning the crucifixion of Jesus. The risen Jesus suddenly joins them on the journey, but they are kept from recognizing him. Their confusion about the meaning of the cross is apparent. They cannot understand how their hopes have been so terribly destroyed by the death of Jesus at the hands of the religious leaders. They have also heard the rumor concerning the empty tomb, but know nothing of its true meaning. Jesus then chides them for their foolish and sluggish response; he criticizes their failure to believe the prophetic promise. He emphasizes the divine necessity of the suffering of the cross as the exclusive way of the Messiah to glory. The risen Christ then interprets the entire Scriptures (the Old Testament of course) as a witness to himself, including all parts of the canon: "Then beginning with Moses and all the prophets, he interpreted to them the things about himself in all the scriptures" (Luke 24:27). Jesus himself is thus not only the true *content* of the biblical witness, but its true *interpreter* as well. Later, the two disciples are amazed at how their hearts burned within them, as Jesus "was opening" the Scriptures to them (cf. v. 32). When all the remaining disciples are eventually gathered, Jesus once again points to the entire canon, "the Law of Moses, the prophets, and the psalms" (v. 44); and once again opens their minds to a true understanding of the Scriptures (v. 45), which find their perfect and complete fulfillment in him. Jesus the risen Lord is the true interpreter of the Scriptures for the gathered community, even as he himself is the true referent for the entire biblical witness.

The church's confession of canon involves both affirmation of the authority of Scripture as norm, and the theological framework for the interpretation of Scripture as content. We have already seen that the authority of Scripture is christologically grounded; now it is crucial to add that the interpretation of Scripture is likewise grounded in the same authority of the exalted Christ. Theological interpretation is given to the church in freedom and responsibility; but interpretation is itself a response to the present rule of Christ over his church. Interpretation is thus a form of encounter; we search the Scriptures, because in them we encounter Christ present in church and world today. We are not simply referred to Christ by the Bible, and then sent back as it were upon our own resources; rather, the Christ who calls us to the Bible, also guides us in theological interpretation of those very Scriptures. We are fully active interpreters, using every skill of interpretation we can summon; yet also in some sense we are also profoundly receptive, waiting upon the Spirit of Christ to lead us from the pages of the text to the One of whom every passage speaks. Theological interpretation means encounter with the risen Christ through serious theological reflection upon the witness of Scripture. Theological interpretation is therefore an exercise in Christian discipleship, practiced in the confessing church, shared by the whole community of faith. Like all Christian discipleship, theological interpretation is an activity of obedience, and takes the form of joyful service to Christ. The energy which draws us to the witness of the Bible, and points us from witness to living reality, is the Spirit of God.

The Bible can obviously be read in any number of contexts. It can be read to provide information on the social world of ancient religion, and is commonly so read on the religious left. It can be read as a source-book for moral values, and is just as commonly so read on the religious right. Confession of canon means reading the Bible in the context of the church's living encounter with the risen Lord, through the gift of the Spirit. When so read, the Bible suddenly turns the "human search for meaning and truth" upside down; it speaks with a voice of stunning power and overwhelming excitement. It no longer addresses the human quest for religion, even true religion; now, it announces the self-revelation of God, which confronts us in the here and now with the life or death decision of faith. It no longer helps us to decide between competing moral claims; now, it brushes aside all competing moral claims, and places before us the living claim of God himself upon the totality of our being in every dimension: mind, will, emotion, body. It no longer offers us a collection of human religious opinions, even right and good opinions; now, it gives us God's own wisdom, which is beyond all human imagination, casting to the ground the utter folly of human pretense in the light of God's sheer grandeur. To borrow a phrase from Karl Barth, read in the context of canon the Bible contains the *strange new world of God*.[15]

Holy Scripture contains the new world of God. Scripture actively speaks with its own voice, summoning all the earth to listen, to learn, to understand. Scripture does not passively wait for human imagination and skill to evoke meanings according to human design. Scripture actively announces the new world of God that transforms the whole of creation. It is not our questions that are necessary in order to solicit biblical answers; rather, Scripture questions us, reducing our answers to nothing, and then giving us an answer that we in no way whatsoever can tell ourselves. The new world of God does not cancel out the need for theological interpretation. But it does certainly redirect the effort of interpretation toward a surprising new goal. We seek God in the Bible, only to discover that God has long since been searching for us. We look for answers in the Bible, only to discover that it is we who are questioned, and we who must give our answer in accountability to Christ. We examine the meaning of our humanity in the Bible, only to discover that God himself has redefined our humanity by entering our space and time as a human being. We look for insight in the Bible, only to discover that the wisdom of God shatters every human claim to moral competence, and enjoins upon us the single-minded devotion of obedience. The Bible inverts the ordinary act of interpretation; as we enter the new world of the Bible it is clear that *we* are being interpreted by Scripture. Paul makes this fully clear in his well-known inversions: "Not that I have already obtained this or have already reached the goal; but I press on to make it my own, because Christ Jesus has made me his own" (Phil 3:12). We search the Scriptures to enter the new world of God; but in so doing we come to discover that the new world of God has already entered our lives as a miraculous and gracious gift, and indeed has already transformed the entire cosmos.

The new world of God contained in the Bible is not a rational, propositional system, constructed according to the canons of human logic. The new world of God in no way owes anything to the canons of human logic. Indeed, before the majesty of God, such an enterprise is nothing short of ludicrous: "He who sits in the heavens laughs; the Lord has them in derision" (Ps 2:4). On the other hand, nor is the new world of God a celebration of postmodern indeterminacy. Meaning in theological interpretation is not the verbal play of the community. Quite the contrary, the new world of God

---

15. Barth, "The Strange New World Within the Bible," in *The Word of God*, 28-50.

invades human life with *all-consuming* determinacy: "Surely, this commandment that I am commanding you today is not too hard for you, nor is it too far away. It is not in heaven . . . nor is it beyond the sea. No, the word is very near to you; it is in your mouth and in your heart for you to observe" (Deut 30:11–14). Theological determinacy does not mean a simplistic approval of univocal meaning; it means rather that the multivalent Scriptures all point, without remainder, to one referent, which is Jesus Christ.

The church's guide in entering the new world of God is the theological framework of Scripture itself in its final form. Confession of canon not only means affirmation of Scripture as norm; canon also establishes the framework for the interpretation of Scripture. We now know—given the tools of historical research—what Luther could not know: that behind the final form of Scripture lies a lengthy history of growth in oral and written stages. We also know—what Luther and classical Christians knew intuitively, though they could not say why—that the Bible was shaped by the community of Israel and the early church over a lengthy process to bear confession to the living reality of God in Jesus Christ. The final, canonical form of Scripture is an *interpreted* text. That is to say, in each book, in each passage, in each section of the canon, a theological framework is present that actively guides faithful interpretation among those who share the faith of Israel and the early church. Confession of the authority of Scripture in the Christian community not only means the willingness to abide by the norm of this text; it also means to interpret this text within the context of the theological framework that is constitutive of canon. The final form of the Scriptural witness is not the same as the final level of redactional activity; the final form is the theological shape of the witness as a whole, the history of which is often obscure, but the effect of which is describable and definitive for church doctrine. The details of how each book of the Bible is theologically shaped for use in the community belong to biblical studies, not doctrine; however, doctrine insists that the theological framework of Scripture in its final form is normative for the church, and cannot be bypassed where living witness to Christ is sought in the Bible. The theological framework of Scripture does not forestall active interpretation, nor replace it; it is a framework only, with positive and negative checks. Nevertheless the canonical shape of Scripture alone offers the only basis upon which interpretation is faithful, relevant, and fruitful for the church and the world.[16]

---

16. For the theological framework of Scripture see Childs, *BTONT*, 107–322.

As one small example of the theological framework that affirmation of the canonical authority of Scripture enjoins upon us, we return to the issue raised by Luther. Is there one gospel, or four gospels? Again, we now know what Luther could not: that behind the present shape of the fourfold gospel collection lies a lengthy process of growth in oral and written tradition, some of which can be discerned historically, but much of which remains obscure. The *effect* of that shaping activity however is quite clear, and appears in the titles of the four Gospels. Luther surely assumed that each title was simply given to the Gospel by the person who "wrote" it; we now know the titles were assigned only in the collecting process. Yet the titles are essential, and paradoxically confirm Luther's very point. Each title is "The Gospel according to X." Not *Matthew's* Gospel, *Mark's* Gospel, and so forth; but the one Gospel according to (*kata*) Matthew, according to Mark, and so forth. There is one gospel, even though it is rendered by four different evangelists. The fact that the titles were not part of the original Gospels, but added by later editors, does not detract from the strength of Luther's point, but *emphasizes* it. The early church is saying this in its theological shaping: there is latitude in how you understand the gospel, in that it is given in four separate renderings; however do not be mistaken, there is only one gospel, and it is for that one gospel that you must search, as you interpret the divine word.

It at least bears mention: both the religious left and the religious right are agreed in following the tradition of Ernesti, which separates Scripture as norm, from Scripture as theological framework. Schleiermacher both solidifies and refines Ernesti's basic point: interpretation of Scripture is but the special application of a general approach to texts based on common understanding of human language and thought (*Hermeneutik*). What then becomes of the *content* of church doctrine? For Schleiermacher, that content is identical to the views of the contemporary church of each age, *not* the theological framework of Scripture: "The interpretation of Christian faith which validates itself (*was sich...geltend macht*) in each age as having been evoked by Scripture is the development, suited to that moment (*diesem Moment angemessene*), of the genuine original interpretation of Christ and His work, and constitutes the common Christian orthodoxy for that time and place."[17] The *norm* is Scripture; the *content* is the contemporary understanding of Scripture based on general principles of understanding. Absent entirely from this approach is the church's vision of Scripture as an

---

17. Schleiermacher, *Christian Faith*, 606.

interpreted text that, while not determining every conclusion, nevertheless *guides* all valid interpretation toward a profitable and faithful goal. When Wayne Meeks wants to use a common cultural-historical approach to the New Testament to find the "Jesus who made history,"[18] and concludes that the Jesus of the cross and resurrection can only be *part* of an "ultimate story" that will "include much else as well, far beyond our imagining,"[19] he surely brings the religious left full circle: with no attachment to the authority of Scripture as *content*, it becomes difficult to see what is left of the authority of Scripture as *norm*.

Is it so different on the religious right? One would perhaps think so. Yet the divorce between norm and content is equally striking, and remains firmly in place. According to Richard Bauckham, the role of the Gospels is to "put us in close touch with the eyewitnesses of the history of Jesus."[20] The events that the eyewitness testimony relate in the Gospels are "exceptional events," and belong in a class of such events such as the Holocaust: a class that needs to be weighed by modern historians according to the merits of exceptional testimony.[21] By the general category of testimony, Bauckham means (following the definition of Kevin Vanhoozer) a "speech act" of witness which counts as "evidence" based on "relevant competence or credentials."[22] How are we to respond? First, according to the theological framework of the gospels themselves, the role of the gospel has nothing to do with putting us in touch with *"evidence"*—a modern general historical category—but with proclaiming the *truth* which sets us free. The gospel narrative *begins* with an affirmation of the eschatological age fully present in the advent of Jesus Christ the Son of God (Mark 1:1). This is not evidence for something else; this is not a claim to be evaluated; this is *kerygma*, proclamation to be *believed*, for Christ himself continues present in that very proclamation. Second, the evangelists do not present eyewitness testimony merely because they are nearer to the events than later writers; after all, many people saw Jesus, standing *right in front of him*, and could see nothing more than a Jewish carpenter's son from Nazareth. The evangelists speak because they are *called*, because they are *commissioned* to speak by the risen Christ: "you will be my witnesses" (Acts 1:8). Only the commission matters.

18. Meeks, *Christ*, 21.
19. Ibid., 139.
20. Bauckham, *Eyewitnesses*, 472.
21. Ibid., 506.
22. Ibid., 473.

Third, the event of the gospel is not in a category of "exceptional events"; it is not in any category at all. God's act in Jesus Christ for the redemption of the world happened in time and space, but it is utterly without *any* analogy whatsoever; and those who approach it—even in order to *prove* it—by using the general axioms of historical understanding will necessarily distort it. God's reconciliation of the cosmos in Jesus Christ is not an "exceptional event" among other "exceptional events," however much the historian may wish it so; God's act is the *one* eternal purpose of life and love for all existence. And finally, the call of the gospel now is certainly not to weigh the *evidence* of eyewitnesses and decide on their historical reliability; the Reformers would call that *fides historica* (mere faith in facts, not saving faith in Christ), which is no faith at all. The call of the gospel rather is to leave everything, absolutely *everything* behind—even familiar ways of looking at the world around us—and to follow him.

b. The Subject Matter of Scripture

We have seen that Scripture is a *witness* to a reality; now we must take another step in our theological analysis, and reflect more directly upon the *reality* to which the witness of Scripture points.

"There is one body and one Spirit, just as you were called to the one hope of our calling, one Lord, one faith, one baptism, one God and Father of all, who is above all and through all and in all" (Eph 4:4-5). Calvin makes the essential grammatical point that draws out the preeminent focus on divine unity in this passage: "Whenever you read this word 'one' here understand it as emphatic . . . The unity of faith, which is here mentioned, depends on the one eternal truth of God, on which it is founded."[23] As we consider the question of the true subject matter of Scripture in the context of church doctrine, our first point is simply this: there is only one subject matter in the whole of the Bible. Everywhere and always church theology has held the same confession, even though the manner of making it has changed based on the mode of expression and tools available.

A brief sampling will help: already Ignatius of Antioch in his Letter to the Ephesians (early second century) speaks of God's one "plan" (*oikonomia*) attested in Scripture, embodied in the life, death, and resurrection of Jesus Christ, God's New Man (*kainos anthropos*).[24] Gregory of Nyssa points

---

23. Calvin, *CNTC* 11, 172-73.
24. Cf. Holmes, *Apostolic Fathers*, 197, 199.

out that the same, self-identical object (*skopos*) of the Bible is always present, even though the mode of teaching (*tropos tes didsaskalias*) often demands a variety of different approaches, depending on the context.[25] Cyril of Alexandria speaks of the "mind of the holy Scriptures" which everywhere discloses the unimaginable mystery of Christ.[26] According to John of Damascus, the whole Bible refers to one living divine reality: "It is one and the same God whom both the Old and the New Testament proclaims, who is praised and glorified in the Trinity . . . For He Himself worked out our salvation for which all Scripture and all mystery exists."[27] According to Thomas Aquinas all texts of the Bible are about God, to God, and from God: "either because they are God Himself (*ipse Deus*); or because they refer to God as their beginning and end (*ad principium et finem*)."[28] According to Flacius Illyricus, all Scripture has one coherent viewpoint (*argumentum*) and one subject-matter (*scopus*), which is "the Lord Jesus himself."[29] According to the early Lutheran theologian Jacob Heerbrand the question "Who is the subject-matter (*scopus*) of theology and of the whole of Sacred Scripture," is to be answered: "Christ, the Son of God and Man, born of the Virgin Mary, who was crucified, suffered, and died for our sins, and rose again for our justification."[30] Johann Gerhard will shorten that same Lutheran insight to a simple declarative confession: "The subject . . . is Christ."[31] On the Reformed side, Ursinus declares without ambiguity: Christ is the substance (*summa*) and ground (*fundamentum*) of the entire Scriptures."[32] While the Leiden *Synopsis* argues that despite the variety of Old and New Testament, there is one (*unica*) substance, one will of God, one redemptive promise.[33] This is of course a brief sampling from a vast literature, all of which points to the same conclusion: according to the ecumenical church—Eastern Orthodox, Roman Catholic, Protestant—the whole Bible points to one divine reality.

The entire Scriptures point to Jesus Christ. Jesus Christ is the one reality of which the Bible speaks, the one referent of every part of the Christian

25. Gregory of Nyssa, *LCC* III, 268.
26. Cyril of Alexandria, *Unity of Christ*, 88.
27. John of Damascus, *Orthodox Faith*, 89.
28. Aquinas, *ST* I, 5.
29. Flacius, *De Ratione*, 34–35.
30. Heerbrand, *Compendium*, 1.
31. Gerhard, *Loci* 1, 19.
32. Ursinus, *Commentary*, 3.
33. Bavinck, *Synopsis*, 6.

canon. The Law of God points to him; Christ alone is the true interpreter of the Ten Commandments, which are the eternal expression of his claim upon all who follow him. The prophets point to him, who is the true fulfillment of God's every promise to the church and to the world. The writings declare the wisdom that is embodied in his word and will alone. The Gospels proclaim him, whose earthly life, death, and resurrection, are the one redemptive purpose of God for all creation. The epistles testify to him, the crucified and risen Christ, who guides his community in the world. God is known only in him; for to know Christ is to know God, and to know God is to know Christ. Creation is known only through Christ, by whom all things were made. Reconciliation is accomplished only in him, in whom all things that exist are joined together in one. Redemption is realized only in him, who is the one hope of all the ends of the earth. Jesus Christ is the new world of God, the firstborn of God's new creation. It is important to sharpen our perception of a point that in traditional affirmations of the unitary subject-matter of the Bible is often left unspoken, though clearly it is assumed. We do not first distinguish between the witness of the text and the subject matter of which it speaks on literary grounds, and only then come to affirm the christological substance of the Bible. Rather, it is because we know that the entire Scriptures point to Christ that church doctrine steadfastly insists upon a rigorous theological movement from witness to reality. "In the beginning was the Word, and the Word was with God, and the Word was God" (John 1:1); because Jesus Christ is the one Word of God, the one true light that shines in the darkness, we necessarily draw attention to the issue of the subject matter of Scripture as an essential matter for Christian theology.

Church doctrine therefore resists all forms of biblicism, whether on the left or the right. Biblicism refuses to distinguish between the witness and the subject matter; in the end it thus completely undercuts the essential Christian witness to the unitary christological substance of the Bible. Both left and right of course intend to do greater honor to the Bible in refusing to move from the text to that divine reality to which the text refers, whether in the name of an inerrant set of self-consistent propositions (on the right) or an intratextual world (on the left). But the Bible itself is a treasure chest, in which full honor is given to the *treasure* that it contains. Jesus himself chides those who look to the Scriptures, but miss the subject-matter: "You search the scriptures because you think that in them you have eternal life; and it is they that testify on my behalf" (John 5:39). To move from witness to subject matter is not to leave the witness behind, but to follow, like the star of Bethlehem, until finding the One upon whom its light shines.

The Bible is one divine book, but in Two Testaments, Old and New. The subject matter of the Bible is therefore grasped only in the dialectical form of Old and New Testament. Both the Old and the New Testaments are equally authoritative for church doctrine. Early in its history, the church rejected Marcionism, which attempts to cut the New Testament free from the Old Testament witness; in modern times, classic Protestant liberalism makes the same error. Schleiermacher, for example, states categorically: "The Old Testament Scriptures owe their place in our Bible partly to the appeals the New Testament Scriptures make to them, partly to the historical connexion of Christian worship with the Jewish synagogue; but the Old Testament Scriptures do not on that account share the normative dignity or the inspiration of the New."[34] By sharp contrast, church doctrine, standing in the mainstream of Christian witness from the very beginning, accepts and affirms the full and equal authority and inspiration of both Testaments.[35]

More recently, the effort has been made among postmodern liberalism to affirm the Old Testament, but only as the "Hebrew Bible"; i.e., to affirm it, yet while at the same time denying the ontological christological witness of the Old Testament characteristic of church doctrine. Strangely enough this move is often made purportedly to honor the Christian relation to Judaism; and indeed, an ontological bond between Christians and Jews remains central to Christian faith. However, it is ironic that *no* Jewish tradition refers to their sacred Scripture, the Tanakh, as "the Hebrew Bible," which remains a neutral category of history of religions, certainly not a Jewish or Christian theological construct. Again by sharp contrast, while the church insists upon the absolute necessity of hearing the Old Testament according to its literal sense, the scandal of the gospel is that precisely the Old Testament in its literal sense is a witness to Christ. The Old Testament makes a direct, existential claim upon the church as the instrument through which Christ makes himself known. Different theological strategies are available

---

34. Schleiermacher, *Christian Faith*, 608.

35. It should perhaps be pointed out that Schleiermacher, the "pietist of a higher order," is anticipated here by Spener, who likewise recommends frequent reading of the New Testament (not the Bible) in the Christian household. See his *Pia Desideria*, 88. No one can accuse Pietism of doctrinal Marcionism to be sure; but there is a kind of *functional* Marcionism wherever the Old Testament is dismissed as marginalized for the Christian community.

for realizing that confession; but the confession of an ontological reference in the Old Testament to Christ is a basic confession of Christian orthodoxy that can never be abandoned.

On other hand, church doctrine can perhaps offer here a small measure of clarity at precisely this point by its distinction between witness and subject matter. The ontological reference of the Old Testament to Christ is not at the level of the verbal sense; church doctrine has no stake in outmoded and unconvincing "proof-texts" from Old Testament prophecy, which characterize the mishearing of the Old Testament on the religious right, as if the reference to Christ can be rationalistically derived from the text apart from the response of faith. The church's reading of the Old Testament is not folded into the rationalistic apologetics of evangelicalism, by the so-called "proofs from prophecy." Rather, as a basic confession of faith in the risen Christ, church doctrine searches for the ontological reference of the Old Testament at the level of the *subject matter* to which it truthfully points. At the level of the verbal sense of the witness, the suffering servant of Isaiah refers to a mysterious figure not identified fully within the text: is it Israel? Is it an individual? At the level of the subject matter—the living reality of whom the text speaks—the church recognizes in the figure of the suffering servant, who bore our infirmities and carried our diseases, precisely him who died for the sins of the whole world.

The classic dialectical formula of Augustine remains definitive for church doctrine: "In the Old Testament the New is concealed, in the New the Old is revealed."[36] On the one hand, we read the Old Testament in light of the New. As Christians, we come to the Old Testament searching for witness to Jesus Christ; we come, that is to say, on the basis of our confession of faith in Jesus Christ, seeking to learn more of him. On the other hand, it is equally true and important that we read the New Testament only in light of the Old. The Old Testament does not simply provide historical background to the New Testament; nor does the Old Testament need to be Christianized in order to count as Christian witness. We fully affirm and insist upon the absolute theological integrity of the Old Testament as an independent witness within the Christian canon, which can never be simply collapsed into the New. Christ himself is the true norm of Christian faith and practice, not the New Testament's interpretation of the Old Testament. There is no higher theological vantage point beyond this dialectical relation of the two Testaments. Church doctrine is certainly not the same as New

---

36. Quoted in Kelly, *Early Christian Doctrines*, 69.

Testament theology of the Old Testament. Such a construction dissolves the dialectic, and therefore loses the mystery of faith. Jesus Christ is the one subject matter of both Testaments; yet only in the dialectical form that is realized ever anew in direct theological interpretation.

Despite the dialectical relation of the Testaments, there is one coherent subject matter in the entire Bible. That is not the same as affirming that any one individual biblical author or text comprises or comprehends that unitary subject matter; again, it is essential to distinguish between the witness of the text and the reality to which it points. Beyond the intentionality of any particular text or author, there is a unitary subject matter of the whole Bible, grounded in the one divine purpose of redemptive love for all humanity. Church doctrine, as carried out in the community of faith, is therefore set apart from the general history of religions, in which the exclusive interest is in charting the development of diverse religious ideas and practices over time within their social and cultural setting. Others may read the Bible that way (which is entirely legitimate), but as confessing Christians we do not; we do not reach the conclusion of one subject matter after an apologetic search through the Scriptures, but rather begin with the affirmation of unity as we approach the Scriptures within the Christian confession of faith. There is one Word of God, Jesus Christ; therefore we read the Bible open to the coherent whole that it presents. We look for theological themes that unite the various parts of the canon, despite the differing genres in which these themes are imbedded. "With all wisdom and insight he has made known to us the mystery of his will, according to his good pleasure that he set forth in Christ, as a plan for the fullness of time, to gather up all things in him, things in heaven and things on earth" (Eph 1:8–10). God's one eternal redemptive purpose of love for all humanity unites the message of the Bible, and indeed the entire cosmos.

On the other hand, we should not try to fit the abundant variety of biblical witness into an artificial, rational system. It is one thing to interpret the Bible holistically; it is another to substitute for the biblical witness a rational system of revealed propositions supposedly derived from Scripture. There are clearly dissonances in the Bible, and those dissonances must be preserved for the sake of truth. Charles Hodge, for example, establishes as a firm rule of interpretation the rational coherence of the Bible based upon the logical law of non-contradiction: "If a passage admits of different interpretations, that only can be the true one which agrees with what the Bible teaches elsewhere on the same subject."[37] Hodge's approach seriously reduces the multiple voices of Scripture to a single rational formula, which in fact distorts and silences the genuine subject matter, undercutting the very authority of Scripture he is purporting to preserve. Christian doctrine is not a rational system of truths abstracted from the Bible; Christian doctrine rather is a holistic theological interpretation of the Bible focused upon the true reality of its subject matter. Without losing sight of the confessional affirmation of unity, church doctrine always seeks to preserve the rich variety of biblical witness for the sake of the subtle nuances of the faith we cherish. Christian faith is inherently complex, and its infinite beauty and wisdom cannot be reduced to a simplistic rational formula. The biblical message is rendered in rich polyphony, not monotony, often unfolding even in dissonant voices, which must be fully appreciated in every respect. "Open my eyes, so that I may behold wondrous things out of your law . . . I run the way of your commandments, for you enlarge my understanding . . . I have seen a limit to all perfection, but your commandment is exceedingly broad . . . (Ps 119:18, 32, 96). "How weighty to me are your thoughts, O God! How vast is the sum of them! I try to count them—they are more than the sand . . ." (Ps 139:17–18). The appropriate response to the unitary biblical subject matter in all its density and counter-valence is open-minded wonder, not a legalistic and artificial "consistency."

The larger theological coherence of the biblical subject matter is narrative in shape. The narrative shape of church doctrine is hardly a new insight. Already in his classic treatise *The City of God*, Augustine handled the full range of church theology according to a loose temporal reflection on the history of the city of God. Perhaps more surprisingly, but certainly no less significantly, the medieval theologian Thomas Aquinas stands out among his scholastic contemporaries for the biblical narrative cast he gives to the science of theology. The overall structure of the *Summa Theologiae* unfolds along a threefold narrative line, which moves from God as the one goal of all creation, to the journey that makes its way to God, to finally the road that each must walk along that journey. The core of his presentation of church doctrine is clearly biblical, with Aristotle providing the conceptual language for analysis. More recently, the structure of the *Church Dogmatics* of Karl Barth also clearly follows a basic narrative line from Creation to Redemption. Despite the completely different eras of these three theologians, and indeed the very different resources each used for theological analysis,

---

37. Hodge, *Systematic Theology* I, 187.

there is a family resemblance of basic approach organized around the narrative shape of doctrine. Why is that resemblance there? It is there because they all read the same Bible. There is a narrative shape to theology because there is a narrative shape to the biblical witness. The Bible attests the event of God's creating, reconciling, and redeeming love; therefore the theological shape of church doctrine is narrative in form. Melanchthon speaks for church doctrine in all communions: "(God) put his doctrine in the form of a story (*historia*) . . . Thus the books of the prophets and apostles, arranged as they are, constitute a complete and beautiful story, and a story is a good means of teaching."[38]

The subject matter of the Bible is the one divine narrative that encompasses all reality. The biblical narrative of God has a beginning, and an ending; time comes into being with creation, and is dissolved in the final consummation of all things in eternal joy. The same narrative unfolds in both Testaments of Scripture. The Bible does not contain two stories, the story of Israel in the Old Testament, and the story of the church in the New Testament. While recognizing the variety of God's hidden ways, church doctrine straightforwardly rejects such a bifurcated view, in light of the clear biblical confession that the God of Israel is the Father of our Lord Jesus Christ. At issue therefore is the unity of creation and redemption already enshrined in *The Apostles Creed*: "I believe in (*Credo in*) God the Father Almighty, Creator of heaven and earth; And in (*Et in*) Jesus Christ, his only Son, our Lord . . ."[39] While there is only one story of God in the Bible, Christian doctrine has from the beginning recognized different economies in the biblical story. The patriarchs lived during a time of preparation for God's coming salvation, awaiting eagerly the fulfillment of the promise; the time of the Exodus was a celebration of the Old Covenant under the leadership of Moses; the Gospels bear witness to the radically new reality of God's Incarnation in Jesus Christ; the early church lives under the New Covenant sealed in the death of Christ; Christian hope focuses on the promised return of Christ and the final consummation still to come. God's story is one; yet the economy of God's purpose is varied.

The unity of the biblical story does not swallow up the manifold and mysterious variety of God's ways, which are preserved in the biblical witness: "Long ago God spoke to our ancestors in many and various ways by the prophets, but in these last days he has spoken to us by a Son . . ." (Heb

---

38. Melanchthon, *Loci Communes* (1555), xlvi, xlviii.
39. Pelikan and Hotchkiss, eds., *CCFCT* I, 669.

1:1–2). Nevertheless, church doctrine likewise asserts that the one triune God governs the entire story in its totality. The Trinity is the God of the biblical story; there is no other. Moreover, the sequence of the story is not an historical sequence; there is movement back and forth in the divine economy that transcends the limits of historical time. The God of the Bible, as Ezekiel makes clear, moves in all directions simultaneously: "As I looked at the living creatures, I saw a wheel on the earth beside the living creatures, one for each of the four of them . . . When they moved, they moved in any of the four directions without veering as they moved" (Ezek 1:15, 17). All parts of the Bible therefore continue to serve as authoritative witness to the divine will, echoing and re-echoing the truths necessary for discerning their dynamic interrelationship. Furthermore, the entire biblical narrative points to the future consummation of the coming reign of God, which is not the extension of historical time but the new time of God's universal reign. The whole narrative always points forward, and therefore faith is completely oriented toward the future, never to the past. And finally, while the economy of God is manifold, the purpose of God is one: Jesus Christ is God's one redemptive purpose for the whole cosmos. Jesus Christ is the beginning of the story, Jesus Christ is the ending of the story, Jesus Christ is the center of the story: "I am the Alpha and the Omega, the first and the last, the beginning and the end" (Rev 22:13).

Classical theology could think univocally about biblical narrative; the events told in the Bible simply happened, and can be read by all right off the pages of the text. We now must think dialectically, not univocally. On the one hand God alone created space and time; God himself, without being any less God, entered the spatio-temporal world he created, in order to redeem it from the inside. The Bible is a narrative because redemption is a divine *event*. The Bible is not about ontology, or anthropology, or about a fictive universe; the Bible is a record of, a witness to, this divine event. To retreat from this confession is to retreat from the gospel itself; God reveals himself in real space and time. On the other hand, redemption in the Bible is a *divine* event. While it happened in space and time, nothing is left of spatio-temporal access but the residue, like the burial clothes in the tomb of the risen Christ. God reveals himself *in* history; but God cannot be known *from* history. The God of the Bible is known only from the proclaimed word heard in faith. This dialectic of history cannot be removed, no matter how much offense it causes; for the offense of the gospel is concealed within this dialectic, like the babe lying in the manger, unseen by the wider world.

c. Dimensions of Theological Interpretation

There are three basic dimensions of theological interpretation. We speak intentionally of dimensions rather than stages, for there is not a simple logical progression from the one to the other; rather, at any given moment of church doctrine, any one or all three dimensions are being explored in the service of the gospel.

The first dimension is *explication*, or theological description. Explication means describing the *literal sense* of the text according to its own inner theological shape. On the surface, explication may seem the simplest of the three dimensions; in reality, it is equally difficult, and in fact requires sustained and energetic openness and critical discernment. It is not enough simply to chart the historical-grammatical meaning of the text, as customarily espoused by the religious right; it is not enough simply to offer a description of the social world in which the text is imbedded, as now commonly argued on the religious left; in fact, both of these approaches are at best distractions, and at worst evasions of the true task of explication. Explication of the text means hearing the witness of the Bible according to its own canonical form, which is built into the text by the community of faith that handed it on to be used by future generations of the community. There is not a single canonical stamp to the whole Bible, nor a single device for rendering its witness for the future life of the community. Every *book* is different; every *part* of the canon is different. There is, however, a comprehensive shaping mechanism at work throughout the entire Bible, which can be carefully and objectively described, and which guides the explication of every passage (such as the titles of the four Gospels, as mentioned above). The first dimension of theological interpretation is to hear the text within its canonical context, which is determinative for all Christian theology. Explication focuses the attention of the church upon the plain sense of the final form of the Scriptures, which guides all *theological* interpretation.

Two questions emerge concerning the issue of the literal sense of Scripture. The first is the issue of clarity: is the plain sense of the text clear for everyone to see? Our example above illustrates the issue: it is obvious to everyone now informed by historical consciousness that the titles of the four Gospels have been added later by the community; is it obvious to everyone that the canonical intention of those titles has its effect in rendering the fourfold gospel as *one* gospel? Thankfully, Martin Luther wrestles brilliantly with this issue in his debate with Erasmus, and quickly summarizing his argument will provide the needed distinction. In *The Bondage of the*

Will, Luther carefully and vigorously argues for the fundamental clarity of Scripture against the historical-grammatical method of Erasmus. What emerges in Luther's argument is the difference between an *obvious* surface reading on the one hand, and the inherent *clarity* of the literal sense of Scripture on the other. Several crucial points are brought out in Luther's position. First, the clarity of Scripture is related to its subject matter, and still leaves room for obscure and difficult passages that are hard to comprehend: "The subject matter of the Scripture, therefore, is all quite accessible, even though some texts are still obscure owing to our ignorance of the terms. Truly it is stupid and impious, when we know that the subject matter of Scripture has all been placed in the clearest light, to call it obscure on account of a few obscure words."[40] Second, and more basic, there is a distinction between internal and external clarity. The *internal* clarity is the genuine substance of the gospel known only where the Spirit works the miracle of faith: "If you speak of the internal clarity, no man perceives one iota of what is in the Scriptures unless he has the Spirit of God."[41] The *external* clarity is the universal proclamation of the gospel in the living word of the sermon, which is freely announced to all humanity: "If, on the other hand, you speak of the external clarity, nothing at all is left obscure or ambiguous, but everything there is in the Scriptures has been brought out by the Word into the most definite light, and published to all the world."[42] Thirdly, the clarity of Scripture is grounded exclusively and completely in the power of the risen Christ, who illuminates the entirety of the biblical witness: "For what sublimer thing can remain hidden in the Scriptures, now that the seals have been broken, the stone rolled from the door of the sepulcher . . . and the supreme mystery brought to light . . . Are not these things known and sung even in the highways and the byways?"[43] Following Luther, we maintain then that the objective sense of Scripture is *clear* (external clarity), but not *obvious* (internal clarity). The literal sense of the text is the plain sense of Scripture; and yet only those who stand with the faith of the community are in a position to see with open eyes the light of Christ that shines in every word with utter clarity. There is a response of faith required in order to see the clarity of the biblical word; nevertheless, the word is there, and it is crystal clear, beyond all evasion and misunderstanding. Nor is the message

---

40. Luther, *LW* 33, 26.
41. Ibid., 28.
42. Ibid.
43. Ibid., 26.

of the Bible a Gnostic secret, kept hidden except only in relation to an inner cabal of the spiritually endowed, or to those possessing the right tools of learned expertise. The genuine clarity of Scripture is a function of the plain sense of the final form of the text, which speaks a message deeply familiar to every ordinary Christian who turns to the Bible seeking the bread of life.

The second question raised by the objective sense of the final form of Scripture is simply this: is not the final form of the text just as human, just as fragile, just as ideologically motivated, as every other level of biblical tradition oral and written? Our answer to that question—often raised against the new vision of Scripture as canon introduced by Childs and here applied to the concerns of church doctrine—is simple and straightforward. Yes: every book of the Bible, every passage, every single verse, is utterly human, utterly fragile, and shot through with the ideological motivations that infect all human speech and action. The Bible would have it no other way: "But we have this treasure in clay jars, so that it may be made clear that this extraordinary power belongs to God and does not come from us (2 Cor 4: 7). The religious left—which of course always chooses *its* favorite passages as the true spiritual core—is wrong; it is *all* human, even the "progressive" passages. The religious right—which of course routinely identifies modern conservative values as the basic thrust of the Bible—is equally wrong; it is *all* human, even the "conservative" passages. Only when we come to that full realization can we then make our confession, as the church of the living Lord Jesus Christ: namely, through the active presence of the Holy Spirit then and now, this all-too-human book, as shaped by Israel and the early church in its final form, *is* the word of God, and *becomes* the word of God again and again. We mean this completely literally, in no way metaphorically. These human words are God's words; God's words are these human words. God says what the Bible says; he said it then, he says it ever fresh, ever anew, in the present moment. If God became a helpless infant on Christmas morning without being any less God, surely God speaks through the words of human beings, with such unmistakable clarity and splendid majesty that God's *own voice* is heard. Let all the world be silent before him.

The second dimension of theological interpretation is *reflection*. Reflection is the effort to expand the literal sense of the text into the *figurative* sense. The figurative sense is based on the literal; nevertheless, the figurative sense transcends the literal in reflecting on the passage in the light of the message of the Bible as a whole. Paul speaks of the veil of misunderstanding that is removed by Christ; he speaks of the guidance of the Spirit, which leads us to behold the glory of Christ with unveiled faces, as though reflected in the mirror of Scripture; he speaks of the transformation which comes from encountering the Lord through the work of the Spirit (2 Cor 3: 12-18). The figurative sense is the gift of the Spirit that brings freedom to behold the exalted Christ in the mirror of Scripture, a freedom given by the Spirit of Christ alone, and not in any way based on natural human capacity: "for this comes from the Lord, the Spirit" (2 Cor 3:18). Reflection means seeking to understand the biblical witness in the light of the subject matter of which it speaks. The figurative sense is grounded in the intention of the Holy Spirit, and may not be present in the intention of any one biblical author. The intention of the Holy Spirit alone is normative. Flacius Illyricus rightly observes: "The Holy Spirit is at the same time both the author and interpreter of Scripture" (*Spiritus Sanctus est autor simul, et explicator Scripturae*).[44] The figurative sense is not an exercise in free creativity, but a full acknowledgment of the abundant creativity of the divine Spirit.

Furthermore, to speak of the figurative sense is to speak of multiple meanings for biblical texts. God speaks through the words of the Bible; but the same God also speaks through the metaphors that these words contain. God speaks the literal truth of the biblical witness; but the same God also speaks the figurative meanings that the literal truth unveils. Church doctrine should not allow itself to be captured in a static schema of reflection, such as the medieval fourfold method of literal, allegorical, anagogical, and tropological (the *quadriga*). However, it must surely resist an overly rationalistic conception of biblical truth, as if God never uses metaphor to instruct his church. For example, according to Ernesti, every word of the Bible must be assigned a single meaning based on the "notion of the thing" (*notio rei*) that it represents; and for that reason, not only all allegory, but even the Reformation idea of the analogy of faith must be utterly rejected from all genuine exegesis.[45] But why cannot the words of God bear more than one meaning? Why cannot the Spirit of God use the witness of Scripture metaphorically, as well as literally? Are we not summoned by God himself to "sing to the Lord a new song" (Ps 98:1)? Indeed, we cannot refuse to hear the metaphors of God's voice, and are challenged by the Bible itself to hear them as divine wisdom: "Give ear, O my people, to my teaching; incline your ears to the words of my mouth. I will open my mouth in a parable; I will utter dark sayings from of old . . ." (Ps 78:1-2). The

---

44. Flacius, *De Ratione*, 30.
45. Ernesti, *Institutio*, 15.

God of the Bible is a *direct* God; the same God is an *indirect* God, whose active and dynamic word must be attended with faithful imagination. Augustine summarizes the issue: "For what could God have more generously and abundantly provided in the divine writings than that the same words might be understood in various ways which other no less divine witnesses approve?"[46] While there are multiple meanings in Scripture, there is only one referent; all valid meanings point to Jesus Christ, and are measured exclusively by his sovereign reality.

Reflection as a dimension of theological interpretation involves a variety of theological techniques. First is the technique of intertextuality, in which the words of one passage are illuminated by other passages. Resonances are created by the canonical form of the biblical witness, in which echoes of truth are created among the varieties of biblical language. Now, church doctrine is bound to the Hebrew and Greek text of the Bible. Verbal resonances accidentally unleashed by translation need to be carefully checked against the original language. Moreover, intertextuality does not mean free verbal play; the whole point of intertextual reading is to return to the biblical witness in the light of the subject matter, in such a way that the subject matter comes more clearly into focus. The subject matter, not the words, controls the aim of reflection, as Augustine shrewdly observes: "it is a mark of good and distinguished minds to love the truth within words and not the words."[47] Still, reading the text in the light of the subject matter means looking for illumination created by the juxtaposition of different texts. We yearn, with George Herbert: "Oh that I knew how all thy lights combine, and the configurations of their glory! . . . This book of stars lights to eternal bliss."[48]

Second, theological reflection moves backwards and forwards along the narrative line of God's event of creation and redemption in the Bible. Prophecy and fulfillment are to be sought and found, and yet prophecy *remains* promise to garner fresh hope; the dialectical movement from Old to New, but also from New back to Old is to be considered; narrative patterns of events are to be noticed and probed, such that not only events mean something, but so too do the connections that obtain between events; the unitary ontological reference of biblical narrative is to be established, while at the same time the unique witness of each narrative is to be treasured as

---

46. Augustine, *Doctrine*, 102.
47. Ibid., 136.
48. Herbert, *Poems*, 49.

one pearl on the string of divine truth. All of these techniques together are often called "typology," but the validity is not in the name given to the approach but in the theological results.

And third, theological reflection means tracing the patterns of biblical *themes* across the variety of individual witnesses. That is not the same as rendering the Bible into a theological system; the unity of the themes is not guaranteed by logical consistency, but rather grounded in the one exalted Lord of all reality. Nevertheless, the *coherence* of church doctrine is not a free creation of the church; rather, the coherence of church doctrine is a pale human reflection of the divine *harmony* that is reflected in the witness of the Bible. Theological reflection is in its own limited way an inquiry into the radiant beauty of divine truth: "One thing I asked of the Lord, that will I seek after; to live in the house of the Lord all the days of my life, to behold the beauty of the Lord, and to inquire in his temple" (Ps 27:4).

The third dimension of theological interpretation is *appropriation*. Church doctrine discerns the truth of God's will only in the contemporary moment, never by retreating into the past; appropriation therefore seeks to lay bare the *active sense* of Scripture. Karl Barth rightly captures the special commitment of dogmatic theology to the direct claim of Scripture upon the present life of the church: "Dogmatics as such does not ask what the apostles and prophets said but what we must say on the basis of the prophets and apostles."[49] The Word is not a dead letter but a living, active, comforting, judging power within church and society; church doctrine necessarily ventures, in the risk of faith, to discern critically the content of the active voice of God in the world today through the living medium of Scripture. Despite the glorious heritage of church tradition, there is no escaping the responsibility of the present moment. Truths that have long been known and cherished by the community of faith must be relearned, and renewed in the language of the contemporary world. The language of faith must be spoken by a new generation, in ways that speak to the exigencies of the present day community of faith. And indeed new truths drawn from Scripture—truths not yet discovered even by the best efforts of the church in the past—await patient but urgent elaboration and application. The truth of God's will shines brightly in the Scriptures; but there is a response of faith required in the present day in order to see what is there to see.

The danger, of course, is constantly real of subsuming the force of biblical truth under the ideologies of the present. That is why the theological

---

49. Barth, *CD* I/1, 16.

shape of Scripture is the only definitive guide to appropriation. There are times when the vaunted needs of the present must simply give way before the superior and coercive force of the biblical word, which reigns supreme in the church. Still, even the theological shape of the Bible leaves room for a response, and indeed demands contemporary responsibility. In the Parable of the Talents (Matt 25:14-30; Luke 19:11-27), Jesus affirms the venture of faith exercised by the two who invest their talents, regardless of the varying outcome; by sharp contrast, he thoroughly condemns the excessive caution of the third, who simply hides his talent in the ground for fear of offending his master. Fear is no excuse; for proper fear should have impelled him to action. Even a minimal investment would have been better than nothing: "You wicked and lazy slave! You knew, did you, that I reap where I did not sow, and gather where I did not scatter? Then you ought to have invested my money with the bankers . . ." (Matt 25:26-27). We cannot escape the responsibility of the present moment. Reverence for Christ is the true motive for appropriation, without which theological interpretation remains woefully incomplete. The God of the Bible is a literal God, and a figurative God; he is also an *active* God, who simply will not stand idly by until his Word is heard and received in the immediacy of absolute decision.

Now, it has become common in many ecclesial circles to respond to the decaying influence of theological liberalism on church life by a new theology of *repristination*. For some it is a return to one or other of the traditions of medieval scholasticism; for others a return to the church fathers; for still others a return to the Reformers; for still others a return to the giants of Anglo-Catholicism, or to Protestant scholasticism, or to one or more great figures in Eastern Orthodoxy. No one can deny that there is much to learn from the history of church doctrine of all periods, as the references in the present work make fully evident. Nevertheless, the church of today *cannot*, and *must* not, simply rest upon the gains of the past, however important it is to sustain insights already won. To do so would be simply to bury our talent in the earth, thus inviting the severe censure of the Lord whom we serve. The church of today can only discover the truth, not by *returning* to the past, but by *turning* to Scripture afresh in our contemporary world. If explication leads us from the witness of the text to the true reality of which it speaks; and reflection returns to the text in the light of the reality; appropriation seeks to discern the all-consuming relevance of the divine reality in our *own* time and place. In the Bible, truth and relevance are always joined in a dynamic unity: "faithfulness will spring up from the ground, and righteousness will look down from the sky" (Ps 85:11). There is no genuine relevance without truth; but nor is there genuine truth without relevance. Church doctrine is above all things *useful*, for it alone contains the joyous freedom of authentic life. We can only read Scripture rightly in the struggle of faith, which can only take place in the present, seeking with all our being to hear the divine message of Scripture. Yet the response demanded flows from the divine gift of understanding, which comes to us only in the miracle of grace, and is in no sense the exercise of human capacity.

All three dimensions of theological interpretation have their appropriate context only in the practicing community of faith. The Bible is not "like any other book"; the Bible is the living word of God, which speaks with the divine voice of majesty and truth. The comforting and demanding tones of the biblical witness are rightly heard only in the common life of the church of Jesus Christ. Only in the context of worship, surrounded by the hymns of the faith, carried by the rhythms of liturgy resounding throughout the hushed silence of the gathered community, are the words of Scripture known for what they truly are: the light of God's will for all humanity. Only in the context of the hard work of Christian practice, and especially active and concrete care for the poor, do the biblical words carry the full weight of authority for definitive guidance in Christian discipleship. And above all, only in faithful prayer: calling upon God for help, waiting upon God for insight, asking for the promised gift of God's Spirit, do we find the appropriate attitude in which the Scriptures of the church truly become God's living word *to us*, and indeed *to me*. God's living word in Scripture directly claims the church today; God's living word in Scripture directly claims my life; God's living word in Scripture directly claims the whole world; only in the context of prayer do the scales fall from our eyes. Only in the context of prayer do we say in our minds and hearts, with the church of all ages: "Open my eyes, so that I may behold wondrous things out of your law . . . so I will bless you as long as I live; I will lift up my hands and call on your name . . . lead me to the rock that is higher than I . . . O send out your light and your truth; let them lead me . . . O Lord my God, you are very great . . . Let the words of my mouth and the meditation of my heart be acceptable to you, O Lord, my rock and my redeemer" (Pss 119:18; 63:4; 61:2; 43:3; 104:1; 19:14).

d. Faith Seeking Understanding

We now weave the various threads of this chapter into a comprehensive approach: theological interpretation of Scripture in the context of church doctrine means *faith seeking understanding.*

In chapter 1 of his work *Proslogion*, Anselm first invites the reader to remove all unworthy distractions from the proper attitude of theological inquiry: "Come now, insignicant man (*homuncio*), fly for a moment from your affairs, escape for a little while from the tumult of your thoughts. Put aside now your weighty cares and leave your wearisome toils."[50] Whatever else it may be, theological inquiry requires focus upon its divine object alone: "Abandon yourself for a little to God and rest for a little in Him."[51] Indeed, theological inquiry is not speech about God, but speaking *to* God: "Come then, Lord my God, teach my heart where and how to seek You, where and how to find You."[52] Anselm them describes the predicament of all theology thus. Humankind as *creature* was fashioned to *know* God: "In fine, I was made in order to see You";[53] and yet as sinful, *fallen* creature *cannot* know God: "How wretched man's lot is when he has lost that for which he was made!"[54] The solution to the human predicament comes *only* from God's merciful, free, and gracious self-revelation: "Teach me to seek You, and reveal Yourself to me as I seek, because I can neither seek You if You do not teach me how, nor find You unless You reveal Yourself (*nisi te ostendas*)."[55] The conclusion is thus firm and certain: faith in God's revealed will leads to true understanding; whereas human understanding can never find its way to faith in God's revealed will. Concludes Anselm: "For I do not seek to understand so that I may believe; but I believe so that I may understand."[56]

We *believe*, through the sheer miracle of God's unspeakable gift; the task of theology is to come to *understand* what we believe. The *truth* of theology is grounded in its revealed object alone (ontically); the *task* of theology is to discover the inner logic of that truth (noetically). Thus, the *reality*

---

50. Anselm, *Proslogion*, 111.
51. Ibid.
52. Ibid.
53. Ibid.
54. Ibid., 113.
55. Ibid., 115.
56. Ibid.

of truth always precedes (and makes possible) rational human reflection upon its *possibility*. To use the language of Scripture, Christ dwells in our hearts "through faith" (Eph 3:17), which is a free gift and not the result of any exercise of human spiritual capacity; and yet, faith is call to "comprehend, with all the saints, what is the breadth, and length, and height and depth, and to know the love of Christ that surpasses knowledge, so that you may be filled with all the fullness of God" (Eph 3:18–19). Faith comes first, not understanding; and yet understanding feeds faith, as the whole body of Christ grows up into it Head, which is Christ the Lord. Church doctrine aids the church in the task of coming to *understand* what we *believe*.

What role should reason play in theological interpretation of Scripture in the context of church doctrine, if we are indeed to follow the path of faith seeking understanding? Three options suggest themselves. The first is reason as *foundational*; reason provides the criteria of meaning and truth as a critical foundation upon which to build the understanding and affirmation of church doctrine. Such a foundational approach is clearly seen for example in the preface to John Locke's seminal work, *The Reasonableness of Christianity*. There, Locke professes his frustration with the inconsistencies found in the "systems of divinity" with which he is familiar; and pledges an "unbiased," "fair and unprejudiced," rational examination of the content of the Scriptures.[57] These competing "systems of divinity" were of course the various Lutheran, Reformed, Anglican, and Roman Catholic dogmatic treatises flowing from the breakup of Christendom in the sixteenth century. The date of publication of Locke's treatise is 1695, a mere generation after the devastation of the Thirty Years War unleashed mindless religious hatred and bigotry on an unimaginable scale throughout Europe. Emanuel Hirsch argues—rightly in my opinon—that the real catalyst for modern "foundationalism" was not the intrinsic validity of the new modes of scientific and philosphical rationality just then burgeoning in early modern Europe; such new forms of thought were merely the tools used to solve a problem. The real problem itself was the catastrophic collapse of a united Christianity, and the territorial and legal implications of intra-religious warfare.[58] Why not turn to "unbiased reason" when the confessing church had shown itself morally bankrupt on the field of battle? It was and is a fair question.

Nevertheless, despite one's sympathy for the way out foundationalism seems to provide, it must be rejected on theological grounds. It reverses

---

57. Locke, *Reasonableness*, 24.
58. Hirsch, *GNET* I, 3–13.

the relation between the ontic reality of divine truth and the noetic search for human reflection upon that truth, as if human beings can establish the rational basis for revealed truth. From the biblical point of view, that is to turn everything completely and disastrously upside down: as if the lump of clay were to exclaim to the potter, "why have you made me like this?" (Rom 9:20). Human reason has a role to play; but it is not the role of setting conditions, or limits, on what God can or cannot say or will for his world. Foundationalism is not an option for church doctrine, even when it is used by conservative theologians to *prove* the truth or reasonableness of Christianity. All foundationalism—by its very essence—arrogates to human capacity an aptitude of judgment that Scripture absolutely denies: "There is no one who is righteous, not even one, there is no one who has understanding, there is no one who seeks God" (Rom 3:10–11). Paul is of course speaking in the light of the gospel, not from the perspective of a pessimistic anthropology; and he is speaking specifically of *religious* humanity, not a supposed secular humanity. We cannot follow the path of foundationalism, whether to prove or to critique church doctrine; although we are summoned by the circumstances of its rise in early modern times to a renewed commitment to ecumenical goodwill in all things.

The second option—which dominates Protestant scholasticism—is the *organic* use (*usus organicus*) of reason in theological interpretation of Scripture. On this view, reason is the *instrument* through which the meaning and truth of God's will are realized and ordered in human thought. There is, as it were, a harmony between right reason and the teaching of Scripture; so that whatever is Scriptural is reasonable, and whatever is reasonable is Scriptural. No critical distance is thus allowed between ontic truth and noetic truth; they are not the same, but nor can they in any way be separated. Benedict Pictet speaks for a wide range of Lutheran and Reformed scholastic theologians: "In fact, reason and faith, though of a different nature, are not opposed to each other. Hence we maintain that we must not admit anything, even in religious matters, which is contrary to right reason . . . but what we maintain is, that reason cannot and ought not to bring forth any mysteries, as it were, out of its own storehouse; for this is the prerogative of scripture only."[59] Thus, reason is the noetic channel for ontic truth, and provides the proper "fit" for the true teaching of the Bible. Of course, by "reason" the scholastics mean Aristotle; including the principle of contradiction, the distinction between essence and accidents,

59. Pictet, *Theology*, 54.

the ten categories, argument by syllogism, potency and act, the four causes ... etc.[60] Every reader of Protestant scholasticism immediately senses that a wide variety of assumptions are being made—unexamined assumptions in hindsight—about what constitutes rationality. Why for example should "faith" have four causes? Why examine faith from the point of view of Aristotelian metaphysics in the first place? Why not Wittgenstein, or Hegel? Or more broadly (and surely more importantly on the modern mission field) why assume that "reason" must take the shape of *Western* rationality, as all the Protestant scholastics certainly do? Why should an African Christian first have to learn Greek logic and metaphysics in order rightly to understand the Word of God?[61]

However one answers these and similar questions, our rejection of the organic use of reason must be just as definitive as the foundational use. If the foundational use clearly reverses the ontic and the noetic by placing the noetic in the position of judge; the organic use collapses the ontic and the noetic, as if there is no real distance between the truth of God and the human search for truth. According to the Bible, such an assumption is clearly false: "To whom then will you compare me, or who is my equal, says the Holy One" (Isa 40:25). There is *not* a pre-established harmony between human reason and divine truth, for the simple reason that God alone is *God*: "For my thoughts are not your thoughts, nor are your ways my ways, says the Lord. For as the heavens are higher than the earth, so are my ways higher than your ways, and my thoughts that your thoughts" (Isa 55:8-9). There is thus a *qualitative* distinction between the ontic reality of God's eternal truth, and the noetic search for human understanding; minor adjustments this way or that fail to see that human rationality *as a whole* is dust and ashes in comparison with the unspeakable grandeur and

---

60. For a comprehensive presentation of the philosophical tools available to Protestant scholasticism, see the still valuable monograph by Max Wundt, *Die Deutsche Schulmetaphysik des 17. Jahrhunderts.*

61. Pictet is of course Reformed; however the same issue appears in very similar ways in high scholasticism on the Lutheran side. See, for example, concerning Johannes Quenstedt, Jörg Baur, *Die Vernunft zwischen Ontologie und Evangelium*, especially 111-15. It should perhaps be stressed that the same critique of the instrumental use of reason in protestant scholasticism applies whether one is a classic Aristotelian such as Turrettini, or a neo-Aristotelian such as Bartholomaeus Keckermann, or a Ramist such as Polanus, or indeed even a Cartesian such as Franz Burman or Christoph Wittichius. The issue is the organic *use* of reason in theological epistemology, not the particular philosophy applied. For an exhaustive survey, see Wollgast, *Philosophie zwischen Reformation und Aufklarung*, 128-220.

glory of God's revealed will. Human reason *cannot* channel what God alone speaks from on high: "The Lord exists forever; your word is firmly fixed in heaven" (Ps 119:89). The organic use of reason domesticates the divine Word in such a way as to make it fully comfortable, because fully conformable, to the expectations and moral "worldview" of Western humanity. Yet the Word of God is not spoken to make us comfortable: "Indeed, the word of God is living and active, sharper than any two-edged sword, piercing until it divides soul from spirit, joints from marrow; it is able to judge the thoughts and intentions of the hearts" (Heb 4:12). The Word of God shatters the categories of human understanding, placing us face to face with the living reality of God, "to whom we must render an account" (Heb 4:13). He most certainly has no need to render account to us.

The third option—in my judgment, by far the most appropriate to the task of faith seeking understanding—is the *dialectical* use of reason, as practiced by the major Protestant Reformers, including Luther, Melanchthon, and Calvin, among others. For the Reformers, faith in the Word of God makes it absolutely clear that reason is utterly blind and completely unable to grasp the divine will. For example, in the *Heidelberg Disputation* (1518), Luther argues that, according to Scripture, the love of God creates its own object. God does not find a lovable person to love and then love them; God finds an unlovable person, and by loving makes them lovable. And yet this is exactly contrary to the teaching of Aristotle and all philosophy, which assumes that the "power of the soul is passive," and therefore can only react to what it finds in the object. Luther sets up an absolute contrast: "Thus it is also demonstrated that Aristotle's philosophy is contrary to theology since in all things it seeks those things which are its own and receives rather than gives something good."[62] So in this sense, reason is thus antithetical to the Word of God; it argues the opposite of truth. Yet on the other hand, Luther can call Aristotle to his aid. In a passage in his *Commentary on Galatians*, he is making the point that faith always precedes good works. According to Luther, even the "sophists" must admit this to be true, since their beloved Aristotle says the same thing: "For they themselves are forced to grant, as they teach on the basis of Aristotle, that every good work proceeds from choice. If this is true in philosophy, it is much more necessary in theology . . ."[63] Thus for Luther, on the one hand, Aristotle—and with him the whole of rational philosophy—leads only to massive error; and yet on the other

62. Luther, *LW* 31, 57.
63. Luther, *LW* 26, 294.

hand, the same Aristotle and the reason he embodies supports the teaching of divine truth. Such examples abound in the Reformers. Melanchthon can say on the one hand that Aristotle (along with Socrates, Xenophon, Plato, Cicero, and Cato) knows "nothing at all" about God's free forgiveness of sins, which is the heart of the gospel, the very truth by which we live;[64] and yet on the other hand, the same Melanchthon can, upon the occasion of promotion of the Masters, in his capacity as Dean of the arts faculty, give an oration ... in praise of Aristotle! Says Melanchthon: "For truly, without the true system of teaching men are not at all different from beasts. Therefore ... the kind of knowledge that Aristotle taught must be preserved with the greatest zeal. I have spoken."[65] Calvin can state that the human mind is nothing but the "mother of error," whose every contrivance does nothing but "basely corrupt religion."[66] Yet he can also confidently affirm: "When we so condemn human understanding for its perpetual blindness as to leave it no perception of any object whatever, we not only go against God's Word, but also run counter to the experience of common sense."[67] Now, in each of these example—and countless more besides could be adduced—it is *not* a matter of dividing up reason into a good part and a bad part, or a good role and a bad role; still less of arguing for a distinction between reason in unredeemed humanity and reason in redeemed humanity, which became common in Protestant scholasticism. Rather, it is a matter of utterly condemning reason in its *totality* on the one hand (for *all* humanity), and yet affirming its usefulness in theology—from *every* source, pagan or not—on the other. That is the dialectical view; how are we to make sense of it?

For the Reformers, faith seeking understanding is not a process, but an *event*. On the one hand, humanity stands before the cross of Jesus and there learns that its reason is completely useless before the supreme majesty of divine truth concealed in the crucifixion: "Where is the one who is wise? Where is the scribe? Where is the debater of this age? Has not God made foolish the wisdom of this world?" (1 Cor 1:20). Not as an article of human skepticism, but only in the light of the cross, comes the realization that human reason is impotent; it knows nothing, contributes nothing, leads to nothing but a "labyrinth" (Calvin's favorite metaphor) of endless self-enclosed misunderstanding. Religion is not exempt from this impotence; it

---

64. Melanchthon, *Loci Communes* (1555), 6.
65. Melanchthon, *Orations*, 211.
66. Calvin, *LCC* XX, 67, 65.
67. Ibid., 271.

only exacerbates it, fueling human arrogance with the fanaticism of piety. After all, it took enormous rational enterprise to build the Tower of Babel, which was to reach to the very heavens (Gen 11:1–9). That is one side of the dialectic, which cannot ever be removed.

Yet on the other hand, the same humanity stands before the risen Christ in the power of the Spirit. And with the presence of the Spirit comes the call to use all gifts of mind, body, will, and emotion, in the service of the risen Lord: "Do not be conformed to this world, but be transformed by the renewing of your minds, so that you may discern what is the will of God . . ." (Rom 12:2). Under the shadow of the cross, *no* human intellectual resources are fit for the kingdom of God. Yet in the light of the resurrection, *all* human intellectual and cultural resources may be fit for the task of seeking to understand what we believe. There in the same land of Babylon—the land of Shinar (Dan 1:2) where the legendary Tower was once built (Gen 11:2), Daniel and his three friends take what amounts to a graduate degree in foreign cultural studies: they are taught "for three years" the "literature and language of the Chaldeans" (Dan 1:3–7). They must prove their faith in the new world of Babylon; yet they are clearly fully at home in that world, in fact given by God himself a degree of knowledge and understanding far exceeding their peers (Dan 1:20). There is no bridge from the old to the new, no platform or method from the old age of human blindness to the new age of human understanding. The shift is not in any way anthropological—we are still fully human in every way, still fully sinners, saved by grace alone—but eschatological, indeed christological: for it is ultimately the crucified and risen Christ alone who uses our intellect as he sees fit. To quote Luther, Christ himself is "the best dialectician" (*der beste Dialectus*).[68]

---

68. Luther, *LW* 51, 309.

3

Proclamation

IT IS OFTEN SAID: the history of the church is the history of the interpretation of the Bible.[1] We ask: despite some obvious insight, is this affirmation true?

To understand the essence of the community of faith—what it is, and how it grows over time—we must learn, not from the fragile basis of human observation, but from the word of God. The Book of Acts begins with a full description of the ascension of the crucified and risen Christ into heaven (Acts 1:1–11), and the coming of the Spirit upon the gathered disciples at Pentecost (Acts 2:1–13). The ministry of the earthly life of Jesus now lies in the past; a new age, a new time in the purpose of God for the world now begins: and that is the time of the church. What exactly then is the relationship between the earthly life of Jesus—his life, death, and resurrection—and the new time of the church? The earthly story of Jesus has come to an end; the narrative of the gospel comes to a conclusion, and does not extend into the new time of the church. The gospel is about the ministry of Jesus; now, in the Book of Acts, the unfolding of the life of the church begins. Nevertheless, the kingdom of God announced by Jesus does not come to an end with his earthly ministry; for indeed, now the community of disciples are entrusted with the ministry of the kingdom—the same ministry as Christ the Lord. They are witnesses of his resurrection, chosen and sent forth by Christ himself: "you will be my witnesses in Jerusalem, in all Judea and Samaria, and to the ends of the earth" (Acts 1:8). Despite the

---

1. The sentiment is usually associated with the groundbreaking researches of Gerhard Ebeling.

difference in the two eras—the earthly life of Jesus and the new ministry of the church—the divine redemptive purpose remains the same.

So how is the new mission of the church described? A decisive new reality breaks forth into the gathered community, and that is the coming of the Spirit: "All of them were filled with the Holy Spirit and began to speak in other languages, as the Spirit gave them ability" (Acts 2:4). They are sent by Christ to the very ends of the earth; now they are equipped by the Spirit with the languages necessary to speak to all nations of the earth. The Spirit moves the church out into the world to fulfill the commission of Christ. And the witness of the church—the genuine fulfillment of its mission—is through proclamation, through *preaching* the word of God: "When they had prayed, the place in which they were gathered together was shaken; and they were all filled with the Holy Spirit and spoke the word of God with boldness" (Acts 4:31). In fact, the Book of Acts is not a history of the early church, as is often asserted; it is a history of the word of God, a history of the *proclamation* of the gospel: "But many of those who heard the word believed; and they numbered about five thousand" (Acts 4:4); "The word of God continued to spread; the number of the disciples increased in Jerusalem, and a great many of the priests became obedient to the faith" (Acts 6:7); "But the word of God continued to advance and gain adherents" (Acts 12:24). The preaching of Christ is nothing less than the very presence of Christ through the power of his Spirit. The proclaimed word—with a specific teaching and a specific content—is now the place where the risen Christ is encountered, through the power of the Spirit. To follow Christ is to welcome the message (*logos*) (Acts 17:11).

We now amend our opening statement. The history of the church is the history of the *proclamation* of the word of God.

a. Faith from Hearing

We have stated that canon implies three essential dimensions: a normative text, the theological shaping of that text for future use by the community of faith, and the actualization of the text in the contemporary life of the community. The first of these we have treated in Chapter 1 above under the heading of the authority of Scripture, the second in the following chapter under the rubric of theological interpretation of Scripture. It is now time to make good on the third dimension of actualization, which takes place in the Christian community specifically in the form of proclamation. Notice that we include proclamation in our *definition* of canon, not in the *application* of canon to the life of the church. Proclamation of the gospel is not a secondary act of appropriation of the word of God; proclamation of the word of God *is* the word of God in this, the third dimension of canon. Proclamation therefore belongs, not buried in the later sections of church doctrine (where it usually appears under the innocuous heading of the "means of grace"), but in the primary position of the church's theological reflection on canon. The authority of Scripture is the *source* of the church's witness; the theological interpretation of Scripture provides the *content* of that witness; but proclamation of the gospel is the *act* of the witness of the church to the world, and therefore the *goal* of all church doctrine. A radical reversal from the customary design of the theological curriculum is therefore in order: proclamation of the word of God is not a secondary application of the various "higher" labors of church theology and research; church theology and research—including exegesis, church history, and church doctrine—are a secondary aid to the primary event of proclamation of the gospel.

To get a better sense for what is at stake, the profound understanding of proclamation in the early Reformation—both Lutheran and Reformed—provides a useful point of orientation. We begin with Luther, who makes what is perhaps an implicit idea from the time of the early church fully explicit, and in doing so revolutionizes the doctrine of proclamation. Already in the *Didache* (c. 100 A.D.?), the notion is clearly expressed that Christ himself is present in the preaching of the gospel: "My child, remember night and day the one who preaches God's word to you, and honor him as though he were the Lord. For wherever the Lord's nature (*kuriotes*=the Lordship) is preached, there the Lord is."[2] The preaching of the rule of Christ *is* the presence of Christ in the church for the world. By all appearances, this *explicit* insight recedes into the background, and becomes *implicit* at best by the time of medieval scholasticism. The Word becomes merely a source of information—both didactic and practical—concerning supernatural realities. Faith is related to those supernatural realities, not to the Word itself. It is against this background that Luther heard something entirely new in the text of Romans 10:17: "So faith comes from what is heard, and what is heard comes through the word of Christ." Luther describes his new understanding of the oral proclamation of the gospel this way: "For the preaching of the gospel is nothing else than Christ coming to us, or we being brought to him. When you see how he works, however, and how he helps everyone

---

2. Holmes, *Apostolic Fathers*, 349–51.

to whom he comes or who is brought to him, then rest assured that faith is accomplishing this in you and that he is offering your soul exactly the same sort of help and favor through the gospel... Then Christ is yours, presented to you as a gift."[3] The proclaimed word is no longer *information* about what Christ does or can do; the proclaimed word is *Christ himself* active through faith. Because it is his voice, the proclaimed word itself creates, judges, gives life, makes whole again. Faith is no longer related to supernatural realities behind the word; faith is related to the Word itself in which it finds the very redemptive power of Christ.

Several points need to be emphasized in coming to grips with the revolution in the doctrine of proclamation that accompanies—perhaps even makes possible—Reformation theology. The Reformation did not simply bring new *content* to preaching; it brought a fresh understanding to the *nature* of proclamation, and therefore its role in theology. The significance of the living voice of the word; the recognition that faith comes only from hearing (*fides ex auditu*), not from doing; the faith and community creating power of the proclaimed word; the presence of Christ by his Spirit in the living voice of proclamation; of all these together brought proclamation itself into the very center of church doctrine. Proclamation is no longer mere concretizing of the Scriptures for the present day; proclamation is the immediate and active voice of the risen Christ himself, without which faith is impossible, yet through which faith can do all things. Indeed, Gerhard Ebeling can even speak of the in-word-ing (*Inverbation*) of Christ, through which the incarnate Christ is now present in the proclaimed word: "The Word alone makes revelation actual, even in its hiddenness, for me."[4] Furthermore, for Luther preaching itself is an eschatological event in which the exalted Christ himself speaks in and through the words of the preacher. The living voice of the gospel (*viva vox evangelii*) that proclamation entails is nothing less than the voice of Christ himself, hidden in the words of the preacher. For Luther, God himself now says what the preacher says; that is the essence of Christian proclamation. When the Law is proclaimed by the preacher, God himself is casting down; when the gospel is proclaimed, God himself is raising up. The one power of the church is the power of the gospel, which is the preaching of the word of God. Again, no one could have a higher view of the Scriptures than Luther; yet he was fond of pointing out that Christ wrote nothing, but only preached, and commanded his disciples

---

3. Luther, *LW* 35, 121.
4. Ebeling, *Evangelienauslegung*, 362–65.

to preach: "Therefore the church is a mouth-house, not a pen-house [Luther is playing on the word *Bethphage*], for since Christ's advent that Gospel is preached orally which before was hidden in written books. It is the way of the Gospel . . . that it is to be preached and discussed orally with a living voice. The sending (of the disciples) shows that the kingdom of Christ is contained in the public oral office of preaching, which shall not stand nor remain in one place . . . but should go openly, free and untrammeled into the world."[5] The God of the entire universe is hidden from all eyes but is *heard* in the lowly voice of the Sunday sermon. In my judgment, it is fatuous to ask, as for example Jaroslav Pelikan does, whether Luther values the spoken word above the written word;[6] in *both* the same God speaks with one voice, therefore, why is the question even relevant? However, of supreme relevance is the simple point that for Luther, the proclaimed word, like the written word, is the *active* voice of God, hidden in the world. The whole point of possessing the treasure of Scripture is that the gospel it attests might be proclaimed anew. The proclaimed word finally is the very source of the life of the church: "Now, wherever you hear or see this word preached, believed, professed, and lived, do not doubt that the true *ecclesia sancta catholica*, 'a Christian holy people' must be there, even though their number is small . . . God's word cannot be without God's people, and conversely, God's people cannot be without God's word. Otherwise, who would preach or hear it preached, if there were no people of God? And what could or would God's people believe, if there were no word of God?"[7] For Luther, proclamation is clearly not mere application of the word of God; it is God's own creative and sustaining voice, summoning the church and the world to behold his glory alone. To summarize, in the words of Ulrich Asendorf: "Luther's theology therefore is, in a special way, bound together with preaching. Preaching is not a sort of side-theme; rather, this theology itself is essentially proclamation, and must from that standpoint be understood."[8]

A concise and systematic articulation of the early Reformed doctrine of proclamation is offered by Heinrich Bullinger in *The Second Helvetic Confession* of 1566, which offers a position differing very little from Luther. It is highly significant that the issue of proclamation is treated in the opening chapter on Holy Scripture, *Of the Holy Scripture Being the True Word of*

---

5. *Luther's Sermons* 1, 44-45.
6. Pelikan, *TCT* 4, 181.
7. Luther, *LW* 41, 150.
8. Asendorf, *Die Theologie Luthers nach Predigten*, 22.

God (*De Scriptura sancta, vero Dei Verbo*). For Bullinger—as for the other early Reformed (and Lutheran) theologians, confessing faith in Holy Scripture as the Word of God is incomplete unless it likewise *includes* the role of proclamation in the divine economy. God himself certainly spoke to the prophets and apostles according to Bullinger; but just as importantly, the same God himself "still speaks to us through the Holy Scriptures" (*loquitur adhuc nobis per scripturas sanctas*).[9] How does he still speak? Bullinger makes it crystal clear in the strident marginal heading which opens the section on preaching: "The preaching of the Word of God is the Word of God" (*Praedicatio verbi Dei est verbum Dei*).[10] When duly called ministers proclaim the word of God in the gathered community, God himself is speaking through them, and his divine word is announced and received by those gathered. Indeed, this divinely ordained means of communication not only applies to today (*hodie*); the proclamation of the word of God is the source of expectation and anticipation throughout time: "neither any other word of God is to be invented nor is to be expected from heaven..."[11] Bullinger goes on to stress the inward work of the Spirit that accompanies the external preaching of the word; however, he bends over backwards to make it clear that the Spirit works through the external preaching, not apart from it: "For he that illuminates inwardly by giving men the Holy Spirit, the same one, by way of commandment, said unto his disciples, 'Go into all the world, and preach the gospel to the whole creation.'"[12] To say that Bullinger's emphasis on the inner working of the Spirit "exposes" his fundamental "spiritualism,"[13] in my judgment, fails to reckon with his forthright declaration: "Inward Illumination Does Not Eliminate External Preaching" (*Interior illuminatio non tollit externam praedicationem*)[14] At any rate, as the above quotation from Mark 16:15 ("Go into all the world...") shows, Bullinger grounds the doctrine of proclamation squarely in the command

9. Pelikan and Hotchkiss, eds., *CCFCT* II, 460.
10. Ibid.
11. Ibid.
12. Ibid., 461.
13. So Neuser in Andresen, et al., *HDThG* II, 227.
14. Ibid., 461. Neuser is obviously seeking to find an analogue to the debate over the Lord's Supper, in which Luther would hold to the preaching equivalent of the *manducatio oralis*, a kind of objective presence of Christ in the proclaimed word regardless of the response of faith; while Bullinger holds to the preaching equivalent of a *manducatio fidelium*, a true hearing of the word of Christ only by those opened by the Spirit. I am not at all convinced the analogy holds.

of the risen Christ. The issue is not rhetorical—it is not about communicating truths found in an ancient book to a modern audience—but christological: Jesus Christ himself is the author of both the written word and the proclaimed word, throughout all time.

Now, with this brief historical orientation from the early Reformation in mind, our theological argument is simple: the first part of church doctrine on canon *must* include, not only the authority and interpretation of Scripture, but also the *essential* role of proclamation. Canon means the normative role of Scripture; the theological interpretation of Scripture; and the proclamation of the word from Scripture. As so defined, canon is the first topic of theology, but also the basic context of all theology; which means that theology as a whole serves the preaching of the word.

Why did the Reformation understanding lose out in the modern project of theology? Why did proclamation become simply "applied" doctrine, rather than the goal of *all* doctrine? When modern prolegomena to church doctrine took shape in seventeenth-century Protestant scholasticism, the Reformation understanding of Scripture was included, as it should be; however, the early Reformation understanding of proclamation *disappeared* from the opening section on Scripture. Richard Muller is certainly right when he argues for a fundamental continuity in the doctrine of Scripture from the early Reformation through the period of Protestant scholasticism.[15] Otto Ritschl, in is comprehensive section on the Protestant dogma of inspiration (*Inspirationslehre*), is able to chart a fourfold variety of approaches (Melanchthon and his school, Luther and his followers, Calvin and Chemnitz, and Gerhard along with the majority of later Reformed scholastics); however, *all* of them stand by the commitment of the early church and medieval theology to the inspiration of the Bible.[16] The notion of a Reformation view of the Bible which somehow denies or passes over the doctrine of inspiration is an historical myth.[17] Muller is, however, quite in error when he maintains that the shift in *method* from the early Reformation to Protestant scholasticism resulted in no appreciable change

---

15. Muller, in Bagchi, et al., *Reformation Theology*, 143.

16. Ritschl, *DP* 1, 55–193. The great advantage of Ritschl's monumental four-volume study of the history of dogma in the Protestant Reformation and scholasticism, even over some more recent research, is that it covers *both* Lutheran and Reformed theologies together. Studies of each tradition in isolation are no doubt helpful; however, it is obvious that both traditions faced very similar theological issues and used similar tools. Until a new historical synthesis is attained, Ritschl's work remains useful.

17. *Contra* Migliore, *Faith Seeking*, 47, among many others.

in *content*.[18] Proclamation in seventeenth-century Protestant scholasticism becomes mere communication of sound doctrine (*sana doctrina*); entirely *lost* to the horizon of thought in Protestant scholasticism, both Lutheran and Reformed, is the fundamental conviction of the early Reformers that proclamation itself is a *mode* of Christ's own voice, without which theological reflection on Scripture is incomplete, even distorted. The cognitive foundation (*principium cognoscendi*) for Protestant scholasticism is indeed Holy Scripture, as Muller points out;[19] but what Muller fails to make clear is the *radical* change this new cognitive foundation signifies with reference to the Protestant Reformers. For the Reformation, as opposed to scholasticism, faith comes by *hearing*, and hearing comes through the *preaching* of Christ. *Proclamation* is the *principium cognoscendi*, to use the language of scholasticism. In the words of John Calvin: "This is a noteworthy passage on the efficacy of preaching, for Paul declares that faith is produced by preaching . . . Too much power would be paid to a mere mortal if it were said that he had power to regenerate us. The light of faith also is too exalted to be able to be conferred by man. But all these things do not prevent God from acting effectually by the voice of man (*per hominis vocem efficaciter*), so as to create faith in us by his ministry."[20] The early Reformation understanding of proclamation did not *reappear* until the opening volumes of the *Church Dogmatics* of Karl Barth. Karl Barth summarizes, not his own special approach to theology, but the fundamental commitment of church doctrine when he states without restriction or reservation: "By the grace of revelation and its witness, God commits Himself with His eternal Word to the preaching of the Christian Church in such a way that this preaching is not merely a proclamation of human ideas and convictions, but . . . it is God's own proclamation."[21]

b. The Living Word of God

God is known in the world: his name is celebrated; his will is cherished and obeyed; his praises are sung; his splendor and glory are enjoyed among all nations and peoples of the earth. God is known in the world; we now ask *how* God is known?

18. Muller in Bagchi, et al., *Reformation Theology*, 140.
19. Ibid., 143.
20. Calvin, *CNTC* 8, 233.
21. Barth, *CD* I/2, 745–46.

The Bible is a book of preaching. Poised on the edge of the promised land, ready to cross over the Jordan River, the people of Israel are gathered to hear the proclamation of Moses, which constitutes the Book of Deuteronomy: "In the fortieth year, on the first day of the eleventh month, Moses spoke to the Israelites just as the Lord had commanded him to speak to them" (Deut 1:3). Once the conquest and settlement of the land have transpired, Joshua also preaches to the gathered community: "A long time afterward, when the Lord had given rest to Israel from all their enemies all around, and Joshua was old and well advanced in years, Joshua summoned all Israel . . . and said to them . . ." (Josh 23:1–2). Preaching thus encircles the entry into the Promised Land and the promised fulfillment of the divine purpose. When the people later ask for a king, mimicking the countries around them, Samuel the prophet proclaims the divine response: "So Samuel reported all the words of the Lord to the people who were asking him for a king. He said . . ." (1 Sam 8:10–11). God instructs; God celebrates; God warns, by preaching. In his last words, King David announces the word of the Lord: "The spirit of the Lord speaks through me, his word is upon my tongue" (2 Sam 23:2). Once again, the proclamation of the word encircles the beginning of the monarchy, carries it through, until it reaches its highest point with the death of King David. The prophet Elijah challenges the people of God to make the hard choice of obedience, without which they cannot live: "Elijah then came near to all the people, and said, 'How long will you go limping with two different opinions? If the Lord is God, follow him; but if Baal, then follow him'" (1 Kgs 18:21).

The ministry of Jesus is a ministry of proclamation of the gospel in word and deed: "Jesus went throughout Galilee, teaching in their synagogues and proclaiming the good news of the kingdom and curing every disease and every sickness among the people" (Matt 4:23). His most characteristic teaching is gathered together in a single "Sermon on the Mount" (Matt 5–7). The Book of Acts is a history of the word of God, charting the growth and spread of the word throughout the whole world, according to the commission of the risen Christ (Acts 1:8). After the coming of the Spirit on Pentecost, Peter preaches to the gathered crowds (Acts 2:14–36); later Peter preaches to his fellow Israelites gathered at Solomon's Portico (Acts 3:12–26); then Peter preaches while under arrest by the religious authorities, proclaiming the good news of Christ to those very authorities: "There is salvation in no one else, for there is no other name under heaven given among mortals by which we must be saved" (Acts 4:8–12). Stephen, too, is seized by the religious leaders, and in the last act before his martyrdom gives a sermon bearing witness to the sovereign divine purpose fulfilled in Jesus Christ (Acts 7:2–53). Paul preaches numerous sermons on his missionary journeys; preaches to those who have arrested and imprisoned him; and finally from house arrest in Rome preaches to all who visit: "He lived there two whole years at his own expense and welcomed all who came to him, proclaiming the kingdom of God and teaching about the Lord Jesus Christ with all boldness and without hindrance" (Acts 28:30–31). Indeed, the Book of Acts is thus framed, literally, by proclamation. The entire Pauline charge to the new generation can be summarized in a phrase: "proclaim the message" (2 Tim 4:2).

The Bible is a book of proclamation; it is no surprise therefore that the community of faith, which lives under the authority of the Bible, recognizes proclamation as the very center of our common life.

The reality of the exalted Christ and the proclaimed word are in dialectical relation to one another. On the one hand, the proclamation of the gospel is grounded solely in the universal authority of the risen Christ. Jesus Christ, and he alone, is the true content of the gospel, the true substance of all genuine proclamation. We do not preach a conservative or liberal ideology, to which the name of Christ is then subsequently attached; for to do so is to forsake the very task by which we live. We proclaim Christ alone to the nations of the earth, to the radical exclusion of every other message: "For Jews demand signs and Greeks desire wisdom, but we proclaim Christ crucified, a stumbling block to Jews and foolishness to Gentiles, but to those who are the called, both Jews and Greeks, Christ the power of God and the wisdom of God" (1 Cor 1:22). We do not preach Christ as an extension of our own personality or insights, nor as the development of our own projects of successful living or self-affirmation; we preach Christ only in obedient response to the commission that we have received from him. Jesus Christ, the one true content of all Christian proclamation, is the Word of God, besides whom there is no other divine word. We do not preach an absent or distant Lord; on the contrary, Christ himself is present in the contemporary proclamation of the word to the gathered community, even as he always has been: "For where two or three are gathered in my name, I am there among them" (Matt 18:20). Indeed, the voice of the contemporary minister, however shaky and fearful it may at times sound forth, is the living voice of Jesus Christ himself: "Whoever welcomes you welcomes me, and whoever welcomes me welcomes the one who sent me" (Matt 10:40). The voice of preaching is, exclusively by the miracle of grace alone, the voice of Christ himself, echoing throughout the whole creation in every age: "The grass withers, the flower fades; but the word of our God will stand forever ... lift up your voice with strength, O Jerusalem, herald of good tidings ... say to the cities of Judah, 'Here is your God'" (Isa 40:8-9). Jesus Christ is the sole basis and content of proclamation.

But so also is the other side of the dialectical equation true: proclamation is the sole avenue to the knowledge of Jesus Christ. The bond between Christ and the church comes solely through the proclamation of the gospel.[22] Christ is not immediately present to the church; rather, Christ is present through the *message* of the gospel. Indeed, Christ is not immediately present to the world; Christ is present through the *word* of the gospel, which is heard throughout all creation. The word of God is the work of God in the world, and is supremely active. The proclamation of the gospel is the medium by which the exalted Christ governs his church, and declares his will throughout the world. Jesus Christ alone is the true norm of proclamation; but proclamation alone is the true instrument by which Christ is present in all creation: "I bow down toward your holy temple and give thanks to your name for your steadfast love and your faithfulness; for you have exalted your name and your word above everything" (Ps 138:2)—actually, the Hebrew even reads: "you have exalted your word above all your name." At the heart of church doctrine stands the astonishing declaration: the proclaimed word is the living word of God. In so saying we are not escaping the literal world into a metaphorical world of as-if; quite the contrary, the church of Jesus Christ insists without wavering that the proclaimed word is, in the most literal sense possible, the living divine word. Again, we are not affirming some hidden capacity in the depths of metaphorical language to disclose the divine reality, beyond the limits of ordinary speech. Words *per se* reveal nothing about God, whether they are literal or metaphorical, whether they are a locutionary, a perlocutionary, or an illocutionary speech-act. It is only by the miraculous gift of the Holy Spirit that Christian proclamation is rendered the living word of God. Still, through the presence of the Spirit, it is literally true that the proclaimed word is the living

---

22. In its proper place in church doctrine we will add to this formulation not only the sacraments of the Lord's Supper and baptism (the Reformation view of Word and Sacrament), but also the *new humanity* that Christ himself forms in the midst of the global church. In my view, it is not only the right preaching of the gospel and the right celebration of the sacraments, but also indeed the new global humanity as a visible sign of God's purpose for the whole world, which signals the true presence of the church.

divine word. The voice of the preacher is, by the power of the Spirit, the voice of God; the words of the preacher are the words of God; God now says what the preacher says; the words of the preacher are, through the miraculous presence of the Spirit, spoken by the mouth of God. There can be no hesitation of the church in making this assertion, which is at the very basis of the Reformation rediscovery of preaching, and is essential to the church's theological confession of canon. No authentic proclamation is possible, except where the wondrous truth of this equation is recognized, despite the astonishing weakness—even absurdity—of the human dimension. Not because of our abilities or insights, which are empty and void, but only because of the gift of the Spirit, the preached word is God's word to the gathered congregation, and it can only be preached as such, and heard and received as such, where Jesus Christ is worshiped and glorified. Authentic humility recognizes this equation in the fear and trembling of living faith.

The proclamation of the gospel is therefore a fully eschatological *event*, in which the same almighty and eternal transforming power of God, already unleashed in the life, death, and resurrection of Christ, is even now present and fully active, calling for ultimate decision. When Mark speaks of "the beginning of the gospel of Jesus Christ the Son of God" (Mark 1:1), he is not marking the chronological time of Jesus's earthly ministry; he is pointing to the beginning of God's saving event through Christ, whose power continues on into the very present. This beginning, this gospel, this preaching about Christ, *does not end*. The words of the preacher are fully human words, and come forth from all too human lips; nevertheless, by the miracle of God, the words of the preacher are the living voice of God breaking forth into reality with overpowering force. God's eternal redemptive power is channeled through the preaching of Christ to the nations of the earth: "For I am not ashamed of the gospel; it is the power of God for salvation to everyone who has faith, to the Jew first and also to the Greek" (Rom 1:16). The vitality of the proclaimed word gathers the community of faith together, and constitutes the very center of our common life. We are formed and reformed by the proclaimed word, which shapes us with the divine power of wisdom and truth, not according to human purposes, but according to the redemptive purpose of God: "For the message about the cross is foolishness to those who are perishing, but to us who are being saved it is the power of God" (1 Cor 1:18). The proclaimed word reconciles us to God, offering the free gift of divine forgiveness, sealing on our hearts and minds the promise of grace: "All this is from God, who reconciled us to himself through Christ, and has given us the ministry of reconciliation … So we are ambassadors for Christ, since God is making his appeal through us …" (2 Cor 5:18–20). The ministry of reconciliation is precisely the ministry of the word of God's reconciling love in Jesus Christ. The proclaimed word opens the eyes of the blind, disclosing blind-spots that we cannot see in ourselves; the proclaimed word heals proud divisions, and shatters the struggles of power that sever us from Christ; the proclaimed word reaches into the core of our being, touching wounds we ourselves can never touch; the proclaimed word liberates us from crippling anxiety, and sets us free to newness of life; the proclaimed word changes human history, bringing down the mighty and lifting up the lowly. The proclaimed word is the truth by which our lives are measured; the wisdom of God by which our confusion gives way to ultimate clarity; the true bread of life by which we are radically and completely transformed. The proclaimed word is active with all the force of divine action, shaping our lives in ways that we cannot always foresee, and yet always according to the image of Jesus Christ. The proclamation of the word of God cannot and will not fail to accomplish the divine purpose for which it is sent forth: "For as the rain and the snow come down from heaven, and do not return there until they have watered the earth, making it bring forth and sprout, giving seed to the sower and bread to the eater, so shall my word be that goes out from my mouth; it shall not return to me empty, but it shall accomplish that which I purpose …" (Isa 55:10–11).

We return to our opening question of this section: how is God known in the world? Apologists on both the religious left and the religious right strive to *make a space* for God in the world, looking either to the good causes of liberal ideology or the good causes of conservative ideology for meaning and support. When those causes fail, God is apparently absent; when those causes succeed, and the church triumphs, God is there! Church doctrine, by sharp contrast, begins with the shattering recognition that God is *already* known in all the earth; that the proclamation of the gospel is *already* a reality throughout the whole of creation. The truth of God is everywhere manifest, and the reality of God is everywhere demonstrated. How? The proclaimed word of God is God's self-manifestation throughout all the world. The question for humanity is not *whether* God is known; the question for humanity is, in the light of the knowledge of God shining forth in the proclamation of the gospel, how shall we then live? Proclamation is not the answer to our questions; proclamation is the divine question, which summons from us an ultimate answer. The proclamation of the gospel does not leave us to search for an absent *God*, as if he is nowhere to be found; rather, because God is here in the proclamation of the word, we are left with the search for an absent *humanity* in the light of God's terrible mercy. The proclamation of the gospel turns the world upside down, never fitting into the schemes and designs of well-intended humanity, but exposing and destroying every scheme opposed to the living Christ through the offense of the gospel, including so-called "Christian" worldviews. The proclamation of the gospel is radiant light and abundant life for all humanity, bringing to all the earth the knowledge of God, often enough far more radical than any liberal cause, often enough far more traditional than any conservative cause. Proclamation is God's invasion of the comfortable and self-sustaining world of human rebellion, restoring the true order of God in the world. The world is not problematic because knowledge of God is absent; things only become truly problematic for humanity because the knowledge of God is already a present reality through the preaching of the living word of God, which cannot and will not allow evasion and subterfuge. Joy, liberation, comfort, encouragement, healing, challenge, direction; the proclaimed word of God enters human life with the divine force of direct encounter between the living God and the real life of ordinary human beings in all their everyday concrete need, and in all their promise.

The living word of God is effective, with all the transforming power of God himself. However stunning such a confession may appear, the sheer weakness of the weekly sermon is in reality the point of contact between the Lord of all creation and all human life. The proclaimed word is self-authenticating, creating space for itself without appeal to human capacity. The words of the sermon are therefore the embodiment of divine power, as Luther rightly declares: "When we seriously ponder the Word, hear it, and put it to use, such is its power that it never departs without fruit. It always awakens new understanding, new pleasure, and a new spirit of devotion, and it constantly cleanses the heart and its meditations. For these words are not idle or dead, but effective and living."[23] The words of the sermons confront humanity therefore with ultimate decision, involving death . . . or life.

---

23. Luther, *Large Catechism*, 23.

c. Ministry of the Word

Every historic denomination within the universal church has procedures in place for recognizing and ordaining ministers of the Word. Such procedures are necessary for the good order of the church, serving to protect the integrity and legitimacy of the office of minister. Together these procedures constitute the horizontal dimension of the call to ministry, which is the province of church administration. Church doctrine, on the other hand, is concerned with the vertical dimension of the call to ministry. Both dimensions are essential, and equally valid; those whom God has called should be recognized and authorized by the visible church, though I am convinced that no one version of church order is *the* only biblical one. Nevertheless, the proper focus on the horizontal dimension must not be allowed to eclipse the necessary *christological* basis of all Christian ministry.

Saul is there at the death of Stephen, approving the barbaric stoning of the first martyr for Christ (Acts 8:1). Saul leads the way in an active persecution of Christians in Jerusalem, entering the homes of the innocent in order to drag them away to death (Acts 8:3). Inflamed by a righteous zeal for cleansing away the filth of Christian discipleship, Saul approaches the high priest himself for permission to carry the persecution to surrounding towns, where Christians have fled for safety. Armed with letters to the Jewish synagogues in Damascus, Saul makes his way along the road, looking for prisoners to bring back to Jerusalem. As he approaches Damascus, a divine light flashes forth around him. Saul falls to the ground, and hears the voice of the risen Christ: "I am Jesus, whom you are persecuting." Christ commands Saul to go into the city and await further instructions. Blinded, Saul is led by the hand into the city, where he waits for three days without food or drink. A man named Ananias is called by Christ to heal Saul. Ananias finds Saul, lays hands on him, and his sight is restored, the scales falling from his eyes. Saul is baptized, and filled with the Holy Spirit. After eating, to regain his strength, Saul—soon to be known as Paul the apostle—begins his explosive ministry by preaching in Damascus. He proclaims Jesus in the synagogues: "He is the Son of God" (Acts 9:1–22).

The Christian ministry of the word is grounded in the call of God. The ministry of the Word is not a fulfillment of personal ambition; it is not a completion of a human search for meaning and truth; it is not a further development of the various life projects that flow from heart and mind. To be called is to be sent; to be sent is to be chosen; to be chosen is to be seized from above by the power of the risen Christ. There is human decision involved; nevertheless, human decision is but a distant echo of the divine decision, which is grounded exclusively in God's electing love. Jesus Christ himself chooses those whom he sends forth into the world with the message of the gospel. The free decision of Christ is the basis for ministry of the Word. The entire ministry of the Word, from start to finish, stands under the unbreakable order: "You did not choose me but I chose you" (John 15:16). The human response to the call is undertaken by the candidate for ministry; the validity of the call is confirmed by approval of the community of faith; but the authority of the call is grounded solely in the sovereign rule of the risen and exalted Christ over all reality.

Ministry of the Word is service of Jesus Christ. Ministers of the Word are servants of Christ. They go where he sends them, even though their natural desires may be contradicted by the higher call of the gospel. They say what he commands them to say, not what their own reason or experience may lead them to conclude. They speak the truth of the gospel, even when doing so is against their own best interests, and may even result in grave personal loss. As servants of Christ, ministers of the Word do not *lose* their own personality, their own way of living and thinking, their own free approach to life. Indeed, there is nothing more spontaneous and joyous than the freedom of service in the Christian ministry. Nevertheless, the call to the ministry encompasses their entire existence, moving them forward according to the superior claim of Christ, which irresistibly and relentlessly guides the church. The service of Christ is not a contradiction of freedom; indeed, true freedom is found only in the service of Christ. Still, the demand of the gospel is the only basis for ministry. In an era of self-affirmation, there is a vital need to hear the call to ministry in all its self-grounded sovereignty: "Then he said to his disciples, 'The harvest is plentiful, but the laborers are few; therefore ask the Lord of the harvest to send out laborers into his harvest'" (Matt 9:37–38).

Ministry of the Word is also service of the people of God. There is no room in the ministry for arrogant domineering; there is no room for harsh and unyielding inflexibility; there is no room for morally superior condemnation without heartfelt compassion. Instead, the minister of the Word sets an example of humility for all to see: "Do not lord it over those in your charge, but be examples to the flock" (1 Pet 5:3). The ministry of the Word is not given for the purpose of gathering a personal following, or amassing fame and fortune. Televangelism is not the peak of Christian ministry, but its nadir; nothing could be further from the divine call to ministry than the contemporary image of the successful television preacher. Instead, the call to ministry redefines the very meaning of what is means to succeed: "You know that among the Gentiles those whom they recognize as their rulers lord it over them, and their great ones are tyrants over them. But it is not so among you; but whoever wishes to become great among you must be your servant, and whoever wishes to be first among you must be slave of all" (Mark 10:42–43). Mutual service in the community of faith is the genuine sign, not only of those called to the ministry of the gospel, but of all Christians called to serve Christ in responsibility for church and society.

The call to the ministry is never rightly accepted as a burden, but only as an extraordinary adventure; and yet it is not received as one option among others, but rather as a compelling direction from which there is no escape. The call to ministry is not the final product of a quest for self-fulfillment, but radically breaks through the many possible options of life, and points toward only one new direction in life. The word of the Lord comes to Jonah, and he flees; only after God rescues him in the belly of the fish does the word come again: "The word of the Lord came to Jonah a second time, saying, 'Get up, go to Nineveh, that great city, and proclaim to it the message that I tell you'" (Jonah 3:1). Christian ministry is in no way a fulfillment of human potential, but rather a miraculous divine claim.

The energy of the ministry of the Word comes from the gift of the Holy Spirit. Christian ministry is not the exercise of human capacity; by sharp contrast, ministry of the Word is the gift of the Holy Spirit. It is not the only gift; the gifts of the Spirit range far and wide throughout the community of faith, summoning it into being, sending it out into the world, guiding and sustaining its life. However, the ministry of the Word is a gift of the Spirit, given according to the divine purpose. The Spirit alone guides the minister to proclaim the truth of the gospel; the Spirit alone prompts the minister to responsible and relevant witness; the Spirit alone moves the minister to an exemplary life of Christian obedience; the Spirit alone bears fruits through the preached word. The Holy Spirit teaches the minister the true content of Christian witness, based on the words and content of Scripture. The Spirit draws the connections between the Bible and the contemporary world, which drive the proclaimed word home with the force and appeal of divine clarity. The Spirit seals on the hearts and minds of the listeners the insights of the biblical message, brought to them through the Christian ministry. No earthly power can stand against the Spirit, who moves according to the mystery of divine freedom: "The wind blows where it chooses . . . so it is with everyone who is born of the Spirit" (John 3:8).

The conduct of the ministry of the word is undertaken in a profound paradox of faithfulness and freedom. On the one hand, ministers are called in the proclamation of the word to be *faithful* to Holy Scripture. In Paul's farewell address to the elders from the young congregation in Ephesus who came to meet him one last time in Miletus, it is clear that an era is ending. According to Luke, Paul is the last of the apostles; and with his death, the apostolic age will come to an end; the post-apostolic church will commence. Paul stresses that in his own ministry he has been faithful, "proclaiming the message to you and teaching you publicly . . ." (Acts 20:20); he has maintained the continuity of apostolic tradition in all its completeness, not failing to teach "the whole purpose of God" (v. 27); and he has put the welfare of the church above any form of personal gain, having "worked with my hands to support myself and my companions" (v. 34). That is the way of a true apostle; now all future leaders of the church are to abide by the apostolic model that Paul himself has exemplified. They have received the "whole purpose of God" from apostolic authority, which sets the outer boundaries of divine truth; now the new generation of leaders is to build on ("remember," vss. 31, 35) that inheritance; they have observed the apostolic way of life, and must now care for the needy, and "support the weak" (v. 35); they must maintain a faithful ministry of the gospel that is a message of grace, a grace which is "able to build you up and give you the inheritance . . ." (v. 32). That some form of regular ministry is being envisioned by this passage is clear; yet the authority comes through faithfulness to the grace of God's word in the service of the weak.

In sum we speak the prophetic and apostolic word with the full vigor of divine power; but we do so as ministers of the prophetic and apostolic Word, not as prophets or apostles. Walter Brueggemann's widely popular book, *The Prophetic Imagination*, abstracts and traces the history of "prophetic ministry" from Moses to Jesus, and then encourages contemporary ministers to engage in that same abstract "prophetic ministry" amidst "bourgeois" congregations.[24] Against Brueggemann, we must argue that the line of prophets and apostles ends with the canon of Scripture. Ours is not "prophetic ministry," but ministry of the prophetic and apostolic word. Calvin is convincing: "Let this be a firm principle (*firmum axioma*): No other word is to be held as the word of God, and given place as such in the

---

24. Brueggemann, *Prophetic Imagination*, 116.

church, than what is contained first in the Law and the Prophets, then in the writings of the apostles; and the only authorized way of teaching in the church is by the prescription and standard (*praescriptio et norma*) of his Word."[25]

On the other hand, the minister of the Word is an ambassador of Jesus Christ, in the full *freedom* of the divine call. The entire Book of Deuteronomy serves as an example of such freedom. In its canonical form, the book, though clearly composed of several speeches, has the appearance of one long sermon by Moses to the people of Israel gathered on the banks of the Jordan waiting to cross over for the first time into the Promised Land. On the one hand, Moses undertakes to explain the Law (Deut 1:5) to the new generation who were not there to receive it at Mount Sinai; for that first generation have all died during the years of wandering in the wilderness. This is no new law; it is the same law as given by God on Sinai. And yet an entirely *new* application of the legal tradition is offered in the book, involving nothing less than a new interpretation of total response of commitment to God: "You shall love the Lord your God with all your heart, and with all your soul, and with all your might" (Deut 6:5). Clearly, explaining the Law means more than simply imparting information about the content of Sinai legislation; Moses clarifies and interprets the divine will so that the new generation will understand in the new context they are about to enter the full impact of the divine command in the covenant of life. Again, God's purpose has not changed; yet Moses offers a new formulation of that purpose in the specific context of leaving the past behind, and embracing a new future: "So now, Israel, give heed to the statutes and ordinances that I am teaching you to observe, so that you may live to enter and occupy the land that the Lord, the God of your ancestors, is giving you" (Deut 4:1).

Now, as ministers of the gospel we speak the prophetic and apostolic word; yet we speak in the freedom of each new generation, in the context of each new situation, in the light of God's one eternal divine purpose of love for all humanity. In his section on the means of grace, Wayne Grudem makes it clear that the Bible is the primary means of grace in the church. There then follows only a page or two devoted to "teaching the Bible," which includes Bible studies, Sunday school, personal reading of "Christian books" and so forth.[26] It is quite clear for Grudem (as it is likewise, for example, for Charles Hodge), that *there is no doctrine of proclamation*. Preaching, if it

---

25. Calvin, *LCC* XXI, 1155.
26. Grudem, *Systematic Theology*, 952-53.

means anything at all, simply means repeating the words of the Bible, and teaching what they mean. That, I submit, is not the joyous freedom of the gospel that truly reveres the Scriptures, but the false legalism of obsessive biblicism that in the end distorts what it aims to honor. We will let Luther defend the true evangelical freedom of genuine proclamation: "A preacher should not . . . ask for forgiveness of sins when he has preached (if he is a true preacher) . . . Here it is unnecessary, even bad, to pray for forgiveness of sins, as if one had not taught truly, for it is God's word and not my word, and God ought not and cannot forgive it, but only confirm, praise, and crown it, saying, 'You have taught truly, for I have spoken through you and the word is mine.' Whoever cannot boast like that about his preaching, let him give up preaching, for he truly lies and slanders God."[27]

To conclude: I have purposely spoken of a paradox of faithfulness and freedom, not a continuum. It is not as though proclamation needs to find a midpoint somehow between freedom on the one end of a line, and faithfulness on the other end. Rather, the paradox of preaching—which is the mysterious paradox of grace itself—is that the very point at which absolute faithfulness is found, there God's own gift of complete and total freedom opens the way.

d. The Language of Faith

The Sunday sermon teaches the language of faith to the gathered community of God's people. There is no more challenging task, drawing forth every ounce of energy and creative imagination; there is no more rewarding labor, confronting the lives of ordinary human beings with the word of life that makes us whole; there is no more daunting endeavor, which summons from those who practice it the highest reaches of intellectual vitality. Teaching the language of faith is hard work; teaching the language of faith is extraordinary joy; teaching the language of faith is astonishing wonder. On the right is conservative ideology, which allows for an easy lapse into a moralistic "worldview"; on the left is liberal ideology, which allows for an equally easy lapse into the rhetoric of self-affirming liberation; but there up ahead is the narrow path that leads to life, and the minister is called to guide the congregation along that path from one week to the next. The call to teach the language of faith to each new generation of the church is extended

---

27. Luther in *Against Hanswurst*, LW 41, 216.

to those who are its intellectual, moral, and spiritual leaders, so infinitely precious is the treasure of the gospel which that language embodies.

The language of faith is drawn from Scripture according to the theological shape of its final form. The various techniques of historical reconstruction using the mode of ostensive reference are a sure method of obscuring the luminous clarity of the language of faith. The issue is not *whether* to use the tools of historical criticism; the issue is *how* to use them in the service of Christian proclamation. The Bible certainly requires preaching in order to bring home the genuine content of its message; Scripture does not preach itself. Nevertheless, Scripture is shaped to be preached, and the theological shape of its final form is definitive and normative. Canon is the sole definitive context from which the language of faith is learned and taught from Scripture. Canon sets boundaries outside of which the gospel is not rightly preached, yet also incorporates legitimate diversity and flexibility to protect against a rigid and stifling legalism. Only by following the canonical guidelines built into the theological structure of the biblical witness does proclamation rightly focus in a balanced way on the radically new promise of the gospel message. The final form leaves the various biblical genres intact, and authentic proclamation follows Scripture in preserving those various genres: narrative is to be retold with dramatic power, epistolary argument is to be rehearsed with dialectical skill, prophetic speech is to be annunciated with all the explosive force of direct divine address, wisdom is to be handled with appropriate meditative reflection, and so forth. The final form of the text leaves a variety of genres, and that means that preaching must be ever flexible in form; and yet the purpose of God is one in all these genres, and only by following the theological shape of the text can proclamation faithfully discern and communicate the one divine purpose with theological subtlety and skill. The pathways to disaster are easy and manifold; the narrow way of true life is hard, and it takes absolute devotion to truth in order to find it and show it to others.

There is delicate interplay between clarity and subtlety in genuine Christian proclamation. The language of faith is always clear; the preaching of the Word should therefore always be lucid in form and content. The basic theological structure of the sermon should be easily grasped by the ordinary listener; the points covered should be easily retained by those who ponder the Word throughout the week. The preaching of the Word is for ordinary people who struggle with the ordinary problems of daily life, and has nothing to do with a philosophical exercise for the merely curious.

Yet on the other hand, the clarity of the language of faith never devolves into over-simplification. There is a subtlety to God's will; a nuance to God's word; a complexity to God's command; therefore, the language of faith must reflect that intricacy.

The oversimplifications of the gospel by the various fads and gimmicks of our time obscure rather than illuminate the language of faith. Surely our time sadly excels in the oversimplification of the gospel. Perhaps because of the pervasive influence of mass media, we in our time are in the unique position of standing out in the history of the church for the unheralded range of possibilities for trivialization of the gospel! The mass marketing of consumer Christianity has brought with it a wide variety of skillful distractions from the word of truth; distractions that have the ring of truth, but that in fact are hollow and misleading. Athanasius had his Arius, with the skillful jingle "there was a time when he was not"; Luther had his Tetzel, with his "when the money clinks into the chest, the soul flies out of purgatory"; but thanks to the mass marketing of Christianity, we today have a thousand varieties of suitable trivializations to choose from! Each new year brings the latest fad; each new season brings the latest gimmick; each new publishing cycle brings the latest trivialization. It is one thing to protect and nourish the true simplicity of the gospel for ordinary people, which is required of all who teach the language of faith; it is quite another to allow trendy marketing to substitute for the refined beauty of biblical wisdom. Yet combining simplicity with subtlety can be done, because it has been done many times over; reading the great preachers of the church firsthand provides the surest touch. Those who teach the language of faith are called by Christ to be "wise as serpents and innocent as doves" (Matt 10:16).

It goes without saying that those who teach the language of faith must themselves first learn it from Holy Scripture. To proclaim the Word of God from Scripture requires deep immersion in the Scriptures as a regular part of daily life. In a time of astonishing biblical illiteracy in the church, those who proclaim the Word must lead the church in knowing the contents of Scripture with profound familiarity. Commitment to preaching therefore brings with it lifelong exposure to Scripture, on a daily basis. There can be no substitute for regular, disciplined, reflective, and attentive reading of the Bible, not as a religious classic, but as God's Word to the church and to me. Such reading should be a regular part of every Christian's daily routine, as a member of the household of faith. How much more, then, should those who teach the language of faith to the people of God, be themselves immersed in the sacred writings from which we draw the bread of life itself?

The language of faith addresses the practical reality of everyday life in the contemporary world. Genuine proclamation does not deal in moral principles; there are no moral principles in the Bible in abstraction from the living Christ. A moralistic approach to preaching may highlight the exalted personal morality of the preacher, but it will not point to the Lord of all human moral life, the true Judge of the living and the dead. Rather, the language of faith involves the concrete, practical claims of the gospel, which show us how to live responsibly in church and society; how to cherish the truth of the gospel while maintaining goodwill toward all; how to contribute to the common good by individual service; how to hate the sin, but still deeply love the sinner; how to live and let live, under the sovereign gift of divine forgiveness. The language of faith is not moralistic but pragmatic, illuminating the everyday life of the ordinary Christian in the everyday world: "Your word is a lamp to my feet, and a light to my path" (Ps 119:105). The goal of all preaching is practical obedience to Christ in the concrete world of everyday life.

At the heart of preaching is a stunning paradox. On the one hand, we inherit the language of faith from generations of the church in the past. We are under sacred obligation to protect and defend the tradition we have received, and to hand on that tradition to the new generation. On the other hand, we live only in our contemporary world, not in the worlds of the past. We are also under sacred obligation to articulate the truth of the gospel in words and concepts appropriate to the present day. Without tradition we cannot be truthful; without contemporaneity we cannot be relevant. Thankfully, truth and relevance are not in tension with one another, as if we must negotiate back and forth between them. For the truth of the gospel only strikes home in the relevance of the present. Every preacher concentrates the full power of truth on the single moment of the present, under the authority of Jesus Christ: "See, now is the acceptable time; see, now is the day of salvation!" (2 Cor 6:2). Above all, preaching serves the eternal Now of God's direct claim upon human existence in the contemporary world, in every respect.

The topics of preaching should be as wide as the Scriptures. One permanent value of the lectionary is that is calls us to preach from all parts of the canon; simply choosing the Gospel reading on a routine basis is an evasion of Christian proclamation, as is preaching from the New Testament to the exclusion of the Old. Among the concerns of preaching must surely be the length and breadth of human emotion. The language of emotion is extraordinarily rich in the Bible; here are fears and joys, troubles and sorrows, hopes and dreams, deepest anxieties and exalted joys. Here is intense suffering, but also unspeakable delight; here is terrible sadness but also ultimate fulfillment. Here in the Bible disappointments are sounded, agonies are voiced, triumphs are celebrated. The language of faith includes the wide range of human emotion. Preaching the word means touching with sympathy the heart of human feeling, yet without the sentimental trap of pious religiosity. The contemporary minister of the Word must know well the human condition; and yet the purpose is not psychological insight, but theological illumination: how do we live in the light of God's amazing rule over all that exists, include the deepest feelings of the human heart?

Application of the language of faith to the present generation requires flexible and creative use of the imagination. Imagination draws connections between the new world of the Bible and the contemporary world in which we live. We are not apostles or prophets; our challenge is to proclaim the apostolic word, not a new word of our own invention. However, the challenge of the gospel includes endless figurative application of God's new world to the everyday life of ordinary Christians in our common life today. The language of faith is always *contemporary* language. Creative imagination is the channel through which God's Spirit leads every new generation of the church in learning the language of faith. Often it is the metaphors of the Bible that provide the key link; a sterile propositionalism will simply look right past the astonishing range of biblical metaphor, and inevitably devolve into pious trivialities. Yet there is trap to be avoided: while we proclaim the language of faith only in the common idiom of the contemporary world, we do not confirm the assumptions of that world. The language of faith always speaks a fresh word, which turns the world of common human experience upside down. The first are last; the poor are filled, while the rich are sent away empty; the weak and unworthy are chosen, while the mighty are cast aside. That may not be how the "world" works, but it is how *God* works in the world.

Imagination guides proclamation to the unexpected, which overturns and invites anew; imagination hears the notes of ultimate decision in the Bible, and never shrinks from sounding those notes with clarity and persuasive power; imagination works by suggestion, never by spelling out the obvious with labored and tedious drudgery; imagination presents the challenge of the gospel with only one goal, which is the total transformation of every listener, and indeed the whole creation; imagination stresses the positive content of the gospel, without falling into the pagan myth of positive thinking; imagination fosters the gift of self-awareness, which comes only through the mirror of the living Word; imagination proclaims the Word in a spirit of wonder, which never becomes familiar, and never lapses into stale custom; imagination does not translate the biblical world into our ordinary world, but rather leads the congregation to enter the new world of God to which Scripture bears witness, only to find that God's strange new world *is* the true mystery of our world today; imagination points, not to the personality of the preacher, but to the sovereign claim of the living Lord to whom we belong in life and in death. The only genuine test for the success of true proclamation is not the size of the congregation, nor the entertainment value provided, nor even the responses of approval from the listeners, however welcome they may be; the only test is the radically reoriented *lives* of those who learn anew the language of faith from the proclaimed Word.

The only effective power of proclamation is the divine power of the Spirit of God, without which preaching is null and void. The Spirit opens the heart and mind of the one who proclaims; the Spirit opens the hearts and minds of those who hear; the Spirit draws the connection between the biblical world and the world of today. The Spirit guides each new generation of the church to discern the present work of Jesus Christ, who alone is the true content of the language of faith. May God send forth his promised Spirit anew that we may know the risen and exalted Lord, and thereby come alive, as if for the first time!

4

The Trinity

MATTHEW'S GOSPEL CONCLUDES WITH an astonishing encounter between the risen Christ and his disciples (Matt 28:16–20). Jesus the crucified is risen from the dead. The risen Christ appears to the disciples, and tells them to go to Galilee. There they will see him, far away from the hostility and turmoil surrounding the event of the cross. The eleven disciples—Judas the betrayer is no longer among them—ascend a mountain. There, in quiet solitude apart, they see Jesus, the risen Lord.

Their response is confused and erratic. Intense joy and paralyzing fear are both in their hearts at the same time. Some of the disciples worship Jesus. But others still struggle with doubt. Even for the disciples, the resurrection is an utterly inconceivable miracle. And what is more, Jesus never offers visible signs to assure their doubt. Even seeing Jesus with their own two eyes does not take away their doubt. The answer to doubt lies in hearing, understanding, and obeying the word of the exalted Christ, not in seeing. Doubt is overcome only by *hearing* and *doing*.

Jesus declares to the disciples that all authority in heaven and earth has now been given to him. It is an astounding statement. Every single Old Testament promise is now fulfilled in him. Christ the risen Lord now rules all reality, the entire cosmos. No force is independent of his absolute control, even evil itself; no unseen power stands outside his universal rule over the entire creation. The whole universe now serves the risen Christ. Now, this passage is not looking forward to the final consummation. Rather, already, now, in the present, Christ rules the cosmos. All peoples and all powers are even now subject to his absolute authority over all reality. The final words of Christ in the Gospel of Matthew are not a *farewell* to the disciples. His words flow rather from his exaltation over the universe. They are words of *enthronement*, in which the full power of the risen Christ the Lord is extended over all that is.

But what does the exaltation of Christ mean for the disciples? Because the rule of Christ is now universal; so now the compassion of Christ reaches out to all humanity. The universal love of Christ calls forth a new reality among God's people: and that is mission. *Mission* is the new order of life appropriate to the rule of Christ.

Christ gives his commission to the disciples, often called the great commission. He tells his eleven disciples to go throughout all the nations of the earth, making disciples wherever they go. During his earthly life, the ministry of Jesus was restricted to the lost sheep of Israel. Now, in light of his unlimited authority over creation, the mission of the disciples is universal. They are sent by Christ to all peoples on earth. Their task is to make disciples wherever they go. They are to baptize in the triune name of God. And they are to teach others to obey everything that Christ himself has commanded. The past tense is important. The commands of the risen Christ that the disciples are to teach are not different commands than they have already received during his earthly life. Rather, the same commands that they have already learned from Jesus during his earthly life, they are now to take with them to all places on earth. The commands remain the same; the words of the earthly Jesus are the one normative rule for all time. What is new is not the message they bring; what is new is the universal extension of that one message to all humanity. Through the power of his command the exalted Christ himself is always present. Wherever his commands are remembered and obeyed, there is Christ himself active among them forever.

Orthodoxy in church doctrine is not a set of timeless propositions, arranged according to a rational system once-for-all. Orthodoxy, rather, is a theological framework of Christian truth, a framework that embraces a variety of theological confessions. Characteristic of this framework is the theological shape of orthodoxy; the inner logic of church doctrine is controlled by the divine subject matter that it reflects, without trying to define or grasp it. Regardless of the particular approach of any theological confession, the inner logic of the substance of church doctrine requires a theological form of reflection. This is clearly not a new insight; Phillip Melanchthon, for example, bears eloquent testimony to the demanding attentiveness to proper order necessary for the labor of dogmatic theology:

"Thus, it is very necessary, in every art and teaching, to note all the principal pieces—beginning, middle, and end—and carefully to consider how each and every piece fits with the others . . . and the teacher and the hearer must accustom themselves to comprehend this in a very orderly totality."[1] The inner logic of church doctrine is not based on the purported needs of the human mind for systematic thinking, but rather upon the inner truth of God's reality.

The doctrine of the Trinity belongs, not in the second part on God, but already in the opening part of church doctrine on canon. Why make this deliberate move, which reverses the characteristic ordering of much traditional theology? Three points need to be stressed at the outset. First, we are not the first to make it. In traditional theology, John of Damascus in the *Exposition of the Orthodox Faith*; Peter Lombard in *The Sentences*; Bonaventure in *The Breviloquium* all begin with the doctrine of the Trinity. In modern theology, Karl Barth very intentionally places the doctrine of the Trinity in the prolegomena to his *Church Dogmatics*. In my judgment, the decision to move the doctrine of the Trinity to the opening part of dogmatic theology is more than simply an individual theological preference; it corresponds rather to the nature of the subject matter itself. The second point flows from the waters of our baptism: the Trinity belongs in the part on canon because the Trinity is the true God, besides whom there is no other, into whose very name we are baptized, whose triune Reality therefore names our very existence. The Trinity is the Christian doctrine of God. The Trinity is God himself; God himself is the Trinity. The church does not arrive at the doctrine of the Trinity after independent philosophical speculation on the nature of "theism"; the God of "theism" is a nameless concept, and therefore an idol, while the biblical God is a name, the name into which we are all baptized. The doctrine of the Trinity belongs therefore in the first part of church doctrine, for it provides the church with a rule of faith by which its speech and life are constantly to be tested. And third, the triune *name* of God and the fundamental *mission* of the church are bound together as one. We cannot even begin to think about the mission of the church in our global society without raising the issue of God's triune name, according to the commission of Christ; nor can we reflect theologically upon the triune name of God without stressing the global reality of the mission of the church. The doctrine of the Trinity and the global mission of

---

1. Melanchthon, *Loci Communes*, xlvi.

the church are joined inextricably together under the authority of the risen and exalted Lord.

a. Unity in Diversity

The *doctrine* of the Trinity is not contained explicitly in Scripture; the mainstream of the Christian church has never taught otherwise. However, the triune *reality* of God to which Scripture bears living witness is such that the doctrine of the Trinity is a true and necessary testimony of the church. There are elements of unity in God, according to the biblical witness; there are also elements of diversity in God, according to the same biblical witness. The unity does not exclude the diversity; the diversity does not compromise the unity. Indeed, the unity is realized only in the diversity; while the diversity is grounded only in the unity. The church doctrine of the Trinity is not an attempt to capture the living God in a rationalistic formula. Rather, the doctrine of the Trinity is a faithful and true response to the astonishing unity and diversity of the God of the Bible, whom we confess as Lord of all.

According to Scripture, God is one; God is a unity. God is not solitary; God is not an abstract monad; God is not isolated. God is however a unity, whose reality is unique and exclusive. There is only one God; God alone is God; there is no other God but God. The classic passage of Scripture celebrating and strictly enjoining the confession of God's unity is of course the declaration of Moses in Deuteronomy 6:4 known as the *shema*, shared by Jews and Christians alike: "Hear, O Israel: The Lord our God, the Lord is one." God is singular; there are not many gods, but one God. The recognition of diversity in God by the Christian doctrine of the Trinity does not in the least compromise the truth of God's unity. At the very heart of the Christian awareness of the Trinity comes the same declaration of God's unity. Jesus states without ambiguity, "the Father and I are one" (John 10: 30). Christians do not retreat even a single inch from the confession of God's unity, which we share with the Jewish tradition; indeed, which we inherited from it, our ancestors in the faith.

Several implications follow from the Christian affirmation of God's unity. First, both Testaments stress the *exclusive* divinity of God; the true God alone is God, shattering the idols of the nations. According to Isaiah, the true God declares: "I am the Lord, and there is no other; besides me there is no god . . ." (Isa 45:5). The New Testament underscores the exact same confession: "there is no God but one" (1 Cor 8:4). Whether in the ancient form of polytheism, or the modern form of pluralism, all idolatry is absolutely rejected by the Christian confession of God's unity. The Christian doctrine of the Trinity may be in sharp disagreement with the Jewish view of God in certain respects; however, both are joined together as one in resisting the false gods of pluralism, which are no gods: "For all the gods of the peoples are idols, but the Lord made the heavens" (Ps 96:5).

Second, the unity of God means that God is *one of a kind*. We do not come to the biblical God with a general idea of the divine, then argue to have our notion of God confirmed. Abstract ideas of God brought *to* Scripture are rejected as worthless in the light of God's self-defined and self-declared reality. The point is nicely captured in the traditional phrase of Christian Trinitarian doctrine: *Deus non est in genere*, God is not in any genus. There is not a larger grouping—known as "Gods of the world"—under which the Christian God is found as one among others. God's unwillingness to share the concept of divinity with any other is made clear by the sovereign self-affirmation of God: "for I the Lord your God am a jealous God" (Deut 5:9).

And third, the unity of God is a divinely self-revealed truth, and is not in any way an achievement of human reason and experience. We know that God is one because God has told us so in his Word. Both the unity of God and the diversity of God are known, equally, only from the divine Word. Philosophical concepts of "unity" derived elsewhere fail to achieve the true unity of the biblical God. Here we must part company with A. A. Hodge, who wrongly claims to find the true unity of God elsewhere: "The whole creation, between the outermost range of telescopic and of microscopic observation, is manifestly one indivisible system . . . if an effect proves the prior operation of a cause, and if traces of design prove a designer, then singleness of plan and operation in that design and its exclusion prove that the designer is ONE."[2] Hodge may have found a concept of cosmological unity, but he most certainly has not found the biblical God, the God of Abraham, Isaac, and Jacob, the God and Father of our Lord Jesus Christ. By sharp contrast, the true God of the Bible withholds only for himself the right to define the terms which are used to denote his reality: "To whom then will you compare me, or who is my equal? says the Holy One" (Isa 40:25); "I am the Lord, that is my name; my glory I give to no other, nor my praise to idols. See, the former things have come to pass, and new things I now declare; before they spring forth, I tell you of them" (Isa 42:8–9). We do not worship cosmological unity, nor the purported cause thereof; we

---

2. Hodge, *Outlines*, 138–39.

worship the one revealed God, who alone made the heavens and the earth, yet who infinitely transcends the creation he has made. The unity of God is an article of faith, based on God's self-manifestation; it is not a human insight based on rational reflection concerning the structure of the universe.

The biblical God is a unity; yet the biblical God is also a diversity. There is self-differentiation within the unitary God of the Bible. The diversity of God in no way compromises the unity; on the contrary, the unity is only realized in the diversity. The one God is God in three ways; the one God is God here, and now there, and now there again; yet in such a way as to confirm, rather than deny, the unity.

God is the Revealer. God is he who makes himself known in the world. God is not required to reveal himself in order to be God;[3] yet in the freedom of divine love, God is he who reveals himself before all creation. God reveals himself in his acts: "O give thanks to the Lord, call on his name, make known his deeds among the peoples. Sing to him, sing praises to him; tell of all his wonderful works" (Ps 105:1-2).

God is not only the Revealer; God is the Revealed. God does not hand over knowledge of himself to another; God is in fact the One revealed. God is he who is freely revealed to all the earth. Revelation in the Bible never becomes a state or a possession; God's revelation is always an active divine *event*. God is always active in revelation as the One who is revealed, and who is therefore concealed even in revealing. The burning bush is the fire of God's active presence, God himself both concealed and yet revealed in the world: "When the Lord saw that he had turned aside to see, God called to him out of the bush, 'Moses! Moses!' And he said, 'Here I am.' Then he said, 'Come no closer! Remove the sandals from your feet, for the place on which you are standing is holy ground'" (Exod 3:4-5). Jesus Christ himself is God *revealed*, the exact image of God: "Long ago God spoke to our ancestors in many and various ways by the prophets, but in these last days he has spoken to us by a Son . . . He is the reflection of God's glory and the exact imprint of God's very being . . ." (Heb 1:1-3); yet also *concealed*, as many

---

3. We therefore cannot and must not accept Hegel's definition of God: "God is himself self-consciousness, differentiating itself in itself. Since God, as this differentiating of itself in itself, is consciousness, so is he, as consciousness, such that he gives himself as object for what we call the side of consciousness. With the consciousness of God we arrive at one side, which we have called religion." Thus religion itself—the finite subject—becomes a moment in the unfolding life of the divine infinite. To that the church can only say: no; *finitum non capax infiniti* (the finite is not capable of the infinite). See Hegel, *The Christian Religion*, 2. On Hegel's conception of Christianity, see Hirsch, *GNET* V, 231-68.

stood right in front of him and failed to recognize who he was: "Woe to you, Chorazin! Woe to you, Bethsaida! For if the deeds of power done in you had been done in Tyre and Sidon, they would have repented long ago, sitting in sackcloth and ashes." (Luke 10:13). God is revealed in the world he has made, yet hidden even in his self-revelation.

God is the Revealer; God is the Revealed; God is also the Revelation. God does not leave humanity to its own resources in receiving the self-revelation of God. God completes the action of self-manifestation by filling human life, rendering human persons capable of accepting what they have received. In themselves, they can receive nothing: "I was ready to be sought out by those who did not ask, to be found by those who did not seek me. I said, 'Here I am, here I am,' to a nation that did not call on my name" (Isa 65:1). But through the superior action of God, God's self-disclosure reaches home: "Arise, shine, for your light has come, and the glory of the Lord has risen upon you ... Nations shall come to your light, and kings to the brightness of your dawn" (Isa 60:1, 3). God becomes the Revelation by filling humankind: "All of them were filled with the Holy Spirit and began to speak in other languages, as the Spirit gave them ability" (Acts 2:4). Again, there are not three gods in the Bible, but One: yet the one God is he who Reveals, he who is Revealed, he who is the Revelation. God reveals himself as Lord; that is: God is the *subject* of revelation, the *act* of revelation, and the *effect* of revelation.

Several implications follow from the biblical witness to the diversity of God. First, God is a personal reality; God is a living Person. God is not a moral value, nor a political-cultural ideal, nor an impersonal force, but a person. To speak of God as a person is not to speak metaphorically, but literally; we learn the meaning of the word "person" from God's own personal action. God as person is not an anthropomorphism, but a true witness to the living God: "Understand, O dullest of the people; fools, when will you be wise? He who planted the ear, does he not hear? He who formed the eye, does he not see? He who disciplines the nations, he who teaches knowledge to humankind, does he not chastise? (Ps 94:8–10). We do first learn from observation of humanity what a "person" is, and then transfer that knowledge to God; rather, we first learn from God's own self-declaration the true nature of personal being, and then come to understand human personal life in light of the knowledge of God.

Second, God is active. Activity is not something that God *does*, but who God *is*: God is he who is active.[4] Action is central to God's very being; God is not a being who acts, but an active being. God's active motion is creative, unrestrained, and moves in all directions simultaneously: "As I looked at the living creatures, I saw a wheel on the earth beside the living creatures, one for each of the four of them . . . When they moved, I heard the sound of their wings like the sound of mighty waters, like the thunder of the Almighty, a sound of tumult like the sound of an army . . ." (Ezek 1:15, 24). God's action is not limited to human awareness, but indeed infinitely transcends it, while yet making itself known in freedom within it.

Third, God is a relationship. Once again, the point is crucial: God is not he who enters into relationship; rather, God *is* a relationship. As Revealer, Revealed, and Revelation, the one God is a relationship. God's unity is established only in God's self-diversity. Orientation toward the other is characteristic of God's very being; love for the other is not something God does as a consequence, but something that God is. Thomas Aquinas carefully argues the point that relation is essential to God, not accidental: "Thus it is manifest that relation really existing in God is really the same as His essence . . . as in relation is meant that regard to its opposite which is not expressed in the name of essence. Thus it is clear that in God relation and essence do not differ from each other, but are one and the same."[5] The self-relation of God is expressed biblically, when read in the light of the full witness of Christian truth, in the divine self-address: "The spirit of the Lord God is upon me, because the Lord has anointed me . . ." (Isa 61:1ff.). Who is the Spirit? Who is the Lord God? Who is the speaking subject? There are not here multiple lords in conversation, but rather the majestic internal address of the divine being, whose unity is nevertheless complete only in the relation of diversity.

It is important to recognize that in speaking of the unity and diversity of God, we are not speaking of the *idea* of "unity and diversity"; God is not an abstract idea, but a concrete reality.[6] The Bible fills out the concrete

---

4. According to the Leiden *Synopsis* (here Thysius), God not only acts external to himself (*ad extra*); God acts internal to himself (*ad intra*). God's actions are not only something that proceed from God, moving outward from God; God acts in his essence (*in essentia sua*). See Bavinck, *Synopsis*, 78.

5. Aquinas, *ST* I, 153.

6. Nor does the Christian doctrine of the Trinity have anything to do with abstract concern for the unity of the ultimate and the concrete in religion, *contra* Paul Tillich, *Systematic Theology* I, 228. For Tillich of course the notion that God is "three" has no

meaning of unity and diversity with specific content: namely, the various patterns of triadic formulae referring to God. In the very passage in which Paul stresses the uniqueness and singularity of God ("there is no God but one"), he then immediately stresses the specific diversity of the Father and the Son, with the emphatic repetition of "one": ". . . there is one God, the Father, from whom are all things and for whom we exist, and one Lord, Jesus Christ, through whom are all things and through whom we exist" (1 Cor 8:6). John carefully differentiates and yet also relates the Father and the Son: "No one has ever seen God. It is God the only Son, who is close to the Father's heart, who has made him known" (John 1:18). Similarly, 1 Timothy makes clear the unity and diversity of the Godhead, including a precise reference to the differing functions: ". . . there is one God; there is also one mediator between God and humankind, Christ Jesus, himself human . . ." (1 Tim 2:5). The triadic formula in the New Testament appears in numerous passages, often of special theological emphasis. Second Corinthians closes with a divine blessing, in which the triadic formula prominently appears: "The grace of the Lord Jesus Christ, the love of God, and the communion of the Holy Spirit be with all of you" (2 Cor 13:13). Similarly, when discussing the astonishing range of spiritual gifts in the church, Paul refers to the theological grounding in the unity and diversity of God himself: "Now there are varieties of gifts, but the same Spirit; and there are varieties of services, but the same Lord; and there are varieties of activities, but it is the same God who activates all of them in everyone" (1 Cor 12:4-6). The repetition of the "same" (*auto, autos, autos*), underscores the unity, while the threefold reference to the Spirit, the Lord, and God, manifests the diversity. The triadic formula can also come in the theological context of apostolic greeting: "To the exiles . . . who have been chosen and destined by God the Father and sanctified by the Spirit to be obedient to Jesus Christ and to be sprinkled with his blood . . ." (1 Pet 1:2). The Risen Christ commissions the disciples to baptize the nations in the triune divine name: "Go therefore and make disciples of all nations, baptizing them in the name of the Father and of the Son and of the Holy Spirit . . ." (Matt 28:19). Already in the Old Testament, the triadic pattern appears; it goes too far to insist that the Trinity appears in the literal sense of the Old Testament, and yet read in the light of the gospel,

---

meaning: "Trinitarian monotheism is not a matter of the number three. It is a qualitative and not a quantitative characterization of God." I daresay for those baptized into the name of the triune God, saying that God is one in three does indeed matter. The diversity in God's unity is not two, or four, but three: Father, Son, and Holy Spirit; for the simple reason that God *is* Father, Son, and Holy Spirit, one God. It matters.

who can deny the clear echo of Trinitarian faith that resounds so forcefully and wondrously: "Holy, Holy, Holy is the Lord of hosts; the whole earth is full of his glory" (Isa 6:3)? The unity and diversity of God in the Bible is not an instance of a general religious or moral idea, but rather a testimony to the living reality of one who is threefold, and yet ever self-identical. We do not worship the general idea of unity in diversity; we worship the Triune God, who is diverse even in unity, one even in diversity.

Once again, several implications follow from the triadic patterns of biblical faith. First, noticing the patterns helps to clarify the point that though the full doctrine of the Trinity is not contained in Scripture, the roots of the doctrine certainly are. The Trinitarian confession of the church is not *eisegesis*, but theological *exegesis*; not arbitrary reading *into* the Bible, but rather drawing *out* of the Bible the true reference of which the biblical texts speak. Theological exegesis of the Bible means Trinitarian exegesis; theological hermeneutics means Trinitarian hermeneutics. While the doctrine of the Trinity is a matter of technical theology, it rightly formulates a central dimension of biblical faith without which the Bible is seriously misunderstood.

Second, the triadic formulae of biblical faith make it clear that the primary issue around which the doctrine of the Trinity is developed—theologically, if not historically, for the historical development is largely unknown—is the divinity of Jesus Christ. Scriptures moves in the direction of the Trinity because of its confession that Jesus is Lord. If Jesus is Lord, what is his relation to the God whom Christians and Jews jointly confess?—that is the question to which the triadic formulae are addressed. The doctrine of the Trinity in the church is therefore seen for what it is: an absolutely essential theological corollary of our basic confession of Christ. According to Scripture, no one can confess Christ, who does not also confess the Trinity; and for that matter, no one truly confesses the Trinity, who does not confess Jesus Christ as Lord of all. Third, it is time to lay to rest once for all the well known Protestant liberal thesis of Adolph Harnack, which ascribes the doctrine of the Trinity to Hellenistic metaphysical speculation that is foreign to the simplicity of biblical faith.[7] As is now far more widely recog-

---

7. "Dogmatic Christianity (the dogmas) in its conception and in its construction was *the work of the Hellenic spirit upon the Gospel soil.*" See Harnack, *History of Dogma*, 5. And not only the liberal, Harnack. Even the usually more traditional, "positive" historian Reinhold Seeberg has only harsh words to say about the achievements of the Cappadocians: "With the gospel in hand, they thought themselves prepared to Christianize philosophy. The dream thus cherished was, however, never realized . . . They paid for

nized, the exact opposite is the case. Hellenistic metaphysical speculation sought to drive the church in the direction of an abstract, transcendental *principle* of Being. The church countered by staking its very existence on the doctrine of the Trinity, precisely in order to *protect* the special quality of the biblical witness to divine unity and diversity, even if it meant violating Hellenistic philosophical "purity." The *doctrine* of the Trinity is not in the Bible; but the *Trinity* is, and for that reason the *doctrine* of the Trinity is biblically sound. Affirming the church doctrine of the Trinity does not mean affirming Hellenistic philosophy; it means affirming the biblical God in concepts borrowed from Hellenistic philosophy but used for a strictly theological purpose in accordance with Scripture—in fact to counter the misunderstanding of God contained in Hellenistic philosophy itself.

b. Act and Being

The doctrine of the Trinity as articulated in the community of faith is based upon the biblical dialectic of act and being in God. God's being is revealed only in his acts; God's acts make known God's very being. Both sides of this theological dialectic are richly displayed in the Bible, and essential to a faithful understanding of the church doctrine of God.

God's being is revealed only in his acts; there is no access to the living reality of God apart from his acts. God makes known his reality only through his action in the world. Eliminated from the outset therefore is any metaphysical or ontological approach to God's reality, based on philosophical reflection on the nature of "Being." When God reveals his name to Moses, God then refers directly to the story of his acts in accordance with the promise given to the patriarchs: "God also said to Moses, Thus you shall say to the Israelites, 'The Lord, the God of your ancestors, the God of Abraham, the God of Isaac, and the God of Jacob, has sent me to you': This is my name forever, and this my title for all generations" (Exod 3:15). Who God is, is defined by how God acts. God cannot be discovered by even the most advanced metaphysical ontology, which leads only to the outer limits of creation, but not to the true reality of God. Nor can God be found by

---

their achievement a high price—the idea of a personal God . . . These Fathers—in league with the world—framed orthodoxy in the Grecian mold." See Seeberg, *Textbook*, 227–33. Like many, I am thoroughly unconvinced. Surely the Cappodocians *saved* the idea of a personal God precisely by articulating the doctrine of the Trinity—*against* the transcendental philosophical world of Greek Hellenism.

the *denial* of the metaphysical possibilities of creation, which leads only to the void hovering as a threat over the goodness of creation (Gen 1:2), not to the living reality of God. Neither the *via positiva* (ontological assertion) nor the *via negativa* (metaphysical denial) lead us to God. God's true being is known only in his acts.

Similarly, when Moses is permitted the exalted vision of God's retreating back, God once again declares his name, and fills out the content of his name with the recitation of his acts: "The Lord descended in the cloud and stood with him there, and proclaimed the name, 'The Lord.' The Lord passed before him, and proclaimed, 'The Lord, the Lord, a God merciful and gracious, slow to anger, and abounding in steadfast love and faithfulness, keeping steadfast love for the thousandth generation, forgiving iniquity and transgression and sin, yet by no means clearing the guilty, but visiting the iniquity of the parents upon the children and the children's children, to the third and fourth generation'" (Exod 34:6-7). The giving of God's name is the unveiling of God's very identity; yet the identity of God is declared exclusively by the character of God's action, and not by the nature of being as such. The focus on God's acts as the key to God's very being reverberates throughout the language of divine praise, according to the Psalms. The adoration of God is strictly tied to the nature of his activity: "Bless the Lord, O my soul, and all that is within me, bless his holy name . . . The Lord works vindication and justice for all who are oppressed. He made known his ways to Moses, his acts to the people of Israel" (Ps 103:1, 6-7). God's majesty is disclosed through glorious action: "Praise the Lord! . . . Great are the works of the Lord, studied by all who delight in them. Full of honor and majesty is his work, and his righteousness endures forever . . . He has shown his people the power of his works . . . The works of his hands are faithful and just . . ." (Ps 111:1, 2, 3, 6, 7). God's action attracts human concern and devotion, guides human conduct, reveals God's nature, and discloses the universal power of God. The apostolic preaching in the book of Acts continues the same tradition of recitation of God's mighty deeds (cf. Acts 7:1-51; 13:13-41). The first side of the biblical dialectic reverberates throughout the Bible: God's being is clearly manifested solely through God's *acts*.

The other side of the biblical dialectic receives equal emphasis in the Bible, and is equally central to the Christian doctrine of the Trinity: God's very *being* is manifested in his acts. There is not the slightest hint in the Bible of a separation between God's being and his acts, as if God's acts were a mask, behind which the unknown God hovers forever concealed. Rather, the very same passages in which God's acts are stressed, likewise stress that God makes known his very being by his action in the world. God not only acts faithfully, God *is* faithful; God not only acts mercifully, God *is* merciful; God not only establishes the covenant; God *is* he who keeps covenant in faithfulness. The story of God's relationship to his people is not simply an interesting tale; rather, through that event, God's people encounter the living reality of God himself, who cannot be evaded.

Biblical texts abound. The same Psalm that focuses upon the divine acts as the clue to God's reality, then proceeds directly to describe that divine reality: "The Lord is merciful and gracious, slow to anger and abounding in steadfast love." God's being is not for philosophical meditation, but directly impinges upon human life: "As a father has compassion for his children, so the Lord has compassion for those who fear him" (Ps 103:8, 13). As Job discovers, God's very reality is disclosed through encounter with his people, and cannot be lightly set aside by pious talk about God: "I had heard of you by the hearing of the ear, but now my eye sees you; therefore I despise myself, and repent in dust and ashes" (Job 42:5-6). The reality of God is to be taken with utmost seriousness, because God is who he is: "O let the evil of the wicked come to an end, but establish the righteous, you who test the minds and hearts, O righteous God . . . God is a righteous judge . . . I will give to the Lord the thanks due to his righteousness . . . (Ps 7:9, 11, 17). He acts a certain way, because of who he is: "For the Lord is righteous; he loves righteous deeds . . ." (Ps 11:7). There can be no escape for God's people into a feigned ignorance of God, as if God's reality is unknown or uncertain: "Have you not known? Have you not heard? Has it not been told you from the beginning? Have you not understood from the foundations of the earth? It is he who sits above the circle of the earth . . . who brings princes to naught, and makes the rulers of the earth as nothing . . . Have you not known? Have you not heard? The Lord is the everlasting God, the Creator of the ends of the earth" (Isa 40:21, 22, 23, 28). God's action confronts Israel with nothing less than the life or death reality of God himself: "Therefore thus I will do to you, O Israel; because I will do this to you, prepare to meet your God, O Israel!" (Amos 4:12). The New Testament simply continues the Old Testament tradition in insisting that God's central act in Jesus Christ makes known God's very being. The letter to the Colossians stresses that Jesus Christ is the very image of God, in whom the "fullness of God was pleased to dwell" (Col 1:15, 19); while the opening theme of the Letter to the Romans announces that in the gospel of Jesus Christ "the righteousness of God is revealed through faith for faith" (Rom 1:17). In his acts of creation, reconciliation, and redemption, God makes known the true reality of his identity.

We now stand back from the witness of Scripture to reflect theologically upon the subject matter to which the whole Scripture points. Jesus Christ is the true dialectical unity of God's act and God's being. Jesus Christ is the one *act* of God's self-manifestation for the whole world; Jesus Christ is the true *being* of God, of the same essence with the Father. Because we follow Jesus Christ, we can look for God's being nowhere but in his act; because we follow Jesus Christ, we discover nothing less than God's very being in God's act. For us, God's being and God's act remain dialectically related, concealed in the freedom of God; but for God they are the same, for Jesus Christ is the unity of God's act and God's being: ". . . that is, in Christ God was reconciling the world to himself . . ." (2 Cor 5:19).

For Trinitarian doctrine the dialectical relation of divine being and divine act is decisive. Based upon the dialectic of act and being, church doctrine affirms both the *economic* Trinity and the *ontological* Trinity. The economic Trinity is the church's recognition that God acts in a threefold form in the world, as Creator, Reconciler, Redeemer. God acts to create the world; God acts to reconcile the world; God acts to redeem the world; therefore we confess the threefold reality of the one God in his action toward his creation. There are not three gods; but one God, who acts in threefold form in the world.

We also confess with equal seriousness the ontological Trinity. God not only acts in threefold form; God is, in the eternal life of his own being, the Trinity. We do not dismiss or ignore the economic Trinity; nevertheless, nor can we in the slightest degree fail to affirm the ontological Trinity. The entire gospel of Jesus Christ rests upon this one point: God is the Trinity, not only in his acts toward the world, but in his own eternal reality. There is no other God but the Trinity. The Trinity is not a symbol for an unknown god standing in the background; the Trinity is the eternal God, besides whom and before whom and outside of whom there is no other. God acts in time as Creator, Reconciler, and Redeemer, because God is in eternity the Father, the Son, and the Holy Spirit. Before time itself, above time, and after time, God is the Trinity: Father, Son, and Holy Spirit. God's eternal being is the Trinity; the Trinity is God's eternal being. God's triune action in time makes known God's triune being in eternity. Therefore we can and must say without reservation or qualification: God is the Trinity, Father, Son, and Holy Spirit. The economic Trinity is the only noetic basis for our understanding of the ontological Trinity; while the ontological Trinity is the only ontic basis for God's threefold action as the economic Trinity.

c. The Triune God

God has a name. As Christians, we are all baptized in the name of the Father, and the Son, and the Holy Spirit; we are baptized into God's one name, which all Christians share and confess together. Our baptism is not an act of self-identification, but rather an act of joyful and obedient response to the call of the exalted Christ: "Go therefore and make disciples of all nations, baptizing them in the name of the Father and of the Son and of the Holy Spirit . . ." (Matt 28:19). God does not have many names, from which we have for our own reasons chosen one in particular; God has one glorious name, which we are graciously invited to share. Nor is God nameless, until we name him. We have not named God, based on the resources of our own inner life; rather, God has made known the splendor of his name to all the nations: "Make a joyful noise to God, all the earth; sing the glory of his name . . . all the earth worships you . . . [T]hey . . . sing praises to your name" (Ps 66:1–4). God's name is God's self-revealed identity, given in the act of direct encounter with God; his name is to be cherished and celebrated by the community of faith. God's triune name claims our ultimate and exclusive loyalty, and confers upon us our very identity as Christians. God's name does not change with the passing seasons of human life, nor is it subject to the changing contexts of human history. We do not understand God's name in the light of history; rather, we understand all history in the light of God's glorious name. God's name binds us together into one people throughout all creation, and indeed throughout all time.

It is traditional in the *Western* church to arrive at the diversity of God only through the unity; while in the *Eastern* church, the unity is achieved only by means of the diversity. Must we here make a fundamental decision in Trinitarian doctrine? I am convinced, instead, that both directions reflect biblical insight, and are to be joined together in the ecumenical faith of the church. Logic may force a choice between the two; but here logic must give way to the superior force of God's own self-defined being.

Now, in order to assert the doctrine of the Trinity, the church has long made use of several technical concepts—many borrowed from ancient philosophy—not found in the Bible. From the very beginning of this use, the criticism has been mounted against the mainstream of church teaching that it is unbiblical, because it is not framed in biblical words. The criticism itself is based on the error of biblicism, which fails to make any distinction between the words of the Bible and the reality of which it speaks. While we cannot separate word from reality, nor can we simply collapse them into one another; for that reason, we not only wrestle with the words of Scripture, we also strive to articulate the true substance to which they testify. And there is no reason whatsoever why words not found in Scripture cannot be used in order to affirm that substance, as long as the words prove useful and illuminating. Calvin—certainly by all accounts a scrupulous and careful student of the Bible second to none—eloquently defends the need occasionally to use non-biblical words and concepts in theology, precisely in order to illuminate biblical truths: "But what prevents us from explaining in clearer words those matters in Scripture which perplex and hinder our understanding, yet which conscientiously and faithfully serve the truth of Scripture itself, and are made use of sparingly and modestly and on due occasion?"[8] Technical theological concepts—even those not found in the Bible itself—are not only sometimes useful, but are often necessary precisely in the service of biblical truth.

Three concepts in particular have long been used in the church doctrine of the Trinity: essence, person, and mode of being. In all three cases, the point is not to reinterpret Christian truth in the light of these philosophical concepts; the point rather is to use these concepts to help express more clearly the truth of the gospel. None is wholly adequate to that task. Augustine's point is well taken, that we choose concepts knowing their inadequacy full well: "Yet, when the question is asked, What three? human language labors altogether under great poverty of speech. The answer, however, is given, three 'persons,' not that it might be completely spoken, but that it might not be left wholly unspoken."[9] Still, despite the poverty of language in the face of God's eternal glory, we speak the doctrine of the Trinity because we *must* speak, in response to the sovereign claim of the divine reality upon our thought and speech. I see no reason to exchange the traditional concepts for others, as long as it is realized that the philosophical concept serves biblical truth, rather than the reverse. Here two points are in order.

8. Calvin, *LCC* XX, 124.
9. Augustine, *On the Trinity*, 124.

First, the concept of essence that the church uses to denote the unity of God is still certainly usable, as long as it is filled out, not by abstract metaphysical speculation, but by the concrete story of God in the Bible. On the one hand, "essence" is not an invitation to abstract philosophical reasoning concerning the meaning of being; the Trinity is not grounded in philosophical ontology. On the other hand, why cannot this respectable philosophical concept be used theologically in the service of the gospel, in order to speak—however haltingly—about the stunning and mysterious reality of divine unity? And second, the concept of person was always used in the ancient sense of a reality that subsists of itself. There was not, until the modern period, any connotation of personality, including the characteristic feature of individual self-consciousness. While we can speak of the three divine persons, it is absolutely crucial not to imply three divine personalities; for there are not three centers of self-consciousness in God, but One. For that reason, I prefer the Greek category mode of being, which refers to the same theological reality, but without the unnecessary implication of distinct self-consciousness.

How then do we speak truthfully of the Triune God in the church of Jesus Christ? We know the diversity of God only by means of the unity. Only by truly understanding God's one eternal essence do we rightly worship the three divine modes of being. There are not three gods but one God. There is no conflict or competition within God, for there are not three divine wills, but one divine will. The unity of God is not compromised by our christological confession, but full confirmed: "For there is one God; there is also one Mediator between God and humankind, Christ Jesus, himself human . . ." (1 Tim 2:5).

On the other hand, only by rightly comprehending the diversity of God do we genuinely grasp the unity. God's three modes of being are not manifestations of undifferentiated unity; rather, God's unity is only truly expressed in three eternal, coequal, coordinate modes of being. Unity is not isolation; unity rather is the *communion* of genuine otherness in God. Again, our christological confession encloses the diversity in infinite blessing: "The grace of the Lord Jesus Christ, the love of God, and the communion of the Holy Spirit be with you all" (2 Cor 13:13). Surely West and East, East and West are joined in the full chorus of the gospel.

God's redeeming love for all the world is the act of the triune God. In all of God's acts, the triune God is active: *opera dei ad extra sunt indivisa*. There are not three separate divine actors, but one divine Actor. On the other hand, church doctrine recognizes within Scripture a certain ordering of our language about God that cannot rightly be ignored or confused. While it is right to speak of redemption as the act of the Trinity, it is not right to say that the Father suffered for our sins; while it is right to affirm the presence of the Triune God among us, it is not right to say that the Son was poured out upon the early church at Pentecost; and again, while it is right and necessary to assert that the three modes of being are coequal in dignity and divinity in every respect, it is not right to say that the Father is the Word of the Son. Rather, the Son suffered for our sins; the Spirit was given at Pentecost; the Son is the Word of the Father. There is an inner order to the life of God; and yet God is not divisible but one. The Christian doctrine of *appropriation* is an attempt to reflect upon this inherent mystery of God's being. We ascribe to the Father, the Son, and the Spirit, the actions appropriate to their roles in the divine economy. Yet we do not divide the action of God into three; we affirm one divine action in threefold form. Moreover, while we appropriate, we do not separate. God the Father is Creator of heaven and earth; yet all things came into existence through Jesus Christ (cf. John 1:3), and the Spirit of God renews the face of the earth (cf. Ps 104:30). Church doctrine does not enclose God within artificial human definition; it points truthfully rather to the living God, who wondrously declares the true nature of his triune identity.

To speak of God as triune is not first to separate, and then to bring together. The living God is not a mathematical formula, but a personal reality; indeed the reality of God defines the true meaning of "person." The Father, the Son, and the Holy Spirit are three eternal modes of divine being, comprised in one divine essence. The Father is fully God; the Son is fully God; the Spirit is fully God; and yet there are not three gods, but one true God. The essence of God is fully in the Father; the essence of God is fully in the Son; the essence of God is fully in the Spirit; yet there are not three essences, but one divine essence. The one essence of God cannot be abstracted from the diverse modes of being; for God's essence is concretely realized only in the diversity of God's inner life. Church doctrine speaks of the *perichoresis*; that is, of the coinherence of God's eternal modes of being. Each of the one is in the other: the Father is in the Son, the Son is in the Spirit, the Spirit is the bond of peace and joy between the Father and the Son. As Gregory Nazianzus asserts: God is "undivided in divided persons."[10] The sheer beauty of divine love is the ultimate interpenetration

---

10. Kelly, *Early Christian Doctrines*, 264.

of the three divine modes of being while yet preserving the threefold form of divine life. All subordination is radically excluded from the Christian doctrine of the Trinity. Following the Cappadocians, we must speak rather of the divine coordination (*sustoixia*); yet coordination, not in the sense of an external arrangement, but in the sense of an eternal mutual presence. At this juncture, church doctrine can only yield to the higher language of Christian worship: "Holy, Holy, Holy, though the darkness hide Thee, though the eye of sinfulness Thy glory may not see, only thou art holy; there is none beside Thee, perfect in power, in love and purity."[11]

God is an eternal relationship of love. The Father is God; the Son is God, the Holy Spirit is God; and yet there are not three gods, but one God. Moreover, while we necessarily appropriate certain actions of God to the various modes of divine being, we also assert that God is one actor, accomplishing one creative and redemptive action. And through the affirmation of coinherence, we point toward the mysterious interpenetration of divine loving, which joins unity to diversity, diversity to unity. How then are we to distinguish the three modes of being from one another? Since Augustine, the answer from church theology has been the doctrine of *relations*. The three modes of divine being are distinguished from one another by their different relations to each other, specifically relations of eternal origin. Even here, our definitions must be governed by the substance, rather than the reverse; while we speak of relations of origin in God, there is no temporal element implied whatsoever. Divine self-otherness is eternal in every respect. Nor is there any form of subordination implied, in any way; divine relations are all coordinate, not subordinate. Nevertheless, the relations of origin within God are real, and distinguish the three modes of being from one another. Noetically, the divine relations are made known to us through the actions of God in time; ontically, God's action in time is a replication of eternal divine relations within the Godhead.

Jesus Christ the Son of God is sent by the Father into the world for the sake of his redeeming love: "For God so loved the world that he gave his only Son, so that everyone who believes in him may not perish but may have eternal life. Indeed, God did not send the Son into the world to condemn the world, but in order that the world might be saved through him" (John 3:16–17). The Son did not send the Father; rather, the Father sent the Son. Jesus Christ the Son of God is born of the virgin Mary, conceived by the Holy Spirit: "The angel said to her, 'The Holy Spirit will come upon

---

11. *Holy, Holy, Holy!* Hymn by Reginald Heber.

you, and the power of the Most High will overshadow you; therefore the child to be born will be holy; he will be called the Son of God'" (Luke 1:35). The Father is not born; the Son of God is born, a babe, in Bethlehem. Even so, God the eternal Son is eternally begotten of the Father. Before all time; before all worlds; in the eternity of God's inner life, the Son is begotten of the Father, while the Father is unbegotten. The doctrine of the church is careful to say "begotten" not "made"; to speak of the Father making the Son is to imply that the Son is a creature, which is false doctrine. The Son is not a creature, but fully divine in every way, of the same substance (*homoousion*) with the Father; and yet the Son is distinguished from the Father by being begotten of him.

On Pentecost, the Holy Spirit is poured out upon the gathered community, in fulfillment of God's promise: ". . . this is what was spoken through the prophet Joel: 'In the last days it will be, God declares, that I will pour out my Spirit upon all flesh . . .'" (Acts 2:17). The Holy Spirit is sent by the Father: "And I will ask the Father, and he will give you another Advocate, to be with you forever" (John 14:15). Yet elsewhere, it is said that the Spirit is sent in the name of Christ (John 14:26), and indeed by Christ, along with the Father: "When the Advocate comes, whom I will send to you from the Father, the Spirit of truth who comes from the Father, he will testify on my behalf" (John 15:26). Jesus himself sends the Spirit: "Nevertheless I tell you the truth: it is to your advantage that I go away, for if I do not go away, the Advocate will not come to you; but if I go, I will send him to you" (John 16:7). The Spirit does not send the Father or the Son; rather, the Spirit is sent by the Father and the Son. Once again, God's action in time is a window of perspective into God's eternal self-relation. The Holy Spirit eternally proceeds from the Father and the Son. Language must yield to glorious reality; the twofold procession of the Spirit is not temporal in any way, but eternal. Nor is there in any sense a connotation of subordination, for we worship and glorify the Spirit in the church along with Father and Son. The Spirit eternally proceeds from the Father and the Son. Just as the Spirit is the bond of peace in the community of faith in time (Eph 4:3); so the Spirit is the bond of love and peace in God's own eternal inner life.

God is one essence in three modes of being (or persons); thus we confess with all who call upon his name, in life and in death.

d. Nicene Faith

In 325 the ecumenical church gathered at Nicaea in the midst of extreme theological crisis—the first such ecumenical council. Official persecution of Christians in the Roman Empire had only recently ended; it is indeed humbling to realize that "many of the participants at Nicaea bore the wounds and disfigurements of torture."[12] The primary purpose of the gathering was to confess the faith of the church against the teaching of Arius, which was sweeping over wide segments of the church, and threatening the unity of the faith; and the secondary purpose was to combat Sabellianism, the view that Father, Son, and Spirit constitute several modes of appearance—masks—behind which only one divine being truly exists in eternity. A creed was formulated to clarify the true content of the faith, and specifically to confess the eternal divine nature of Christ, and the unity in diversity of the divine persons. Again in 381 the ecumenical church gathered at Constantinople—the second ecumenical council—as the crisis continued. The section on Christ in the original Creed of Nicaea is expanded; and even more significantly, a section on the divinity of the Holy Spirit as a coequal member of the Trinity is added. This creed adopted in 381, now widely known as the Nicene Creed, brought to final maturity the Trinitarian theology of the early church. It is recognized as an authoritative expression of the true faith of the church by Roman Catholicism, Eastern Orthodoxy, the Oriental Orthodox Churches, and by all members of the World Council of Churches. As an ecumenical creed of the universal church, the Nicene Creed expresses our common faith concerning the true reality of God.

Now, in the light of the Trinitarian mission of the gospel (Matt 28: 18-20) with which we opened this chapter, I suggest that there are three prominent issues for contemporary theological reflection on the church doctrine of the Trinity. Simply affirming our faith is not enough, even when the words used to make that affirmation are not only unobjectionable but time honored and universal in their validity for all who call upon the risen Lord. It is essential furthermore to come to *understand* what we have affirmed, that we might honor, not only with our voices, but with our hearts and minds, indeed our entire being, him whose name is poured over us in the waters of life.

First, we must inquire whether the heresies negated by the Nicene faith of the early church have their analogies in modern theology. As is well

---

12. Pelikan and Hotchkiss, eds., *CCFCT* I, 156.

known, the creeds of the early church are largely negative in their formulation; that is, they do not recommend only one specific theology, so much as they set legitimate boundaries to what counts as orthodox confession within the church of Jesus Christ. Are those boundaries being crossed in our time as well? Are there any signs of either Arianism, or Sabellianism, whether they appear on the religious right or the religious left?

The religious right—despite its clear and well-intentioned efforts to the contrary—falls short of the full glory of Nicene confession. The standard approach on the religious right is to define God in terms of philosophical reflection on "theism," and only then to add on the Christian doctrine of the Trinity after that definition is already complete. Wayne Grudem for example follows the now standard approach, with chapters on the existence of God (ch. 9), the knowability of God (ch. 10), and the character of God (ch. 11), before even considering the Trinity.[13] We must ask: what God is being proven to exist? What God is being shown to be knowable? What God is being described according to his character? An abstract God of theism that brackets and explains the Triune God of the Christian faith, while not technically equivalent to the teaching of Sabellius, in fact falls outside the Nicene commitment to the absolute priority of God's eternal triune reality. God is not "God" first and then the Trinity second; God is the Trinity, first and last. The Bible knows nothing of the abstract philosophical god of theism; it knows only the Triune God, who rules all things: "Holy, holy, holy, the Lord God the Almighty, who was and is and is to come" (Rev 4:8).

Furthermore, while strict Arianism is carefully avoided on the religious right, in fact the language of *subordinationism* is allowed back into the doctrine of the Trinity in direct contradiction to the confessing faith of the church. To be sure, the essential equality of the three persons is openly professed; but so also is subordination in relation to "personal subsistence and consequent order of operation."[14] According to Grudem, unless the Son is subordinate to the Father, the persons of the Trinity cannot be distinguished from one another.[15] Now, the earliest church fathers often used the language of subordination in describing the inner life of God. But by the time of the Nicene Creed clarity had emerged concerning what had once been confused; "subordination" gave way to the Cappadocian (originally Athanasian) language of "coordination." The inner life of God is a coor-

---

13. Grudem, *Systematic Theology*, 141–261.
14. Hodge, *Outlines*, 193.
15. Grudem, *Systematic Theology*, 251.

dinate unity, not a subordinate hierarchy. The members of the Trinity are distinguished not by super- and sub-ordination, but by genetic relations; the result is unambiguously three coequal, coeternal, mutual persons of the one essential God. The Athanasian Creed is absolutely unambiguous: "And in this Trinity there is nothing before or after, nothing greater or less (*nihil maius aut minus*), but all three persons are coeternal with each other and coequal (*coaequales*)."[16] When Jesus says: the Father is greater than I (John 14:28), the reference is not to the status of the Son in the eternity of God's inner life, but the humility of the Incarnate One, who serves the Father's will. The persistence of subordinationist language on the religious right, while not Arianism strictly speaking, is nevertheless a deeply troubling departure from the Nicene faith of the church founded on the witness of Holy Scripture.

On the other hand, the religious left can scarcely be recommended for their careful affirmation of the Nicene faith of the church. At roughly the same time that Charles Hodge was reintroducing subordinationist language in the doctrine of the Trinity, Friedrich Schleiermacher was arguing, with Sabellius, for a god of undifferentiated unity behind the three modes of divine being. Schleiermacher famously removes the doctrine of the Trinity from dogmatics proper, and assigns it the role of an appendix. He does so on that the ground that the doctrine of the Trinity wrongly refers to God's reality, God in himself, not to religious experience: "We have only to do with the God-consciousness given in our self-consciousness along with our consciousness of the world; hence we have no formula for the being of God in Himself as distinct from the being of God in the world . . ."[17] We cannot rightly speak of God as he is in himself if we are to follow the method set out in his philosophical prolegomena to dogmatics; we can only use language of God as he is given to religious self-consciousness. The Trinity is therefore religiously meaningless speculation. Albrecht Ritschl likewise rejects the Trinity on similar grounds, reducing the name of God accordingly: "The complete name of God which corresponds to the Christian revelation is 'The God and Father of our Lord Jesus Christ.'"[18] Tillich follows a similar line of argument, rendering the three modes of being as diverse symbols of what concerns us ultimately: ". . . it is not the number 'three' which is decisive in Trinitarian thinking but the unity in a manifoldness of divine

---

16. Pelikan and Hotchkiss, eds., *CCFCT* I, 675-77.
17. Schleiermacher, *Christian Faith*, 748.
18. Ritschl, *Three Essays*, 224.

self-manifestations."[19] Or again, Sally McFague makes the same argument, in which the three persons are alternative "paradigms" of God, among numerous other "paradigms": "We *believe* . . . that a particular paradigm is *one* appropriate way to express what can never be fully or adequately expressed . . ."[20] Against the religious left—no less reluctantly but no less firmly than against the religious right—we must confess that God has a name, and has made known his true reality in his name, which radiates his splendid glory to all creation: "Enter his gates with thanksgiving, and his courts with praise. Give thanks to him, bless his name" (Ps 100:4).

Similarly, on the religious left the issue of Arianism has not gone away—perhaps it never will, as some heresies seem to have a nearly ontological life in the struggle of the confessing faith. I am referring to the long and multifarious "search for the historical Jesus." Most recently, Marcus Borg has argued for a "pre-Easter Jesus" as opposed to a "post-Easter" Jesus, and has offered a portrait of what such a historical character is in historical factuality like. The life and message of Jesus have nothing to do with heaven, nothing to do with the "afterlife;"[21] all references to the kingdom of God in the teaching of the true historical Jesus have exclusively to do with "transformation of life in this world" and nothing at all to do with a "world beyond death;"[22] the life of the "age to come" consists only in knowing God "in the present," and has nothing to do with a future yet to be;[23] Jesus was led to his death because he was a prophet like the Old Testament prophets who was a "radical critic of the domination system."[24] What the life of Jesus is most certainly *not* is the story of Jesus's identity as God's only Son whose "sacrifice for sin makes forgiveness possible."[25] In my judgment, an extended rebuttal of Borg's picture of the life of Jesus is unnecessary in this context for the simple reason that it has already been written. While the techniques of modern critical study of the New Testament have changed, the resulting picture of the life of Jesus on the religious left from Hermann Samuel Reimarus, to David Friedrich Strauss, to the many "Liberal Lives of Jesus" in the late nineteenth century, and on through to Marcus Borg

19. Tillich, *Systematic Theology* III, 293.
20. In Hodgson and King, eds., *Christian Theology*, 382.
21. Borg, *Jesus*, 13.
22. Ibid., 144.
23. Ibid.
24. Ibid., 163.
25. Ibid., 162.

has remained remarkably consistent. The story of this movement has been exhaustively examined by Albert Schweitzer, and his conclusion applies as directly to Borg as it does to the many who preceded him: "The Jesus of Nazareth who came forward publicly as the Messiah, who preached the ethic of the Kingdom of God, who founded the Kingdom of Heaven on earth, and died to give His work its final consecration, never had any existence. He is a figure designed by rationalism, endowed with life by liberalism, and clothed by modern theology in an historical garb."[26] Schweitzer's profound condemnation can scarcely be improved.

The second issue concerns what has come to be called the "social analogy" of the Trinity, usually associated with Jürgen Moltmann and Colin Gunton, but now widely represented in contemporary theology. I will follow the standard presentation by Migliore.[27] Just as human life is inherently communal, so God himself is "essentially communal." There is an eternal "trinitarian hospitality" among the three members of the Trinity — found especially in ancient Eastern thinking (so the claim goes) — a "divine dance" among the three.[28] Because of this innate divine hospitality, all life among human beings is inherently communal. Usually, the social analogy is set against the so-called "psychological analogy" of the Latin St. Augustine, which is eschewed as inherently individualistic and therefore anti-Trinitarian. What are we to make of this new turn?

In my judgment, two essays have dealt a devastating blow to the "social analogy" of the Trinity, and radically call into question its appropriateness for confessing the Nicene faith. The first is an historical critique by Sarah Coakley, "Persons in the 'Social' Doctrine of the Trinity: A Critique of Current Analytic Discussion."[29] Coakley — herself an accomplished patristic scholar — points out that the current "social" Trinity essentially posits a "closely embraced community of divine individuals," a view that in her opinion has "embarrassingly tritheistic overtones."[30] Furthermore, while the "social" Trinity calls upon the likes of Gregory of Nyssa for support, in

---

26. In Schweitzer, *Quest*, 398.

27. Migliore, *Faith Seeking*, 79-80.

28. For what it is worth, the highly emotional descriptions of a divine dance, of divine inner longing and yearning, certainly have their precedents; I am thinking for example of the highly erotically charged language of Zinzendorf, for whom all theologically knowledge rests upon the awakening of human emotion. See Hirsch, *GNET* II, 401-11, esp. 406.

29. In Davis, et al., eds., *The Trinity*, 123-44.

30. Ibid., 127.

fact "his trinitarianism subscribes to none of the features just described" as characteristic of the "social" Trinity.[31] For Gregory, God is a *communion* of persons, not a *community* of persons.[32] Thus, from the point of view of a patristic scholar, the attempt to link the so-called "social analogy" with ancient church doctrine is in fact highly misleading. The "social" analogy is a leap into tritheism.

The second essay is by Karen Kilby, "Perichoresis and Projection: Problems with the Social Doctrine of the Trinity."[33] Kilby comes at the matter from an analytic point of view, but reaches the same conclusion as Coakley from the historical. Kilby summarizes the "social" view of the Trinity: "most basically social theorists propose that Christians should not imagine God on the model of some individual person or thing which has three sides, aspects, dimensions or modes of being; God is instead to be thought of as a collective, a group, or a society, bound together by the mutual love, accord and self-giving of its members."[34] Like Coakley, Kilby thus (rightly in my opinion) stresses the difference between God as living communion, and God as social community. Then, Kilby carefully unpacks the logic of the view, concluding that is in fact not a true *analogy* of God, but rather a *projection*. First, Christians decide what it is to be basically human (human being is being in society); then, they project that image onto God (divine being is being in society); and finally, they use that projected image as an ethical ground for human integrity (living in integrity is living with social integrity). "Projection, then, is particularly problematic . . . because what is projected onto God is immediately reflected back onto the world, and this reverse projection is said to be what is in fact *important* about the doctrine."[35] Indeed, Ludwig Feuerbach could not have said it any better!

I am convinced that the so-called "social analogy" of the Trinity—despite its popularity—has to be rejected as false doctrine in the light of the Nicene faith of the church. First, God is not a community of love, but a communion of love; God is not a *social* unity, but an *essential* unity. The persons of the divine Trinity do not have individual wills, individual minds, individual purposes, which then come together in the "dance of life"; the triune God has one will, one mind, one purpose, while yet remaining

---

31. Ibid., 130.
32. Ibid., 134, emphasis hers.
33. Kilby in *New Blackfriars*, 432-45.
34. Ibid., 433.
35. Ibid., 443.

eternally threefold. As the Athanasian Creed rightly summarizes, "The Father is eternal, the Son eternal, the Holy Spirit eternal. Yet there are not three eternals, but one eternal; just as there are not three increates or three infinites, but one increate and one infinite."[36] The so-called "social analogy" fails—and fails rather dramatically—to achieve the divine unity. Second, it is hard to ignore the politicized language which permeates the "social analogy"; as if we have an individualistic capitalist God on the one side (the "Latin") vying for attention against the now in vogue socialist communitarian God (the "Eastern"). We have already pointed out the historical misinformation that lies behind both of these characterizations of patristic doctrine. However that may be, against *both* the capitalist god and the socialist god, it needs to be asserted with utter clarity, that the triune God is *God*; he is not a plaything for human political maneuvering, even with the best of intentions. God is not a projection of political tribalism, whether on the left or on the right; he is the incomparable Lord of nations: "Even the nations are like a drop from a bucket, and are accounted as dust on the scales; see, he takes up the isles like fine dust" (Isa 40:15). How can mere *dust* say to the eternal God: "you are like me!"? And third, while human life is indeed to be conformed to the reality of God—"Be perfect, therefore as your heavenly Father is perfect" (Matt 5:48)—God makes known his will, not through a speculative *analogy* of his being (*analogia entis*), but through the concrete medium of his *commandments*: "teaching them to obey everything that I have commanded you" (Matt 28:20).

Now, I believe there *is* a proper analogy to be stressed in the doctrine of the Trinity, but it comes from God to us, not from us to him: and that is the analogy of grace (*analogia gratiae*). Just as God is in himself an eternal communion of love; so God in his free and unmerited kindness wills to establish a relationship—a communion of love—with all humankind. God is love (1 John 4:16); and for that very reason God so loves the world . . . (John 3:16): that is the true analogy of grace, coming down with absolute certainty from above.

The third issue is of course the very wording of the Nicene Creed itself. Should we confess that the Holy Spirit proceeds from the Father; or that the Holy Spirit proceeds from the Father *and the Son* (*Filioque*). Grudem calls the doctrinal issue of the Filioque "obscure,"[37] which in my opinion hardly qualifies as a helpful observation. Kallistos Ware, by contrast, refers

---

36. Pelikan and Hotchkiss, eds., *CCFCT*, 676.
37. In Grudem, *Systematic Theology*, 247.

to the matter as "technical, but not trivial,"[38] a far more well-balanced and judicious evaluation surely. At any rate, the history of the theological and ecclesiological issues surrounding the doctrine of the Filioque can be readily found in competent studies, and need not be repeated here.[39] For us, the issue can be stated thus: is there fresh light to be shed on the Filioque controversy in the light of the present situation of the church, in particular the astounding and miraculous growth in globalization of the church starting in the last decades of the twentieth century? In my judgment there is; I believe that the Filioque should be retained in the Creed in light of the fresh work of God in our midst.

My theological argument is based on the text with which we opened this chapter, and now bring it to a close (Matt 28:18–20), which speaks so dramatically and explosively of the enthronement of the risen and exalted Christ to rule over all reality; of the unrestricted mission of the disciples to carry the gospel to all nations and peoples; of the command to baptize in the triune name of God; and of the promised presence of Christ among his gathered disciples for all time. We are witnessing with our own eyes a "paradigm shift" in the life of the church in light of the globalization of the community of faith. When it comes to the gospel, North America and Europe are clearly the third world; Africa and Latin America are without doubt the first world. The gospel has quite literally turned the world upside down. The paradigm shift in the church must surely be reflected in a paradigm shift in theology. The era of mediating the message of Scripture through Western European experience, before it can reach global experience, is simply over. The *Scriptures* carry the gospel directly from the risen Lord to every nation and culture. There is no "first world natural theology" to stand as a filter through which the good news must first be mediated. Nor, in my opinion, is the answer to now look for a new "third world natural theology" to act as a new filter. The answer lies, rather, in the eternal mystery of God: in the relation between the Spirit and the Son both in time and eternity.

The Spirit not only proceeds from the (Father and) the Son in time (John 16:7, "I will send him to you"); the Spirit proceeds from the (Father and) the Son in eternity. Jesus Christ himself is the one and only basis for human response to God in time; Jesus Christ is the one and only basis for

---

38. In Cunliffe-Jones, ed., *History*, 218.

39. The best current monograph is probably *The Filioque*, by A. Edward Siecienski, which has the enormous merit of following a single narrative line from the early church right up to the present.

human response to God likewise in all eternity, in the eternal life of God. Not Aristotle; not Western metaphysics; not Wittgenstein; not the middle class ideals of bourgeois western democracy, however noble these may be; Jesus Christ alone is the one basis in time and eternity for human response to God. Christ, through the miraculous and creative power of Word and Spirit, is *immediately* present to all peoples, tribes, nations, societies, and cultures, without mediation through the sieve of any dominant cultural norms. How do we know this? Because we confess that the Spirit proceeds from the Father and the Son; and thereby affirm that the human response to God is freed by the Spirit for direct and immediate presence to Christ. In sum, I believe that the Filioque is ultimately a necessary implication of Christian *mission*, as well as the true theological possibility for it. It should be retained, not because we are told that it should from on high;[40] nor because it is simply there and there is no reason to remove it; but because it is true, and bears in its truth the liberation of all humanity to receive the fresh word of God's eternal love.

---

40. I mean the Pope of course (not God). In this regard, I agree fully with the criticism of the uncharitable conduct of the Latin church by Photius. See Pelikan, *TCT* 2, 183–98.

5

The Divine Imperative

WHEN THE FIRST WORLD War broke out Karl Barth remained committed to the theological liberalism in which he had been trained. The experience of the war would bring Barth extreme distress, brought on by utter disappointment in the unanimous and vigorous support of the war by his esteemed theological professors in Germany, for whom Christianity had become little more than an expression of the basest tribal nationalism. Yet it is also clear that long before the war started, Barth was searching. The profound and onerous work of discovery took place in Safenwil, a small village in Switzerland, where Barth was pastor for ten years, 1911–1921. While there, Barth not only found a new theology; he found a *new world* in the Bible. His discovery was presented to a church gathering in the fall of 1916.[1]

In this brilliant and fundamentally groundbreaking essay Barth asks the simplest of theological questions: "What is there within the Bible" (*Was steht in der Bibel?*).[2] Barth continues by recounting narratives of the divine call in the Bible, which are grounded in no anthropological possibility, but solely in the sovereign divine claim. Again, the question: "What is there behind all this (*dahinter*), that labors for expression" (*will . . . zum Vorsheim kommen*)?[3] Barth has clearly struggled long and hard before reaching the stunning conclusion: "within the Bible there is a strange, *new world*,

---

1. Barth, "The Strange New World" in *The Word of God*, 28–50.
2. Ibid., 28. Just like paradigm shifts in science, it is often simple theological questions which lead to monumental shifts in theological discourse; such as, Luther's: how can I find a gracious God?
3. Ibid., 32.

the world of God."⁴ Barth quickly points out that the new world of God in the Bible immediately makes extraordinary demands upon the reader: "We must openly confess that we are reaching far beyond ourselves. But that is just the point: if we wish to come to grips with the contents of the Bible, we must dare to reach far beyond ourselves. The content of the Bible (*Der Inhalt der Bibel*) admits of nothing less."⁵ In fact, reading the Bible is not an act of self-transcendence, but a miraculous transformation from above: "It is the Bible itself, it is the straight inexorable logic of its on-march (*Zusammenhang*: here perhaps "the whole story, with all its ins and outs together") which drives us out beyond ourselves and invites us, without regard to our worthiness or unworthiness, to reach for the last highest answer . . ."⁶ Because the new world of the Bible—which is the world of God himself—intrudes itself upon our ordinary world, we must let it establish its own criteria of the moral life: "At certain crucial points the Bible amazes us by its remarkable indifference to our conception of good and evil."⁷ In fact, the Bible turns our vaunted moral universe upside down: "Once more we stand before this 'other' (*vor diesem 'Andern'*) new world which begins in the Bible. In it, the chief consideration is not the doings of man, but the doings of God—not the various ways which we may take if we are men of good will, but the power out of which good will must first be created . . ."⁸ Nor can we hide from the sovereign God of the Bible in the false comforts of religion: "It is not right human thoughts about God which form the content of the Bible (*den Inhalt der Bibel*), but the right divine thoughts about men."⁹

In my judgment, Barth is exactly right in this extraordinarily fresh and powerful essay. Now, we cannot retreat behind Barth; to do so is to return to a past that has been left forever behind. We cannot remain with Barth; to do so is to stand still, which is inevitably to lose the gains which have already been made. The only way, is forward . . .

4. Ibid., 33. The title of the talk in German is simply "The New World of God," though the gratuitous addition of "strange" is certainly justified on grounds of the content of the essay. Call it a *translatio ad sensum* . . . not unlike Luther's famous/infamous addition of "*allein*" in the translation of Romans 3:28.

5. Ibid., 33, with my slight emendation of the text to bring out the German more clearly.

6. Ibid., 34.

7. Ibid., 38.

8. Ibid., 39–40.

9. Ibid., 43.

a. The Will of God

We consider first the *form* of the divine command. That is to say, we ask first of all *how* God makes known his will according to the witness of Scripture. We enter straightaway therefore into the vertical dimension of theological ethics, the absolute claim of the sovereign God upon the totality of human life. The God attested in Holy Scripture never reveals himself without making an absolute claim upon the totality of human life. God alone commands, and demands a human response. But how?

Some familiar theological options fall before the majesty of the commanding God made known in Holy Scripture. There is in the Bible no moral intermediary between the sovereign commanding God and the needed human response. God does not speak through rules of the formation of human character; God does not speak through listing virtues and vices; God does not offer abstract moral principles of right and wrong to be applied according to the exigencies of human rational reflection. God does not offer moral or political or cultural agendas for the faithful to adopt and follow. God does not found a moral community, and then permit that moral community to decide for itself the best future direction; nor does he hand over to the individual the determination of what should be done. God does not invite the community of faith to struggle to find its own moral self-identity in his light. God does not give moral values, whether liberal or conservative, and invite the faithful to follow them. God does not define and defend a moral worldview. God does not give statutory principles to be applied by casuistry to the unfolding dramas of human life through rational-judicial application. There is no moral order of natural law in the Bible; it simply does not exist. There are no moral absolutes in the Bible, as if God himself were bound to a moral universe; rather, all that exists—including the determination of right and wrong—is bound exclusively to his decision alone. All of these familiar options—despite their popularity in numerous ecclesiastical circles on both ends of the theological spectrum, liberal and conservative—are entirely absent from the Bible, and therefore cannot and must not serve as the basis for theological ethics in the church of Jesus Christ. All of these options certainly lead to right human thoughts about God; but we care nothing for such opinions, when the Bible offers us nothing less than God's own thoughts about us.

In the Bible—and therefore in church doctrine—the *content* of the message about God cannot be separated from the *claim* that God makes upon human life. There are not "theological" passages in the Bible on the one hand, and then "ethical" passages on the other. To see it that way is precisely to turn theological ethics into an abstraction from the living reality of God, which is the one great error to be avoided at all costs. Who God is, and what he wills for human life, are one message in the Bible; and therefore must constitute one message for church doctrine. God reveals himself in his name; and in that very moment makes a sovereign claim upon human life: "You have seen what I did to the Egyptians, and how I bore you on eagles' wings and brought you to myself. Now therefore, if you obey my voice and keep my covenant, you shall be my treasured possession out of all the peoples of the earth" (Exod 19:4–5). The commanding God revealed his will to his people by his spoken word; the commanding God continues to reveal his will to his people by his spoken word. God actively and effectively communicates his will according to his sovereign good pleasure, grounded solely in his gracious purpose of love.

Several aspects of this vertical dimension—the *how* of the divine command—can now be more closely considered. First of all, the divine revelation of his will takes place within a *community* of faith. Covenant and command always go together. To do right in the Bible is to be righteous; and to be righteous is to be in a right relationship with God. Righteousness is not an abstract, absolute moral norm in the Western sense of legal rules. In the Bible, there are no legal rules that have any authority or validity whatsoever apart from the fact that God wills them; God's living will is everything. And God's will always creates a community in relationship to himself: "Hear, O Israel, the statutes and ordinances that I am addressing to you today; you shall learn them diligently. The Lord our God made a covenant with us at Horeb. Not with our ancestors did the Lord our God make this covenant, but with us, who are all of us here alive today" (Deut 5:2–4). Obedience to the divine command does not create the covenant; rather, the gracious establishing of the covenant provides the divine context for the giving of his command to the community. The indicative of God's merciful action is the sole basis for the imperative of the divine claim toward a human response. Theological ethics take place within a living relationship with God; all dead legalism is radically excluded from the outset.

Second of all, the commands of God are always specific, always *concrete*. To Abram, God gives the sovereign and concrete command: "Go from your country and your kindred and your father's house to the land that I will show you" (Gen 12:1). To Moses, God says: "So come, I will send you to Pharaoh to bring my people, the Israelites, out of Egypt" (Exod 3:

10). In both cases there are questions, concerns, evasions, outright denials; yet the concrete quality of the command simply cannot be evaded. God commands Samuel: "How long will you grieve over Saul? I have rejected him from being king over Israel. Fill your horn with oil and set out; I will send you to Jesse the Bethlehemite, for I have provided for myself a king among his sons" (1 Sam 16:1). The concrete command of God overrides human loyalty, human custom, human moral obligation, and puts us face to face with the living reality of God. To Isaiah, God says: "Go and say to this people: 'Keep listening, but do not comprehend; keep looking, but do not understand'" (Isa 6:9). The concrete commands of God may even put those who are called in an impossible situation, certainly a highly burdensome one; but that is no matter, for faithfulness is everything, success is nothing. To Matthew, Jesus says: "Follow me" (Matt 9:9). There is no preparation for the concrete command of God, no anthropological possibility, no human natural capacity summoned into moral maturity; there is only the old that is passing away, and the new that has even now come through encountering the living reality of God.

And thirdly, the command of God is *clear*, but not *obvious*. The entire Bible simply assumes that the commands of God are not only clearly known with unambiguous clarity but completely doable. To those who hide in the quagmire of pious moral ignorance; who substitute for the true will of God the false religiosity of "thousands of rams" or "ten thousands of rivers of oil," the divine response is unequivocal: "He has told you, O mortal, what is good; and what does the Lord require of you but to do justice, and to love kindness, and to walk humbly with your God?" (Mic 6:6). To those who, hearing the concrete divine command, would hide under the pretext of inability to carry it out, the answer is equally definitive: "Surely this commandment that I am commanding you today is not too hard for you, nor is it too far away . . . No, the word is very near to you; it is in your mouth and in your heart for you to observe" (Deut 30:11-14). Clear yes, but not obvious; intense moral reflection is required to discern the active shape of God's purpose in his commands: ". . . be transformed by the renewing of your minds, so that you may discern what is the will of God—what is good and acceptable and perfect" (Rom 12:2). The command of God is never simply "given"; it is always to be sought again and again, in direct encounter with the One who rules all things: "All must test their work; then that work, rather than their neighbor's work, will become a cause for pride" (Gal 6:4). Thus, we do not reflect morally upon God's will because it is unclear; but precisely because it so clear and certain, we strive to discern the given command of God in the given situation, that his glory may be known in all the earth.

It is instructive—if not somewhat depressing—to recognize how quickly the vertical dimension of the divine command can be discovered in the history of church doctrine, only to be lost so quickly again.[10] For Luther and Calvin, the purpose of the divine commandments serves one purpose only: as the means by which the sovereign God actively communicates his will to the world. In his *Treatise on Good Works* (1520), Luther opens with a resounding declaration identifying good and evil directly with the will of God: "The first thing to know is that there are no good works except those works God has commanded, just as there is no sin except that which God has forbidden."[11] In a single stroke, the entire medieval system of virtues and vices, together with the abstract validity of the "natural law," collapses. All human moral considerations are futile: "Accordingly, we have to learn to recognize good works from the commandments of God, and not from appearance, size, or number of the works themselves, nor from the opinion of men or of human law or custom, as we see has happened and still happens because of our blindness and disregard of the divine commandments."[12] Prayers, fasting, giving of alms, all such good works are pointless and worthless, apart from the active command of God. What makes a work good is simple: it "pleases God";[13] this alone is the test, even if that may sound strange to human reason and experience. Similarly, according to Calvin in the *Institutes of the Christian Religion* (1559), it is essential that the form of the divine command be understood in the light of its purpose or goal. The commandments of God are in fact the best instrument (*optimum organum*) through which to learn the will of God (*Domini voluntas*).[14] For Calvin, the commandments of the Bible are not abstract moral norms; they are the means through which God makes known his will, and only as such can their truth be rightly discerned. The Bible therefore does not contain a *set* of moral rules (*plures*), but only *one rule* (*una regula*) to live by: which is God's one eternal will made known in his commandment.[15] The chief obstacle to obedience is religious piety, which specializes in dreaming up

---

10. For what follows see Gass, *GCE* II, 1–172.
11. Luther, *LW* 44, 23.
12. Ibid., 23.
13. Ibid., 25.
14. Calvin, *LCC* XX, 360.
15. Ibid., 362.

human precepts accorded a religious aura. Even the commands of the Bible can be twisted and distorted; and therefore one primary rule of interpretation is essential: every commandment is to be interpreted in the law of the active will of God. It is in reference to his character (*a cuius ingenio*) "that the nature of the law is to be appraised."[16] To summarize: the command of God has its meaning solely in the context of the active divine will, and not in any human system of religious or moral virtue, which it casts aside as utterly worthless; so the Reformers.

The story is very different within a generation or two. In his *Commentary on the Heidelberg Catechism* (1598, published posthumously by David Paraeus), Zacharias Ursinus moves in the exact opposite direction from that of the Reformers in his consideration of the meaning of the divine command. The Latin term law (*lex*), he informs the reader, is derived from a phrase meaning a public document. Hence, the point of the law in the Old Testament (*Torah*) must mean to publish what therefore cannot be ignored without severe blame.[17] Similarly, the Greek idea of law (*nomos*), means to distribute duties to all; and indeed that is the nature of law for "all rational creatures."[18] So, accordingly, all human and divine laws come under the same category: they are both laws (*leges*) and both therefore share the same general characteristics of all laws: "Laws are divine and human. Human laws are such as are instituted by men . . . Divine laws are such which God has instituted . . ."[19] Notice how far and how quickly we have departed from Luther and Calvin. *They* understood the command solely in the light of *God* and his active will; *Ursinus*—despite excellent observations in his actual exposition of the Decalogue—understands *God's* will in the light of the general *nature* of law as such, divine and human. The reformation (and in my opinion biblical) logic of theological ethics has simply been turned around the exact opposite direction. Then again, in 1626, Johannes Wollebius published his justly famous *Compendium of Christian Theology*, the second half of which is devoted to Christian ethics. With astounding rapidity, Wollebius turns the Reformers on their head, and opens his ethics with a discussion of moral virtue: "Good works are . . . called virtues," which he defines as "all holy desires, thoughts and actions."[20] He lists the

16. Ibid., 373.
17. Ursinus, *Commentary*, 489.
18. Ibid., 490.
19. Ibid.
20. Wollebius, *Compendium*, 191.

various virtues: wisdom, prudence, sincerity, readiness, and constancy; and then goes on to discern in each of the Ten Commandments the particular "virtue" that is taught in each. It is difficult to avoid the impression of legalistic casuistry. For example, in his discussion of the "Works of the Second Commandment," Wollebius describes in detail the distinction between a proper and an improper fast: "A true fast is to be recognized by its quality and its purpose."[21] One immediately senses in his discussion of "proper" fasting how far we are from the world of Luther and Calvin!

We now complete the circle on the Lutheran side. In 1634, Georg Calixt wrote his *Epitome of Moral Theology*. What is new about the book is not that it separates ethics from theology—that had been done as early as Melanchthon—but that it turns ethics from a doctrine concerning the will of God into something entirely different. Not the will of God; but faithful Christian humanity, living a pious and holy life, in a state of grace, is the subject of moral theology.[22] As Wallmann points out, Calixt has reduced theological ethics to a study of ecclesial personhood.[23] Does that not make the threat astonishingly apparent that God's will inevitably becomes a *possession* of the church, and if a possession, surely in the end a *distortion* by the church? And indeed, Calixt goes on to speak of moral theology precisely in terms of ecclesiastical laws (*leges ecclesiasticae*),[24] again in a way so profoundly different from Luther and early Lutheran concern for the sovereignty of Christ in his church. We have to consider, finally, the *Institutes of Moral Theology* (1727) by Franz Buddeus. While Buddeus is clearly intending to align himself with the Reformation,[25] and with Martin Luther in particular,[26] his basic definition of theological ethics shows how far matters have come. According to Buddeus, the object of the study of moral theology is "the growth of regenerate humanity in the spiritual life."[27] Those

---

21. Ibid., 206.

22. Calixt, *Epitome*, 4, in *Ethische Schriften*. To the topic *De subiecto theologiae moralis* Calixt offers the basic definition: "*Per haec, quae hactenus diximus, quondam subiectum sit, haut potest latere. Nempe subiectum hic habemus hominem non infidelium aut convertendum, sed fidelem et conversum* . . . Not the human person without faith, or yet to be converted; but the faithful and converted person is the true subject of moral theology."

23. Wallmann, *Der Theologiebegriff*, 153.

24. Ibid., 113.

25. Buddeus, *Institutio*, 15.

26. Ibid., 13.

27. Ibid., 8. "*Obiectum theologiae moralis, est incrementum hominum regenitorum in vita spirituali.*"

who undertake the study are therefore those who are themselves regenerate, and should be proficient in the "virtues and piety" of spirituality. The role of Scripture is then to teach "Christian prudence" by its examples, its precepts, its teachings, its sermons.[28] We are again surely forced to ask: is that truly what Isaiah means when he says: "You have heard; now see all this; and will you not declare it? From this time forward I make you hear new things, hidden things that you have not known ... [B]efore today you have never heard of them, so that you could not say, 'I already knew them'" (Isa 48:6–7)? Truly, we began with the Reformers talking about the "right divine thoughts concerning humanity"; we have arrived—supposedly on Reformation ground—at the "right human thoughts about God."

We cannot go backwards; we can only go forwards. To do theological ethics in the community of faith in Jesus Christ in the present time means to discover what we have never known before, what we cannot even imagine no matter how hard we try, no matter how much rational experience we may bring to bear, no matter how deep our religious experience may prompt us forward: the sovereign and living will of God, which is his to declare, and never ours to own, but only to obey.

We close this section on the vertical dimension of the divine command with one final, but crucial point. God's will is God's command, actively communicated by God through the medium of Scripture. In making known his will, God lays a total claim upon the whole person, calling for an active and eager embrace of obedience. Yet here we must make a clear distinction: while God's will for human life is clear and certain, the mystery of God's gracious purpose is reserved only for God's own free majesty. God declares his will; yet God retains for himself the gracious purpose of his acts in human life and history. In Scripture, whenever God reveals, he also at the same time conceals. God reveals himself to Moses with astonishing intimacy: "Thus the Lord used to speak to Moses face to face, as one speaks to a friend . . ." (Exod 33:11). God clearly makes his will known. God makes known to Moses his very identity, and declares his name (Exod 33:19). Yet Moses catches only a mere glimpse of God's retreating back, while God shields Moses from seeing his form directly (Exod 33:23). Not even Moses—the friend of God—can see God's face. Through his command, God guides the whole of life according to his gracious purpose for human welfare. Our greatest joy on this earth is to give pleasure to God by the enjoyment of life under his pleasant ordering. Nevertheless, obedience

---

28. Ibid., 10.

to the command is one thing; complete knowledge of God's purpose is quite another. We are not called upon to act because we fully understand God's purpose, for we do not. We are called upon to act because God has commanded us to act; only God knows fully his purpose in his commands. Clearly, there are times when faith is challenged by a seeming contradiction between God's clear command and God's hidden purpose. Abraham is commanded by God to sacrifice Isaac in direct contradiction to God's promise (Gen 22). Here faith can only obey God's command and leave the accomplishment of God's purpose to God alone. "Once God has spoken; twice have I heard this: that power belongs to God . . ." (Ps 62:11). To obey is to do the will of God, leaving in God's hands the accomplishment of his wondrous purpose.

b. The Commandments of God

We ask, second of all, concerning the *means* of the divine command. That is to say, we inquire concerning the medium through which God communicates his will to the world. We have spoken of the vertical dimension of theological ethics; now—without retreating for a moment from the significance of the vertical dimension—we must with equal force and clarity focus upon the horizontal dimension.

We begin with the most comprehensive answer: Holy Scripture is the one means through which God actively communicates his will to the church and world. The Bible not only tells us *how* God commands (the vertical dimension); the Bible is the one exclusive *medium* through which God in his sovereign freedom continues to make known his will afresh in each new generation of the community of faith. Thus, Holy Scripture is not only the *source* of all theological ethics, from which Christians long derived the insight and direction in the life they seek; Holy Scripture is likewise the one *norm* for theological ethics, to which the Christian community has long turned—east and west, north and south—for true guidance in every exigency of life and death. Here in the Scriptures of the church God has declared his will; here through the Scriptures of the church God still declares his will. By affirming the Scriptures of the church as canon, the confessing community acknowledges that here God not only declares to us the Word of truth that sets us free; here God binds us to himself in service to one another. Here in the Scriptures we hear the Word of grace that makes us whole; here we also hear the Word of command, which claims our whole existence in outer service to others, especially the weak and vulnerable. Thus, our answer to the horizontal dimension is not complicated or confused (though it will have to be clarified and unfolded); our answer is univocal: Holy Scripture alone is the means through which God makes known his sovereign will to the community of faith, which shines like a light in the world.

We now explore the meaning of the horizontal dimension of theological ethics more fully. As the normative canon of faith and action, Holy Scripture is the one source for the knowledge of God's active will in the church. The Bible is not an abstract book of moral propositions; the Bible is the unique means through which we encounter the living reality of God, who lays absolute claim upon all dimensions of human existence. We believe in the guidance of the Spirit, without which not a single page, not a single letter of Scripture can be rightly understand; without whose guidance not a single step of Christian discipleship can be confidently taken. Yet we confess—with the church universal—that the Spirit works with and through the Word of Scripture to guide every new generation of the church, sometimes along well-worn paths of Christian service, other times along surprising new ways of obedience never yet seen or known in the community of faith.

Indeed, it is precisely the role of Scripture as canon—which means not only the normative function, but also the theologically shaped message of Scripture as well as its true content—to preserve and transmit the ethical witness of Scripture in such a way that it is an ever-present power and voice. What Paul, say, once wrote to the struggling Christian congregation in Corinth about love (1 Cor 13) is preserved and shaped by the canon of Scripture in such a way that through it, God teaches *every new generation* of his people the true meaning of love. The "original voice" of Paul is not lost or overridden; but it is carefully shaped and transmitted theologically as a witness to the living reality of God, who even *now* speaks these very words of love to the global Christian community of the present. Thus, the role of canon, in the horizontal dimension of theological ethics, is not to limit what God can and does say, or to mute in any way the sovereign freedom of God's command in its vertical dimension; the role of Scripture as canon rather is simply to point to the *place* where God's sovereign and majestic voice is heard in the world. Nor does the canon of Scripture limit the freedom of God to the narrow concerns of the church. Indeed, Scripture itself explicitly forbids such an assumption, as Jesus makes clear in the Sermon on the Mount: "Not everyone who says to me, 'Lord, Lord,' will enter the kingdom of heaven, but only the one who does the will of my Father in heaven" (Matt 7:21). To speak of theological ethics in terms of "ecclesial personhood" is clearly to miss entirely the majesty of Scripture. On the other hand, the bold affirmation of Scripture is equally clear: all ethical truth whatsoever is encompassed within the glory of God's revealed will: "The law of the Lord is perfect . . . the decrees of the Lord are sure . . . the precepts of the Lord are right . . . .the ordinances of the Lord are true" (Ps 19:7-9). According to Scripture, ethical truth far exceeds the narrow concerns of ecclesial humanity; yet on the other hand, all ethical truth is embraced within the infinitely wide arms of the Almighty.

The various legalistic frameworks—virtues and vices, abstract moral values, ethical worldviews, natural law—that are scattered throughout the literature of Christian theological ethics are shattered by the strange new world of God in the Bible. Instead of such moralistic reductionism, one finds . . . astonishing variety. In the Old Testament, there is the brilliant and inexhaustible witness of the narrative tradition. While much of Christian moral tradition has tried to draw simple moral lessons from these stories, they notoriously evade easy ethical description: why indeed did Abraham act this way? Or Isaac? Or Jacob? The community of faith is left to ponder, not necessarily to conclude; and that is essential to the moral maturity of Christian faith, which often finds *us* in situations that are humanly quite unclear, even though in the light of God they can on occasion suddenly become all too clear. There is the witness of the Law of Moses, often enough unfolding in *negative* imperatives that clear a space for action, yet leave freedom for thoughtful response open-ended. There is the ethical witness of the Old Testament prophets, which quite explicitly insists that only direct encounter with the living reality of God—both in judgment and in salvation—gives the needed direction in life. There is the ethical witness of the Psalter, in which the sheer drama of unfolding life in immediate relation to God is portrayed in both the depths of painful struggle and the heights of joyous celebration, reaching directly into the unknown—perhaps even unknowable—depths of the human heart. And finally in the Old Testament, there is the witness of the wisdom literature, searching for the divine will as it is expressed in and shapes the patterns of human experience. In the New Testament, one encounters immediately the preaching of Jesus concerning the kingdom of God, which has already broken into the world through his person and already turned the world of human moral values upside down.

In Paul, all ethics is related to eschatology; the new creation has already come, yet the Christian continues to live out the tension of the not yet, through conformity to Christ. The remaining letters of the New Testament continue to preserve the variety of the biblical witness, often focusing upon the struggle of faith in the face of doubt and persecution.

Now, my point in briefly rehearsing the variety of biblical ethical witness is simply this: any church doctrine of the divine will must be conformed to Scripture, rather than seeking to force Scripture into the alien mold of an external moral principle. When, for example, the late Reformed scholastic theologian Benedict Pictet outlines theological ethics by considering the nature of "virtues and vices," in his *The Marrow of Christian Ethics* (1694), he is certainly continuing a time honored tradition.[29] It will show up again in the nineteenth century on the religious left as the "moral ideals" of the Bible, and in the twentieth century on the religious right as the system of "moral values." Nevertheless, from the point of view of the canon of Scripture—which is the sole norm of ethical witness in the church of Jesus Christ—the astounding *variety* of ethical witness in the Bible renders such moralistic reduction entirely unusable for church doctrine.

On the other hand, in the light of the biblical witness, it is also crystal clear that God does not will many things, but only one thing; that there are not many divine imperatives, but only one divine imperative. God's will is one, throughout all his commandments. We are therefore compelled to ask: are there Scriptural indications of the unity of the divine will amidst the variety of the ethical witness of the Bible? Indeed there are, both in the Old Testament and in the New. In both Old and New Testament there are clear, coherent *summaries* of what God wills for the church and the world. Our purpose in general theological ethics is not to expound these ethical summaries, but simply to identify them, and affirm their continued role in church doctrine.

In the Old Testament the primary summary of God's will is of course contained in the Ten Commandments, or the Decalogue (Exod 20:1–17; Deut 5:6–21). In the Old Testament itself, the Ten Commandments have the role of setting the interpretative context for the remaining legal material, and stand apart as the binding authority in the light of which all others statutes and ordinances are to be understood. Jesus himself clearly affirmed the continuing authority of the Ten Commandments. When asked by the rich young ruler for the way of life, Jesus simply quotes from the Ten

---

29. Pictet, *Medulla Ethicae Christianae*, 28–29.

Commandments as the one eternal expression of God's will: "If you wish to enter life, keep the commandments . . ." (Matt 19:17). The correction Jesus offers the earnest young man is not to add another commandment, or a new ethic, but to put the divine will made known in the Ten Commandments in a *new light*: obedience to God's command means to abandon *everything* out of love for God. Similarly, when the Pharisees substitute moral custom for the fifth commandment to honor father and mother, Jesus explicitly defends the commandment against their moral tradition: "For God said, 'Honor your father and your mother,' . . . [but] for the sake of your tradition, you make void the word of God" (Matt 15:4-6). We must say more about the relation between Christ and the Ten Commandments in the remaining sections of this chapter; but what we say cannot and will not undercut the continuing role of the Decalogue as a summary of the divine will for human life.

In the New Testament, the primary summary of the divine will is of course the Sermon of the Mount (Matt 5-7). In this Sermon, Jesus makes it clear that the divine command reaches down into the depths of the human person, penetrating heart, mind, will, even body. God's will claims the whole of human existence, and cannot be evaded by legalistic manipulation of the divine word. Moreover, the eschatological setting of the Sermon, which begins with the Beatitudes (Matt 5:1-12), stresses the celebration of joy from which all true obedience stems. The final blessing of God is already here ("Blessed *are* . . .") for those who respond to the call of Christ with their whole being. The Lord's Prayer (Matt 6:9-13) stands apart from all the remaining prayers of the Bible both in form and content, in such a way that it provides a summary of every biblical prayer.

In the light of these summaries—set apart in the Bible itself—we will expound theological ethics by following the Ten Commandments, the Lord's Prayer, and the Beatitudes. In doing so, of course we are not alone; the entire history of church doctrine echoes the canonical role of these summaries of the divine will by the prominent role they have played and continue to play in the life of the church. To name but a few from among literally hundreds of examples: the *Catechismus Romanus* (1566), designed to help pastors popularize the Catholic faith as formulated by the Council of Trent, treats the Decalogue in the Third Part, and the Lord's Prayer in the Fourth (and final) part (Part I treats the Apostles Creed, Part II outlines the seven sacraments; thus the Decalogue and Lord's Prayer amount to half the catechism). Its modern counterpart, the *Catechism of the Catholic Church* (1994), published over four centuries later following the astounding advances of Vatican II, nevertheless continues the same formal structure, with the Ten Commandments in Part Three, and the Lord's Prayer in Part Four (Parts One and Two remain formally the same as well). Among Easter Orthodox, the *Confession of Faith* (1625) of Metrophanes Critopoulos affirms the Decalogue: "So upon the elect of God is laid the necessity of keeping these commandments with all their power."[30] Already by the mid-fourth century, the Lord's Prayer is included in the celebration of the Eucharist according to Cyril of Jerusalem: "Then, after these things, we say that Prayer which the Savior delivered to His own disciples, with a pure conscience entitled God our Father, and saying, Our Father, which art in heaven . . . "[31] Among protestants, the list is nearly endless; we will simply point to Luther's *Large Catechism* (1529), which includes both the Ten Commandments (the first section) and the Lord's Prayer (the last section, apart from the appended material on confession), in which the will of God thus frames the entire substance of catechetical instruction.

While the Beatitudes have not played quite so explicit a role in the history of doctrine, their impact is not to be underestimated. In the East, Gregory of Nyssa gave a series of sermons on the Lord's Prayer, but also another on the Beautitudes: "May God the Word open His mouth also for us, and teach us those things which to hear is bliss";[32] the *Catechism of the Catholic Church* has a short section on the Beatitudes, which are named the "heart of Jesus' preaching";[33] while among Protestants, Dietrich Bonhoeffer's unforgettable exposition of the Beatitudes in his *The Cost of Discipleship*, describes the surprising and astounding blessing of God that comes to the disciples simply because they "have obeyed the call of Jesus."[34] I have planned to include the Beatitudes in the ethical portions of this presentation of church doctrine because I am convinced that the element of joy that pervades genuine obedience is essential especially in an age of ideological anger—whether conservative or liberal makes no difference. Obedience to Christ is no burden, but the light of life, the one true source of every satis-

---

30. Pelikan and Hotchkiss, eds., *CCFCT* I, 509.
31. Cyril of Jerusalem, *Catechetical Lectures*, 155.
32. Gregory of Nyssa, *The Beatitudes*, 86.
33. *Catechism*, 426.
34. Bonhoeffer, *Discipleship*, 107.

faction. Among theologians of the church, Thomas Aquinas hits the notes of joy in his short but sublime section on beatitude that opens the second part of the *Summa Theologiae* (IaIIae qq. 1–5), and thus in essence guides his moral theology as a whole; not in the form of obligation, but in the form of human delight. We will differ from Thomas only in putting that note of supreme joy last, leaving it to resound and reverberate . . .

A few final points are in order concerning the horizontal dimension of theological ethics. On the one hand, we must in every way respect and revere the freedom of the Spirit to guide the church through the medium of Scripture according to his own purpose. That means that there is no room for casuistic ethics in the community of faith, no rationalistic bridge between Scripture and the real world of ethical decision today. Thus, when William Ames (in his *The Marrow of Theology*) inserts a complex system of rational moral virtue (II. II) between his outline of genuine obedience on the one side (II.I), and good works on the other (II.III), he is introducing a rational calculus utterly foreign to Scripture; that Ames is a Ramist as opposed to an Aristotelian is immaterial to the issue at hand. The Spirit of God is free to work as he will, speaking through the many voices of the Bible the one divine Voice that guides us along the narrow path of life with inscrutable and unlimited power. No rational calculus can make this happen; only the miracle of God leads and guides his church. Moreover, it is essential to insist once again that figurative meaning—multiple meanings of biblical passages as an extension of the literal sense—are a clear part of theological ethics. Nor is this multivalent dynamic "homiletics" as opposed to doctrine; in fact, the use of imagination in theological ethics is an essential component of disciplined faithfulness to the authority of Scripture under the guidance of the Spirit. On the other hand, while not in any way restricting the freedom of the Spirit, the church confesses to find the Spirit at work in a specific *context*: which is the community of faith at worship, in prayer, through care of the vulnerable. Only those who together sing God's praises suddenly find themselves illuminated by the true light of life. Only those who search together for God in the public prayers of the church, suddenly realize that he is right here, right now, answering our prayers with the gracious gift of his will. Only those who through outer service of the weak and needy engage together in the mission of the church, suddenly find the genuine path of life opened gloriously before them, unmistakable in its clarity and truth.

c. Conformity to Christ

We have asked concerning the *form* of the divine imperative, which is the vertical dimension of theological ethics; we have asked concerning the *means* of the divine imperative, which is the horizontal dimension; we now ask concerning the *content* of the divine imperative, which is in fact the one intersection between the vertical and horizontal dimensions. The one content of the divine command is Jesus Christ. Jesus Christ himself—not a christological principle, but the living person of the risen, glorified, and exalted Lord of all reality—is the one true content of God's command for all human life. Jesus Christ is the sole content of God's one covenant of grace with all humanity. Christ is therefore the vertical dimension of the command: God himself reaching down in free fellowship with humankind through his Son. At the same time, Christ is the horizontal dimension of the command: God himself among us, living and dying for us with God in our place.

Just as Jesus Christ is the one grace of God by which we are set free for newness of life; so he is the one claim of God, by which we are bound to him in joyful obedience. The issue of the christological content of Christian ethics has already been raised for church doctrine with profound insight in the Barmen Declaration (1934). In article 2, the Declaration begins by quoting 1 Cor 1:30: "Christ Jesus, whom God made our wisdom, our righteousness and sanctification and redemption." The point of the quote is to make it clear that Christ is not somehow limited to the grace of God, while the claim of God—the sphere of Christian ethics—is relegated to a separate sphere of reality independent of Christ. No, according to Paul, Christ himself *is* our sanctification, our new direction in life, and not just our justification, our new relation to God through faith. Jesus Christ, the Declaration continues, is not only God's promise of "forgiveness of sins," but with the same sovereign power and truth is also "God's mighty claim" upon the wholeness of human existence. The Declaration then condemns the "false doctrine" of the so-called German Christians, who affirm that there are spheres of life which do not belong to Jesus Christ but to "other lords" (*anderen Herren*).[35] We can only affirm the supreme truth confessed at Barmen: Jesus Christ himself is not only the one grace of God, but also

---

35. All quotes from the Barmen Declaration are in Pelikan and Hotchkiss, eds., *CCFTC* III, 507.

the one true claim of God upon our existence, a claim which we eagerly embrace in life and death. God's grace and God's claim always go together.

We now explore several issues concerning the christological content of Christian ethics. We have spoken of the role of Scripture as canon for the ongoing life of the church in relation to doctrine. There is no need to repeat our affirmation; we need only to stress the theological shape of Scripture as the sole means by which the risen and exalted Christ guides every new generation of the church in *practice*, as in faith. Christ himself, by his Spirit, guides every new generation—facing new circumstances, new cultural and historical situations, new challenges and opportunities—into the fullness of his life and will. Scripture is the sole means for his guidance; yet Scripture in his hands is not a dead letter, nor a legalistic codex, but a living witness of power and renewal for all humanity. Nor are we simply speaking here of the words of Jesus in the New Testament, though of course those words are included in the canonical witness. Rather, the entire Bible—Old and New Testament—is shaped theologically in the light of the risen and exalted Christ, who speaks through these words his living command for the contemporary community of faith and practice. Just so: in ethics as in doctrine, we cannot retreat into the past, though we are profoundly grateful for all who have labored in this vineyard; for Christ claims us now in the *present moment*, and we cannot evade the direct, immediate, concrete, exclusive claim he now makes upon our lives. Those who say: "how can you base your life on a book written millennia ago?" fully misunderstand the dynamic of Christian theological ethics. Those who say: "there is no need for theological ethics, for the Bible is the only ethics we need," fully misunderstand the power unleashed by the Spirit who fills the pages of Scripture with ever new meaning in the ongoing life of the church. Christ is risen; we therefore base our lives on what he *now* says to us through the witness of Scripture. The Bible does not create an ethical worldview; rather Jesus Christ himself speaks through its many and varied voices, that we might hear his one Voice, and render unto him the service we gladly and freely offer.

Flipping the issue around, as it were, we now affirm another crucial point: Jesus Christ himself is the sole ultimate criterion, the sole standard and norm, by which God's will is discerned in the witness of Scripture. Once again, we are not referring to a christological principle; rather the living reality of Jesus Christ himself is the final test by which our words and deeds on the basis of Scripture are judged. Are our words and deeds—spoken and ventured forth on the basis of the biblical witness—truly in accordance with the eternal will of God? The sole criterion of judgment by which this question is raised and answered in the church is the living reality of Christ himself. Christ alone is the true embodiment of God's will; therefore, only in reference to him, are works "good works"; only in reference to him, are actions faithful actions. Are we not arguing in a circle? If Christ teaches us through the Bible; yet Christ alone is the norm of the Bible; then how do we ever know whether are actions are truly his claim upon our lives? We have spoken of the role of the community at worship, at prayer, and in active care for the poor as the necessary context for Christian ethical reflection; yet in the end, there is always a risk of faith. In the end, having done our best, we must leave all in his hands, to whom we must all one day render an account. In the end, we must accept the wager of faith knowing that Christ our Judge died for us, even for us, that we might live for him and with him always.

Theological ethics of the divine command means *fellowship* with Jesus Christ. Above all, credit goes to Dietrich Bonhoeffer for his revolutionary insight: "Here is the sum of the commandments—to live in fellowship with Christ."[36] Christian practice means discipleship: leaving everything—literally everything—behind, in order to follow Jesus Christ. We hear much of course about how Christianity reaffirms "family values"—by which is usually meant the portrait of family live in Victorian culture—but the gospel says differently. The call of the gospel is the highest priority, infinitely outranking every other claim upon human existence. "To another Jesus said, 'Follow me.' But he said, 'Lord first let me go and bury my father.' But Jesus said to him, 'Let the dead bury their own dead; but as for you, go and proclaim the kingdom of God'" (Luke 9:59-60). The call to live in fellowship with Christ radically overturns every customary moral convention, every traditional moral claim, every routine of normal existence, and binds us directly to the sovereign and immediate authority of the risen Christ alone.[37] Discipleship in this sense is not a process but an event: a complete and total break with the past, which is an order of existence already come to

---

36. Bonhoeffer, *Discipleship*, 75.

37. According to the Family Research Council website, its purpose includes advancing traditional family "core values" from a "Christian worldview." Now, there are no core values anywhere in the Bible; there is no worldview anywhere in the Bible; and Christ himself explicitly demands that the traditional claims of family be absolutely overruled in the light of his sovereign call. From the point of view of theological ethics based on the gospel of Jesus Christ as attested in Scripture, such an approach has to be radically abandoned; let the dead bury their own dead.

an end; a complete and total affirmation of the future, which is a new order of existence only leading us forward in fellowship with Christ. The call does not confirm our hopes and dreams and projects in life; the call puts one life to an end, and opens up before our very eyes a whole new order of life in the presence of Life itself. The call is an *event* from the side of God; it therefore requires *decision* from the side of the human person. The call cannot be conveniently incorporated into any moral scheme, whether traditional or progressive; the call radically overturns all moral schemes, and transfers our direction in life to One who is good simply because he is. Here there is no Christian ideal; there is only Christ himself, the light of life, who from now on guides all who follow him in the way of joy and peace.

The call of Christ binds us to his person alone as the one source of life; and yet the call is more than simply a connection to his person. The order of existence we leave behind when we follow Jesus Christ is an order of *inner* self-fulfillment, as if the meaning of life were the ways in which we can adjust the people, objects, and world around us to meet the inner needs we (think to) perceive in ourselves. That life is now over. The new order of life, but in sharp contrast, unfolds as *outer* service of others, and especially the weak and vulnerable in society. To follow Jesus Christ is therefore to share involvement in a new society. To say so is not to politicize the gospel; to say so is to recognize that Christ rules all things, including the *polis*, and therefore calls the Christian community to responsibility for society in the form of those who cannot help themselves. To care for the outsider, the marginalized, the poor, is the basic shape of the call to follow Jesus Christ. Through Christ, the rule of God has already broken into our world, turning the order of life upside down, radically reversing all human moral values; to follow Christ is to meet him, to greet him, in the face of the stranger, the naked, the hungry, the outcast, the sick and dying. Precisely such involvement among the vulnerable in society is the truest joy of those who belong to Christ.[38]

Fellowship with Jesus Christ means participating in his cross. A distinction is necessary between *imitation* of Christ—trying to copy, as it were, the deeds of his earthly life as a mode of piety—and *participation* in the cross of Christ, proclaimed in the gospel. We are to take up our cross and

---

38. Again, it is surely of the essence of liberal theology in the widest sense to speak of the essence of Christianity based on the self-understanding and inner self-actualization of persons. Again, from the point of view of theological ethics based on the gospel of Jesus Christ attested in Scripture, we can only stress that our true purpose in life as followers of Christ lay radically elsewhere—in the concrete needs of Christ our neighbor.

follow him; we are to lose our lives that we might find them; we are to be last, in order that we might be first. What do these mean in the light of the crucified and risen Christ? Acts of "cruciform" piety are exactly the wrong way to be conformed to the image of Christ. Rather, we are called to participate in his suffering and death by giving our lives for one another. "No one has greater love than this, to lay down one's life for one's friends" (John 15:13); to imitate Christ is to participate in the suffering of Christ by giving life itself for the sake of others. In doing so, paradoxically, we do not *lose* the fullness of joy in life; we find it for the first time. Again Bonhoeffer: "To go one's way under the sign of the cross is not misery and desperation, but peace and refreshment for the soul, it is the highest joy."[39] The cross of Christ is no burden to carry; it is the joy of life that makes us whole. "Come to me, all you that are weary and are carrying heavy burdens, and I will give you rest. Take my yoke upon you, and learn from me; for I am gentle and humble in heart, and you will find rest for your souls. For my yoke is easy, and my burden is light" (Matt 11:28–30).

d. The Rule of Love

We conclude now our section on general ethics by considering the *shape* of the divine command. There are times when the church at worship and prayer, in active care for the vulnerable, turns to Scripture seeking the will of God; the boundaries of the divine will are charted; the flexibility of God's wondrous command is clearly discerned; and yet still, the question remains: what shall we do in the present moment? What is God's command to us, through the witness of Scripture, as we seek above all else to be faithful to him alone in word and deed? The shape of the divine command is self-consistent in all ethical contexts; but it is particularly acute in the life of the church when crisis makes ethical decision on the basis of Scripture a burning issue. How exactly does the God of the Bible want us to act? The answer is given in the twofold rule of love.

As every reader of the New Testament knows full well, Jesus engages throughout the Gospels in sharp disagreement with the Pharisees. According to Jesus, their rigid legalism misses the central purpose of God. They put burdens on others that they themselves are unwilling to carry. The error of the Pharisees is hypocrisy: they say one thing in religious self-display toward others, and yet they do something altogether different before God.

---

39. Ibid., 93.

Jesus removes every attempt to evade the living claim of God upon the whole person. He does not set aside the divine command; he radicalizes the divine imperative, in order to show its true meaning for every human being in God's new world.

A direct ethical confrontation finally becomes inevitable (Matt 22: 34-40). The Pharisees move in swarms; setting up an ambush instead of genuine debate. An expert in the Mosaic law comes forward to question Jesus. He is not looking for illumination; he is probing for weakness. He is trying to elicit from Christ a response that can be used against him. "Teacher, which commandment of the law is the greatest?" The Pharisees carefully avoid any attempt to summarize the Law of Moses, or to manifest its essential unity. Laws are laws; there they let the matter rest; all of them ought to be followed with the same force as a uniform set of legal rules. The question is a trap.

Jesus turns the trap into a moment of luminous ethical and moral clarity, guiding the church of all future generations into the truth of his will for the world. The command of God is not simply a list of abstract moral rules, or a handbook of virtues and vices; the command of God is the eternal expression of God's living will. Jesus accepts the binding authority of the Ten Commandments; yet at the same time, with sovereign freedom, Jesus defines their essential divine purpose. Jesus distinguishes between the heart of the matter, and mere externals. Here Jesus is fully in line with all the Old Testament prophets, who chastize Israel for its hardness of heart. With supreme authority, Christ declares the twofold purpose for which God gave all his commandments.

The heart of God's living will is to love God with every dimension of one's existence. To love God with mind, will, emotion; indeed, the whole person, is the greatest commandment. This is the essential that all the commandments teach. This is the priority around which all else is gathered. And there is a second comprehensive imperative: "You shall love your neighbor as yourself." All of the various concrete commandments teach this and only this: how to love God and how to love neighbor. That is their purpose. The twofold rule of love is the *shape* of God's will for all eternity. Everything that the Old Testament (and by extension, the Bible as a whole) teaches rests on these two commands, like a door hanging on its two hinges. The twofold command of love is in fact the key that unlocks the true mystery of God's eternal will for all humanity.

The twofold command of love is implicit in the remaining narrative of the Gospels. For example, what does love for neighbor really mean? The parable of the Good Samaritan (Luke 10:29–37) directly addresses the issue, and in fact expands the point without limits. Love for neighbor does not mean love only for those within one's own religious circle, but explicitly reaches outside the people of God to embrace the foreigner, even the enemy. Similarly, love of neighbor as expounded in this parable completely undercuts any form of an ethic of "intentions." Good intentions could not possibly do the injured stranger one tiny bit of good; only concrete actions of kindness provide any real neighborly help at all. Again, the parable illustrates the terrifying point that religion itself is often enough the most aggressive block to genuine love for neighbor, and therefore the greatest failure to discern the true shape of the divine will. Another example: in the parable of the Unmerciful Servant (Matt 18:23–35) the point is made with crystal clarity that those who have received mercy from God, must learn to show mercy to others; love is to be shown to the neighbor, because love has first to be freely received as a divine gift. In his words, and in his deeds, Jesus embodies the twofold love of God and neighbor that gives shape to the divine imperative as a whole.

The shape of God's will calls us to love him with our entire existence. We are to submit our finite thoughts to his eternal thoughts. It is of course so easy and tempting to do the reverse; to crowd the divine will into the categories and prejudices of human rational logic and experience. Yet love for God compels us to a logic of faith; giving away our prejudices and preconceptions, in order to be further instructed by the divine will according to his good pleasure. Our decisions in life are to reflect the glory of his love. Who does not far too often base personal decision upon a careful calculus of human self-actualization? And yet to do so is to miss the true shape of God's purpose, not only for my humanity, but for all humanity. Our emotions are to reflect the radiant beauty of God's splendor. We are much too hard on ourselves when we should give our hearts room to breathe; we cling in nostalgia to the past, when God calls us forward to a new future. Even our bodies are to be shaped by divine love: care for the body is an essential dimension of Christian love for God. He made us whole; to take care of our physical well-being is a crucial part of what it means to love God alone above all things.

Love for our neighbor means once and for all coming to grips with the new global world in which we live. Our society is a strange paradox. It has never been more interconnected: a touch of a button on a computer, and you can see what is happening in real time at remote locations anywhere in the world. And yet, at the same time, we still live for the most part in tribes. We still live for the most part with people who look like us, think like us, talk like us, live like us. And worse, we expect God to take sides with our tribe against the other tribe. The twofold rule of love turns the world of tribal religion upside down. The God of the gospel is not a tribal God; *he* is not conformed to us, it is *we* who are conformed into his image. The love of God is not for people just like us; God's love embraces every human being upon the face of the earth. God's love does not seek to secure a place in our limited worldview; God's love *shatters* our worldview, and every worldview, setting free the whole creation through the free gift of his merciful kindness. God's love does not hide within the special interests of a party, or faction, or moral agenda; God's love shines forth in broad daylight, reaching out to all nations and peoples of the earth. God's one purpose of love surrounds every human being upon the face of the earth, embracing everyone, leaving out no one.

Love for neighbor means awareness of the concrete. As disciples of Jesus Christ we are called to share concern for a new society. We are the salt of the earth; the light of the world; a city on a hill. At the end of every economic decision; at the end of every political decision; at the end of every foreign policy decision; there is a living person, a real human being of flesh and blood. In the end, it does not matter to us whether that person is a Christian or not; it does not matter whether that person is friend or enemy; it only matters that we are called by the risen Christ himself to show concrete love for our neighbor in need. To share concern for a new society means to put real human persons at the *beginning* of the equation, rather than at the end; to see clearly the real humanity affected by every social and political decision. As followers of Christ it is our special responsibility to see the concrete needs of the *invisible* people in our society and world, even especially those who have been made invisible by moral and religious bigotry.

Genuine love is objective, rather than subjective. A false, subjective love looks to another to find something that I can appreciate; something that is like me, like my way of looking at the world, my cultural or political convictions, my race or gender, my basic concerns in life. A false love then says: you are like me! and that is why I love you. False love is like a lamp, always shining upon others, only able to see the projected images of the self.

Biblical love is not like that; it is objective, like a mirror. It does not create an image of others, but accurately reflects the realty that one meets along the way: people of different cultural and political convictions; people of different race and gender; people with completely different concerns and projects in life; in fact people who may be nothing like us at all. Genuine love says: I love you, simply because you, like me, are created in the image of God. Respect and care for the other in a global society is the only way forward for Christian ethics.

To summarize: Jesus Christ is not only the source and embodiment of the twofold rule of love; he is as well the one true object of that love. Jesus Christ is perfectly divine and perfectly human in the unity of one person. To love God with all our heart, mind, and strength is to love him; to love our neighbor as ourselves is to love him. To love Jesus Christ alone above all things is to fulfill the will of God. When Peter finally encounters the risen Christ on the shore, after his betrayal, Jesus asks him one emphatic question, three times: "Do you love me?" (John 21:15–19). Theological ethics; Christian moral life; discipleship; are about one thing only, and flow from one motive only: which is love for Christ. In him, love for God and love for neighbor meet, and send us out as his witnesses in mission to the whole world . . .

Bibliography

Ames, William. *The Marrow of Theology*. Translated by John Dykstra Eusden. Grand Rapids: Baker, 1997.
Andresen, Carl, et al. *Handbuch der Dogmen-und Theologiegeschichte*. 3 vols. Göttingen: Vandenhoeck & Ruprecht, 1999.
Anselm of Canterbury. *The Major Works*. Oxford: Oxford University Press, 1998.
———. *Proslogion*. Translated by M. J. Charlesworth. Notre Dame, IN: University of Notre Dame Press, 1979.
Aquinas, Thomas. *Summa Theologica*. Allen, TX: Christian Classics, 1981.
Asendorf, Ulrich. *Die Theologie Martin Luthers nach seinen Predigten*. Göttingen: Vandenhoeck & Ruprecht, 1988.
Augustine. *On Christian Doctrine*. Translated by D. W. Robertson. New York: Bobbs-Merrill, 1958.
———. *On the Trinity*. Nicene and Post-Nicene Fathers First Series III. Grand Rapids: Eerdmans, 1998.
Bagchi, David, et al. *The Cambridge Companion to Reformation Theology*. Cambridge: Cambridge University Press, 2004.
Barth, Karl. *Church Dogmatics*. 4 vols. Edinburgh: T & T Clark, 1932 ff.
———. *The Word of God and the Word of Man*. Translated by Douglas Horton. New York: Harper & Row, 1957.
Bauckham, Richard. *Jesus and the Eyewitnesses*. Grand Rapids: Eerdmans, 2006.
Baur, Jörg. *Die Vernunft zwischen Ontologie und Evangelium*. Gütersloh: Gerd Mohn, 1962.
Bavinck, H. *Synopsis Purioris Theologiae*. Leiden: Didericum Donner, 1881.
Bonaventure. *Breviloquium*. Translated by Jóse de Vinck. Paterson, NJ: St. Anthony's Guild, 1963.
Bonhoeffer, Dietrich. *The Cost of Discipleship*. New York: Simon and Schuster, 1995.
———. *Creation and Fall*. New York: Macmillan, 1978.
Borg, Marcus. *Jesus*. New York: HarperCollins, 2006.
Brueggemann, Walter. *The Prophetic Imagination*. 2nd edition. Minneapolis: Fortress, 2001.
Buddeus, Franz. *Institutiones Theologiae Moralis*. Leipzig: Fritsch, 1727.
Calvin, John. *Institutes of the Christian Religion*. Translated by Ford Lewis Battles. Library of Christian Classics, volumes XX and XXI. Philadelphia: Westminster, 1960.
———. *Calvin's New Testament Commentaries*. 12 vols. Grand Rapids: Eerdmans, 1959 ff.

Calixt, Georg. *Ethische Schriften*. Edited by Inge Mager. Göttingen: Vandenhoeck & Ruprecht, 1970.
Catechismus Romanus. Bassani, 1733.
Catechism of the Catholic Church. Vatican City: Libreria Editrice Vaticana, 1994.
Childs, Brevard. *Biblical Theology of the Old and New Testaments*. Minneapolis: Fortress, 1993.
———. *Introduction to the Old Testament as Scripture*. Minneapolis: Fortress, 1979.
———. *The New Testament as Canon*. Valley Forge, PA: Trinity Press International, 1984.
Cunliffe-Jones, Hubert, ed. *History of Christian Doctrine*. Philadelphia: Fortress, 1980.
Cunningham, Mary, et al. *The Cambridge Companion to Orthodox Christian Theology*. Cambridge: Cambridge University Press, 2008.
Cyril of Alexandria. *On the Unity of Christ*. Translated by John McGuckin. Crestwood, NY: St. Vladimir's Seminary Press, 2000.
Cyril of Jerusalem. *Catechetical Lectures*. The Nicene and Post-Nicene Fathers, Second Series VII. Grand Rapids: Eerdmans, 1996.
Davis, Stephen, et al. *The Trinity*. Oxford: Oxford University Press, 1999.
Ebeling, Gerhard. *Evangelische Evangelienauslegung*. München: Christian Kaiser, 1942.
Ernesti, Johann August. *Institutio Interpretis Novi Testamenti*. 5th edition. Leipzig: Weidmann, 1809.
Flacius, Matthias. *De Ratione Cognoscendi Sacras Literas*. Düsseldorf: Stern, 1968.
Frei, Hans. *The Eclipse of Biblical Narrative*. New Haven: Yale University Press, 1974.
Gass, Wilhelm. *Geschichte der Christlichen Ethik* I–II/II. Berlin: G. Reimer, 1881.
Gerhard, Johann. *Loci Theologici*. Leipzig: Hinrichs, 1885.
Gregory of Nazianzus. *The Theological Orations*. Library of Christian Classics III. Philadelphia: Westminster, 1964.
Gregory of Nyssa. *Address on Religious Instruction*. Library of Christian Classics III. Philadelphia: Westminster, 1964.
———. *The Beatitudes*. Translated by Hilda C. Graef. Ancient Christian Writers, vol. 18. New York: Paulist, 1954.
Grudem, Wayne. *Systematic Theology*. Grand Rapids: Zondervan, 1994.
Harnack, Adolf. *Outlines of the History of Dogma*. Translated by E. K. Mitchell. Boston: Beacon, 1957.
Heerbrand, Jacob. *Compendium Theologiae*. Tübingen: George Gruppenbach, 1573.
Hegel, G. W. F. *The Christian Religion*. Translated by Peter Hodgson. Missoula, MT: Scholars, 1979.
Herbert, George. *Poems*. New York: Knopf, 2004.
Hirsch, Emanuel. *Geschichte der Neuern Evangelishen Theologie*. 5 vols. Gütersloh: Gerd Mohn, 1949ff.
———. *Hilfsbuch zum Studium der Dogmatik*. Berlin: Gruyter, 1964.
Hodge, A. A. *Outlines of Theology*. Lafayette, IN: Sovereign Grace, 2002.
Hodge, Charles. *Systematic Theology*. 3 vols. Grand Rapids: Eerdmans, 1973.
Hodgson, Peter C., and Robert H. King, eds. *Christian Theology*. Philadelphia: Fortress, 1982.
Holmes, Michael. *The Apostolic Fathers*. Grand Rapids: Baker Academic, 1992.
Horton, Michael. *The Christian Faith*. Grand Rapids: Zondervan, 2011.
Hutter, Leonhard. *Compendium Locorum Theologicorum*. Edited by Wolfgang Trillhaas. Berlin: Gruyter, 1961.

Jenson, Robert. *Canon and Creed.* Louisville: Westminster John Knox, 2011.
John of Damascus. *The Orthodox Faith.* The Nicene and Post-Nicene Fathers Second Series IX. Grand Rapids: Eerdmans, 1997.
Kelly, J. N. D. *Early Christian Doctrines.* San Francisco: Harper & Row, 1978.
Kelsey, David. *The Uses of Scripture in Recent Theology.* Philadelphia: Fortress, 1975.
Kilby, Karen E. "Perichoresis and Projection: Problems with Social Doctrines of the Trinity." *New Blackfriars* 81:957 (2000) 432–45.
Kuyper, Abraham. *Lectures on Calvinism.* Grand Rapids: Eerdmans, 1931.
Lindbeck, George. *The Nature of Doctrine.* Philadelphia: Westminster, 1984.
Locke, John. *The Reasonableness of Christianity.* Palo Alto, CA: Stanford University Press, 1958.
Lohse, Bernhard. *A Short History of Christian Doctrine.* Translated by F. Ernest Stoeffler. Philadelphia: Fortress, 1966.
Luther, Martin. *Luther's Works* (American Edition). St. Louis and Minneapolis: Concordia and Fortress, 1955 ff.
———. *Complete Sermons of Martin Luther.* 7 vols. Grand Rapids: Baker, 2000.
———. *The Large Catechism.* Translated by Robert H. Fischer. Philadelphia: Fortress, 1959.
———. *Lectures on Romans.* Translated by Wilhelm Pauck. Library of Christian Classics, vol. XV. Philadelphia: Westminster, 1961.
Meeks, Wayne. *Christ Is the Question.* Louisville: Westminster John Knox, 2006.
Melanchthon, Philip. *Loci Communes 1555.* Translated by Clyde Manschreck. New York: Oxford University Press, 1965.
———. *Loci Communes Theologici.* In *Melanchthon and Bucer*, edited by Wilhelm Pauck, 18–152. Library of Christian Classics, vol. XIX. Philadelphia: Westminster, 1969.
———. *Orations on Philosophy and Education.* Translated by Christine F. Salazar. Cambridge: Cambridge University Press, 1999.
Migliore, Daniel. *Faith Seeking Understanding.* 2nd edition. Grand Rapids: Eerdmans, 2004.
Oberman, Heiko. *Forerunners of the Reformation.* Philadelphia: Fortress, 1961.
Origen. *On First Principles.* Translated by G. W. Butterworth. Gloucester: Peter Smith, 1973.
Pictet, Benedict. *Medulla Ethicae Christianae.* Geneva: Sumptibus Societatis, 1712.
———. *Christian Theology.* Translated by Frederick Reyroux. London: Seeley and Sons, 1834.
Pelikan, Jaroslav. *The Christian Tradition.* 5 vols. Chicago: University of Chicago Press, 1975ff.
Pelikan, Jaroslav, and Valerie R. Hotchkiss, eds. *Creeds and Confession of Faith in the Christian Tradition.* 3 vols. New Haven: Yale University Press, 2003.
Quasten, Johannes. *Patrology.* 4 vols. Utrecht: Spectrum, 1975ff.
Quenstedt, Johann Andreas. *De Efficacia Verbi Dei.* Wittenberg: Wendian, 1670.
Ritschl, Albrecht. *Three Essays.* Translated by Philip Hefner. Philadelphia: Fortress, 1972.
Ritschl, Otto. *Dogmengeschichte des Protestantismus.* 4 vols. Leipzig: Hinrichs, 1908 ff.
Schleiermacher, Friedrich. *The Christian Faith.* Philadelphia: Fortress, 1976.
Schweitzer, Albert. *The Quest of the Historical Jesus.* New York: Macmillan, 1968.
Seeberg, Reinhold. *Textbook of the History of Doctrines.* Translated by Charles Hay. Grand Rapids: Baker, 1964.

Siecienski, A. Edward. *The Filioque*. New York: Oxford University Press, 2010.
Spener, Philip Jacob. *Pia Desideria*. Translated by Theodore Tappert. Philadelphia: Fortress, 1964.
Tillich, Paul. *Systematic Theology*. 3 vols. Chicago: The University of Chicago Press, 1967.
Ursinus, Zacharias. *Commentary on the Heidelberg Catechism*. Phillipsburg: Presbyterian and Reformed Publishing, n.d.
Wallman, Johannes. *Der Theologiebegriff bei Johann Gerhard und Georg Calixt*. Tübingen: Mohr, 1961.
Wollebius, Johannes. *Christianae Theologiae Compendium*. Edited by Ernst Bizer. Neukirchen: Kreis Moers, 1935.
Wollgast, Siegfried. *Philosophie in Deutschland zwischen Reformation und Aufklarung*. Berlin: Akademie, 1993.
Wundt, Max. *Die Deutsche Schulmetaphysik des 17. Jahrhunderts*. Tübingen: Mohr, 1939.

www.ingramcontent.com/pod-product-compliance
Lightning Source LLC
Chambersburg PA
CBHW030111170426
43198CB00009B/576